Teaching and Learning

Pedagogy, Curriculum and Culture

Alex Moore

London and New York

First published 2000 by RoutledgeFalmer
11 New Fetter Lane, London EC4P 4EE

Simultaneously published in the USA and Canada
by RoutledgeFalmer
29 West 35th Street, New York, NY 10001

RoutledgeFalmer is an imprint of the Taylor & Francis Group

Typeset in Bembo by
Florence Production Ltd, Stoodleigh, Devon

Printed and bound in Great Britain by
TJ International Ltd, Padstow, Cornwall

British Library Cataloguing in Publication Data
A catalogue record for this book is available from the British Library

Library of Congress Cataloging in Publication Data
A catalogue record for this book has been requested

ISBN 0-7507-1000-4

For Miranda, Jess, Ben and Jack

Contents

List of Figures   viii
Acknowledgements   ix
Series Editor's Preface   xi

1   **Models of Teaching and Learning**   1

2   **Teaching, Learning and Education**   33

3   **Teaching, Learning and Language**   62

4   **Teaching, Learning and Culture**   91

5   **Effective Practice: what makes a good teacher?**   120

6   **Working With and Against Official Policy: pedagogic and curricular alternatives**   149

References   177
Index   188

Figures

1.1	'Mental ages' and the 'ZPD'	17
1.2	Possible pedagogic implications of 'Piagetian' and 'Vygotskyan' perspectives	21
2.1	Official rationales for formal state education	35
2.2	Articulations between purpose and theory of education	37
2.3	Possible unofficial official rationales for formal state education	50
2.4	Key aspects of Enlightenment thinking in the development of state education	52
3.1	The 'How many squares?' problem	68
3.2	Ratio and proportion exercise	69
4.1	Modes of differentiation	108
5.1	The teacher as strategist	141

Acknowledgements

My thanks to Val McGregor, Susan Sidgwick and Elizabeth Plackett, whose advice and wisdom helped me greatly in the writing of Chapter 3: *Teaching, Learning and Language*. Also to Gwyn Edwards for his invaluable help and advice in preparing the sections on Reflective Practice and Action Research in Chapter 5, and to Ron Greer and the staff at Acton High School for allowing me to use their Teaching and Learning policy document to exemplify points on whole-school policies in the same chapter.

Series Editor's Preface

THE KEY ISSUES IN TEACHING AND LEARNING SERIES

Teaching and Learning is one of five titles in the series *Key Issues in Teaching and Learning*, each written by an acknowledged expert or experts in their field. Other volumes explore issues of *Understanding Assessment*, *Understanding Schools and Schooling*, and *Reading Educational Research and Policy*. The books are intended primarily for beginner and newly or recently qualified teachers, but will also be of interest to more experienced teachers attending MA or Professional Development Courses or simply interested in revisiting issues of theory and practice within an ever-changing educational context.

TEACHING AND THEORISING

There is currently no shortage of books about teaching, offering what must sometimes seem a bewildering choice. Many of these books fall into the 'how-to' category, offering practical tips and advice for teachers on a range of matters such as planning for students' learning, managing classroom behaviour, and marking and assessing students' work. Such books have proved very successful over the years, providing beginner-teachers in particular with much of the support and reassurance they need to help them through their early experiences of classroom life, as well as offering useful advice on how to make teaching maximally effective. Increasingly, such books focus on sets of teacher competences – more recently linked to sets of standards – laid down, in the UK, by the Office for Standards in Education (OFSTED) and the Teacher Training Agency (TTA) (see, for instance, OFSTED and TTA 1996). Other books have focused on the teacher's need to be reflective and reflexive (e.g. Schon 1983; 1987; Valli 1992; Elliott 1993; Loughran 1996). These books may still be described as 'advice books', but the advice is of a different kind, tending to encourage the teacher to think more about human relationships in the teaching–learning situation and on the ways in which teaching styles connect to models of learning and learning development.

More predominantly theoretical books about teaching for teachers are perhaps in shorter supply, and those that do exist often address issues in decontextualised ways or in very general terms that do not immediately speak to classroom practitioners or take account of their particular academic backgrounds. There is, furthermore, evidence that, partly through time constraints, some of the most profound works on sociological educational theory, by such commentators as Bourdieu, Foucault and Bernstein, are very little read or discussed on teacher training courses (Moore and Edwards 2000), while the work of developmental psychologists such as Piaget and Vygotsky, which used to feature very prominently on PGCE and BAEd courses, has become increasingly marginalised through a growing emphasis on issues of practical discipline, lesson planning, and meeting National Curriculum requirements.

Teaching and Learning: Pedagogy, Curriculum and Culture, like the other books in this series, seeks to address this imbalance by exploring with teachers a wide range of relevant educational *theory*, rooting this in classroom experience in a way that encourages interrogation and debate, and presenting it in a language that is immediately accessible. The book does not ignore or seek to devalue current trends in educational practice and policy, or the current dominant discourses of competence and reflection (indeed, it is constructed very much with the OFSTED/TTA sets of competences and standards in mind). Rather, it aims to provide readers with the knowledge and skills they will need in order to address and respond to these and other educational discourses in critical, well-informed ways that will enhance both their teaching and their job satisfaction.

With this aim in mind, the book does not tell readers how they should teach; nor does it seek to cram prepackaged, ready-made theory down readers' throats. Instead, it seeks to present issues, questions and dilemmas *about* teaching and learning processes – and curriculum practices – to which it invites teachers to formulate their own responses through guided activities, through discussion with colleagues, through further reading, and, most importantly, through refining their own educational theory in terms of what articulates best with or most effectively challenges their existing philosophies and classroom practice. In doing this, the book seeks to provide a philosophical and theoretical *context* for teachers' developing classroom practice, and to help empower teachers to participate fully in local and national debates about the nature, the purposes and the future of compulsory education both in the UK and elsewhere.

Because of its brief, *Teaching and Learning* makes no claim to cover everything that needs to be covered on its given subject. Rather, it is presented as an individual account that makes moderately detailed selections from current theory, basing those selections on what has proved most useful to the author in his own professional practice and what, in his judgement, will provide the most useful *entry-points* to other teachers for practical and theoretical interrogations of their practice. In this respect, the book is intended not as a competitor or as an alternative to 'how-to' books, or indeed to books that explore specific issues in far greater depth (I am thinking, for example, of David Wood's excellent *How Children Think and Learn* [1988], which explores, in far greater depth than I have been able to, a range of different *models of learning*). It is more appropriately viewed, like the other volumes in the series, as a different – and complementary – *kind* of text: one that takes, as its starting-point, a view that in order to be effective practitioners, and to be able to *continue to develop* as effective practitioners, teachers need a grounding in some of the key theories and issues within which their practice is sited, and need to have a genuine, critical interest in those theories and issues.

Teaching and Learning does not, either, set out to consider *all* aspects of teaching and learning. Because its primary focus is on teaching and learning related to cognitive–linguistic and (to a lesser degree) affective development (what might, taken together, be termed 'academic development'), it does not have a great deal to say about the teaching and learning of interpersonal skills, or of the development of what is sometimes referred to as 'social intelligence', or of the implications for teaching and learning of students' and teachers' *feelings* – including their feelings about what is being learned and taught. This is not because I believe these other areas of learning to be unimportant, or to have nothing to do with teachers or schools. (Indeed, a belief that learning has a primarily social *function* as well as a primarily social *nature* [Nixon *et al.* 1996] underpins everything else that is argued within the book.) Nor does it imply that such issues are not relevant to cognitive–linguistic–affective development. The importance of interpersonal relationships is central, for example, to the work of Vygotsky (1962; 1978) and Bruner (1996), explored in some depth in Chapter 1, while the need for teachers to take account of the emotional context of the classroom – and indeed the part played by the emotions in academic learning – is becoming increasingly recognised (e.g. Britton 1969; Appel 1995; Boler 1999). If *Teaching and Learning* has little to say about these important matters, it is hoped that readers will see this as a pragmatic choice, related to what is manageable within the covers of one volume, rather than as a deliberate marginalisation.

STRUCTURE AND CONTENT OF THE BOOK

Teaching and Learning is presented as six chapters, each of which has a degree of integrity that enables it to be read independently of the other chapters – although deliberate echoes and elaborations of points made in earlier chapters have been included in those that follow. Each chapter starts with a summary, and concludes with suggestions for further reading and areas for thinking and research. While the readings and activities can be undertaken independently, they are designed so that they can also be completed collaboratively, providing the basis for small-group discussions on BAEd, PGCE, MA and Professional Development courses for teachers. As with other volumes in the *Key Issues in Teaching and Learning* series, boxes have been used in the body of the text to highlight particularly important points or useful summaries.

The book begins with a chapter on *Models of Teaching and Learning*, which offers an overview of some of the more influential theories of cognitive–linguistic theory to have emerged this century. The particular focus here is on some of the work of Piaget, Vygotsky and Bruner, and includes an assessment of the similarities and key differences between these thinkers' theories as well as of the implications for teaching.

With reference to historical documents, Chapter 2, *Teaching, Learning and Education*, explores some of the official *purposes* of formal education, and invites readers to consider the extent to which these purposes and associated policies articulate or fail to articulate with the theories of development described in Chapter 1, or indeed with their own favoured models and theories of learning and teaching.

Chapter 3, *Teaching, Learning and Language*, examines the role and significance of teacher and student language in teaching and learning, and in particular the ways in which language can help or hinder learning depending on how it is used.

Chapter 4, *Teaching, Learning and Culture*, develops many of the issues raised in Chapter 3, examining, with the support of classroom-based case-study material, the ways in which cultural bias can operate against the interests of some students and to the benefit of others. It begins to consider some of the approaches teachers might take to counterbalance such systemic cultural bias.

In Chapter 5, *Effective Practice: What makes a Good Teacher?*, the emphasis of the book shifts away from student development and systemic bias towards pedagogy – exploring, and inviting readers to critique, some currently dominant theories and models of 'good teaching' and 'effective practice'. This includes considerations of the ways in which teachers need to be 'competent' as well as being reflective, reflexive, strategic and in possession of good communication skills. The notion of the whole-school policy is also discussed within the context of its ability to support teachers in their pedagogic development and to provide an 'action space' within which teachers can continue to reflect on and debate their own and their school's classroom practice.

The book's final chapter, *Working With and Against Official Policy,* revisits some of the issues raised in Chapter 2: How do teachers handle discrepancies between their own teaching philosophies and practice and those promoted by Government policy? To what extent and in what fashion do pedagogical compromises have to be made because of characteristics of the larger social and educational systems, or because the 'reality' of the classroom militates against the pursuit of preferred practices and goals? What 'action' spaces can teachers find within current bureaucratic and curricular arrangements to promote forms of practice and curriculum content that they feel are under threat? These issues are explored within the context of 'alternative' models of curriculum and pedagogy – including notions of 'accelerated learning' and 'multiple intelligences' – currently being promoted by a range of experts in a variety of fields. Readers are encouraged to consider the ways in which not only curriculum content and style but also their own practice as teachers might usefully develop in the changing social and natural world in which they live. Whereas Chapter 2 principally looked *back*, to the policies and decisions that have shaped and that continue to constrain curriculum and classroom practice, Chapter 6 looks *forward*, to more recent ideas about teaching and learning that may have greater relevance to students and societies in the twenty-first century.

REFERENCES

Appel, S. (1995) 'The Unconscious Subject of Education.' *Discourse* 16(2), 167–190

Boler, M. (1999) *Feeling Power: Emotions and Education.* New York and London: Routledge

Britton, J. (1969) 'Talking To Learn.' In Barnes, D., Britton, J. and Torbe, M. *Language, the Learner and the School.* Harmondsworth: Penguin

Bruner, J. (1996) *The Culture of Education.* Cambridge, Mass: Harvard University Press

Elliott, J. (1993) 'The relationship between "understanding" and "developing" teachers' thinking.' In Elliott, J. (ed.) *Reconstructing Teacher Education.* London: Falmer Press

Goleman, D. (1996) Emotional Intelligence. London: Bloomsbury

Loughran, J. (1996) *Developing Reflective Practice: Learning About Teaching and Learning Through Modelling.* London: Falmer Press

Moore, A. and Edwards, G. (2000) 'Compliance, Resistance and Pragmatism in Pedagogic Identities.' Paper presented at the Annual Conference of the American Educational Research Association, New Orleans, 24–28 April 2000

Nixon, J., Martin, J., McKeown, P. and Ranson, S. (1996) *Encouraging Learning: Towards a Theory of the Learning School.* Buckingham and Philadelphia: Open University Press

OFSTED/TTA (Office for Standards in Education/Teacher Training Agency) (1996) *Framework for the Assessment of Quality and Standards in Initial Teacher Training 1996/97.* London: OFSTED

Schon, D.A. (1983) *The Reflective Practitioner: How the Professionals Think in Action.* New York: Basic Books

Schon, D.A. (1987) *Educating the Reflective Practitioner.* San Francisco: Jossey-Bass

Valli, L. (ed.) (1992) *Reflective Teacher Education.* New York: State University of New York Press

Vygotsky, L.S. (1962) *Thought and Language.* Cambridge, Mass.: M.I.T. Press

Vygotsky, L.S. (1978) *Mind in Society.* Cambridge, Mass.: Harvard University Press

Wood, D. (1988) *How Children Think and Learn.* Oxford: Blackwell

1 Models of Teaching and Learning

This chapter introduces some of the most influential theories of learning and development of recent years. These theories have been used both to support early models of school instruction and to initiate and develop new ones, including models that have come to be labelled 'progressive', 'constructivist' and 'child-centred'. With an initial emphasis on learning rather than teaching, the chapter gives particular emphasis to the complementary developmental theories of Piaget and Vygotsky, foregrounding Vygotsky's sustained argument that all learning is essentially social in nature. Detailed reference is also made to the work of Skinner and Bruner and to the implications of their theories for classroom practice and experience. As the classroom implications of Piaget's and Vygotsky's work are explored, the emphasis of the chapter shifts from learning to teaching. The work of both theorists is considered within the context of National Curricula and current debates about educational priorities and styles of teaching and learning.

THEORIES OF LEARNING AND TEACHING

Every schoolteacher operates according to a theory or theories of learning and within the context of a philosophy of what education should be fundamentally about. The only difference is that sometimes these theories are very consciously held and operated upon by the teacher, perhaps carefully referenced to published theory in the field, while others are held and operated upon rather less consciously, with perhaps little or no reference to published theory.

The central purpose in this first chapter is to consider some of the major published theories of learning and teaching practice that have emerged over the last seventy years or so, and to assess the extent to which these are supported by – or lend support to – (a) central government policy (as manifested, for example, in the National Curriculum), (b) teachers themselves, operating within the terms of their own privately and professionally held views and beliefs as to what constitutes a good education and what effective teaching and learning look like. Of particular interest will be the extent to which the favoured models of teaching and learning espoused by teachers chime or fail to chime with the models advocated explicitly or implicitly in government policy. This theme will be explored in greater detail in the following chapter, when we consider the extent to which favoured models of teaching and learning (both teachers' and governments') articulate with 'official' and 'unofficial' notions of what formal education itself is fundamentally there for. It is hoped that the revisiting of published theory will support teachers in articulating and interrogating their own theory and practice in the social and educational contexts within which they currently operate.

To do full justice to the range of learning theories at teachers' disposal and to the similarities and differences between them is an undertaking immense in its scope. To illustrate this point, we need only allude to the numerous books that have been written by and about one of the major educational theorists of the present century, Jean Piaget. What I shall seek to accomplish in this chapter is not to attempt to provide the reader with a comprehensive tour of current and past educational thinking, but to select a number of relatively recent theorists whose work I consider to be of particular importance or relevance. I shall provide no more than an outline of what I take to be some of the key ideas of these theorists, inviting the reader to explore their work in more detail in whatever way seems most appropriate. In this respect, readers are strongly recommended to go back to original sources: in the end, difficult though some of this reading is, there is no substitute for gaining *first-hand* experience of the work of such writers as Piaget, Vygotsky and Bruner, and of making personal sense of that work in the context of one's own classroom experience. Readers are also recommended to explore texts which deal with aspects of teaching and learning that are specifically *not* included in this chapter – not because I consider them unimportant, but because the breadth of scope of the book has demanded a high degree of selectivity. Jessel, for example (1999), provides a particularly useful and cogent account of the relationship between learning and *study,* referencing this to much of the cognitive theory drawn upon in this chapter.

WHICH THEORIES?

In deciding what makes a theorist 'particularly important or relevant', I had initially intended to select those writers whose work appeared to have been most influential in contributing to, supporting or even determining *public policy* on education. This has remained a central criterion. However, as we shall see in Chapter 2, the presence of *explicit* theory related to the processes of teaching and learning in public policy documents has been generally conspicuous by its absence. Consequently, I have had to make my own judgements as to what elements of whose theories appear to sit most comfortably with official government policy. I am also aware that recent research (e.g. Halpin, Moore *et al.* 1999–2001) suggests that teachers themselves often have surprisingly little explicit knowledge of the ideas of theorists of teaching and learning, being

much more concerned with 'the realities and actualities of classroom experience'. With these reservations in mind, I have used my own judgement and
experience to select those theorists whose work seems to:

- be most obviously embedded in teachers' everyday classroom practice
  and teaching philosophy (even though it may not be identified and
  articulated by teachers);
- support or be supported by the various dominant discourses in teaching
  and learning (for example, the 'levels' approach of the National
  Curriculum in the UK, or the group-work approach still favoured by
  many classroom teachers);
- offer the best routes into the exploration of a range of key issues and
  debates in the field (for instance, the 'student-centred'/'teacher-led'
  debate).

I have avoided theories and theorists – often more recent – where I have
judged that there is insufficient evidence on which to base realistic evaluations of them. These include recent work on accelerated learning and multiple
intelligences – although I shall return to each of these in the final chapter,
when we consider 'alternative' pedagogies and curricula.

While reference to key educational theorists may be absent from much official documentation, there is no doubt that their work has contributed –
selectively and even locally, perhaps – to the educational *zeitgeist*, and that,
although their work cannot claim to predate the teaching philosophies and
classroom practice with which it is typically associated (Piaget's work with
'child-centredness', for example, or Vygotsky's with dialogic teacher–student
relationships) it has often lent credence and implicit support to official policy,
to government-commissioned reports and surveys, and to teachers' own
philosophies and practice. It has also informed – and continues to inform –
courses of and textbooks for initial and continuing teacher *education* (see, for
example, Scott Baumann *et al.* 1997).

THEORY AND THE EDUCATIONAL CONTEXT

Most of the theories of language and learning that we shall be considering in
this chapter can be described as essentially *psychological* in character: that is to
say, they focus on the nature and development of the 'individual mind' in so
far as it may conform to or deviate from certain identifiable and recognisable
'universal patterns' of development. Partly because of this, much of it has
arisen from experimental research carried out with children (typically, with
very young children rather than, say, adolescents) removed from the familiar
social contexts within which they would normally be operating. One consequence of this is that much of the theory tends to overlook what we might
call the *contingent* and *idiosyncratic* aspects of teaching and learning: that is to
say, aspects related to particular school or individual circumstances, to cultural

preferences and biases, to the ongoing role of parents in the developmental process, or to the philosophies, policies and ideologies within and upon which education is constructed. (As we shall see, some of Vygotsky's and some of Bruner's work – especially Bruner's more recent work – provides notable exceptions to this rule.)

A particular difficulty with experimental work of this nature, conducted outside the normal context in which human development occurs (Piaget, for example, did not base his theories on longitudinal observations of children in their homes or their classrooms but on tasks conducted by them under 'experimental conditions') is that it may produce results that are not typically repeated in those normal contexts – a problem exacerbated by the fact that the person carrying out or supervising the experiments may not be accustomed to working with children in everyday social situations and may not have been trained to do so. Margaret Donaldson (1978), as we shall see, has thus cast doubt on some aspects of Piaget's theories by repeating some of his experiments in more 'natural' situations and by using more 'normal' language with which the children are familiar and comfortable.

LEARNING AND BEHAVIOUR: SKINNER'S LAW OF 'POSITIVE REINFORCEMENT'

One theorist whose work continues to reflect not just the ways in which schools and teachers behave towards students but also a growing common-sense view of how development *in general* (i.e. both inside and outside the school setting) occurs and should be managed is Burrhus Frederic Skinner (1953). Much of Skinner's theory revolves around the view that people learn best by being rewarded for 'right responses' or by responses that show evidence of having the potential eventually to *lead to* 'right responses' (sometimes known as 'operant conditioning'). Starting with Thorndike's 'law of positive effect', Skinner elaborates what he calls the 'law of positive reinforcement', which includes the notion that school-students can be trained to replicate certain (adult) behaviours if they come to associate such replication with the occasional (and therefore possible) receipt of tangible rewards. These days, such rewards might include 'merit marks', various forms of public approval, special privileges, and even sweets.

Skinner's theory emphasises not only the importance of a high level of positive reinforcement in the classroom, but also the use of highly structured materials through which students can work step by step towards externally-imposed goals. Because the making of mistakes is thought by Skinner to demoralise or demotivate the learner, interfering with their steady progress, he advocates that such materials should, as far as possible, be '*error free*'. Very structured, 'scripted' lessons, with teachers' words pre-ordained and seldom significantly deviated from, are linked to a very fixed – sometimes loosely referred to as a 'traditional' – discursive pattern of 'Teacher initiates (through, for example, asking a scripted question or providing a simple instruction), student responds'.

Skinner's work – which belongs to a much wider body of work growing out of behavioural theories of learning (for a much fuller account of these, see Bower and Hilgard 1981) – has undoubtedly left its mark in the areas of working with students with learning difficulties (Scott Baumann *et al.* 1997, p. 49) and, in particular, of managing classroom behaviour. In this latter respect, aspects of Skinnerean theory have become an integral and unquestioned part of much of what is now known as 'progressive' classroom practice. We might point, for example, to the practice of rewarding students for 'appropriate' behaviour rather than endlessly and futilely punishing them for 'inappropriate' behaviour, or the 'Skinnerean' notion that before deciding on a programme of instruction for any student the teacher needs to establish, as a baseline, what the student already knows and can do.

> Such common practices as establishing groundrules for behaviour, setting targets, privileging praise, providing meaningful rewards, being clear and open with students about what is unacceptable behaviour and what rewards will consistently follow good behaviour, and the avoidance of unhelpfully vague diagnostic phrases such as 'disruptive' or 'disturbed', may all be seen as sitting comfortably with Skinnerean theory. The theory may also be seen to support an increasingly common practice in schools of establishing a 'rights and responsibilities' policy, whereby students may 'earn' short- or long-term privileges through periods of sustained good behaviour or academic progress.

If Skinner's theory has become regularly applied to the 'pastoral' and 'behavioural' aspects of teaching and learning, its relation to *cognitive–academic* learning and development and to issues of *pedagogy* has generally proved too simplistic to be of enduring value, reminding us that much of the theory was derived in the first instance from experiments with animals. (For a more detailed account of Skinner's behaviourist theory, related to the work of Pavlov, see Wood 1988.) In recent times, many of Skinner's ideas have been overtaken by subtler theories of development, that have emphasised the social, interactive nature of learning (see, for example, Vygotsky 1962, 1978) and the need for students to 'construct' knowledge through experience rather than merely to 'receive' it (that is to say, a 'constructivist' approach to learning and teaching: see also Jessel 1999).

Particular *difficulties* in relating Skinnerean theory to academic-cognitive development and behaviour include:

- the development of a widely held view that making errors and *taking risks* represent an important and fundamental part of learning (Skinner, by contrast, seeks to reduce risk);
- an increasing rejection of school-learning as being principally content-based, and a corresponding privileging of learning *processes* (the

Skinnerean approach may be seen to reduce questions of process to a simple matter of conditioning);

- an increasing interest in the 'invisible', 'unreachable' aspects of learning and progress, to set alongside the more readily observable ones (as we shall see, students are quite capable of getting 'right answers' without having an adequate grasp of the concepts involved, while 'wrong' answers may often mask the hidden development of 'right' processes);

- an understanding that concepts actually *develop* rather than remaining the same (there is no real space in Skinner's theory for the notion of concept development: answers are generally treated as right or wrong, and knowledge as crystallised and finite);

- an increasing understanding that learning is an active, creative business rather than an essentially receptive one;

- a fear that if students work to externally-conferred 'rewards', rather than becoming independent learners who see learning itself as *intrinsically* rewarding, they may lose the *motivation* to learn once the source of the rewards is no longer there (the issue of motivation will be returned to later in this chapter).

Even in the area of managing students' behaviour, Skinner's theory is not without its difficulties, especially in the multicultured classrooms in which many teachers nowadays operate. Specifically, Skinner's work may be criticised as overlooking *cultural* issues related to behaviour, and the fact that a consistently applied set of punishments and rewards may prove inflexible and counterproductive in many classroom situations. (With reference to this point, readers are invited to consider the case, reported in Moore 1995 and elsewhere, of the bilingual student who *respectfully* averts his eyes from the teacher when being chastised, only to be doubly chastised for what is interpreted by the teacher as a gesture of rudeness or defiance. Examples of how bilingual students often fail to invoke teachers' rewards for the effort they put into their *academic work* because it is interpreted as wrong rather than simply different can be found in Moore 1999a and are discussed in Chapter 4 below.)

Skinner's theory may also be criticised for its underplaying of the role of teachers' own behaviours in the teaching and learning processes, tending to limit its considerations in this area to matters of the awarding of punishments and rewards rather than, say, the need for teachers to be reflective and reflexive. It also offers little help to teachers who have to deal with students who simply choose not to 'play the behaviour game' (see, too, Willis 1977): students, that is, who appear not to care whether or not they succeed academically or whether or not they are praised or chastised by the teacher. In this respect, the theory has little to say about 'internal' motivation and personal expectations or goals, and does not take full account of the extent to which an unwillingness or an inability to conform to certain *behaviours* may be confused with a *cognitive* deficiency in the student.

This latter difficulty may be seen as part of a more general concern over Skinner's work, that it does not sufficiently problematise the overlaps and interactions between behaviour and achievement. The awarding of 'pass grades' in public examinations offers a graphic example of this kind of overlap and resultant confusion. On the one hand, the awarding of a good exam grade may be seen as merely representing a recognition or marker of the student's previous achievement. On the other hand, the grade may be seen as an ultimate reward *in itself* for 'doing the right thing' – a reward that can be cashed in for, say, a university place or a prestigious job. In this respect, the exam grade may *itself* be seen as the student's achievement, rather than the effort and thought that have gone into getting it.

JEAN PIAGET: ACTIVE LEARNING

An influential theorist whose work *does* continue to contribute very significantly to debates about cognitive development is Jean Piaget. Unlike Skinner, whose theory often seems to present the learner as malleable material on whom the teacher must work, Piaget's enduring legacy to educational theory is the assertion that human beings are, from early childhood, active, independent meaning-makers who *construct* knowledge rather than 'receive' it. We make connections with our physical and social environments, to be sure, and are in some important senses controlled by them; however, this is a fundamentally *interactive* process involving acts of what Piaget describes as *assimilation* and *accommodation*.

- '*Assimilation*' is the process by which the learner incorporates, as it were, elements of the physical world into the logic of his or her own developing and existing understandings or 'interpretative categories' (Barnes 1976, p. 22). A simple example of assimilation, observable in very young children, is the incorporation of everyday household objects such as slippers, hairbrushes or empty jars into play activity, whereby those objects come to represent for the child some other thing (a cave, a forest, a person, and so forth). People continue to 'assimilate' as they grow older. However, assimilation becomes increasingly associated with our developing understandings of the world and the ways in which we conduct ourselves in society. Too much assimilation, and we may become rather ineffective learners, interpreting every new event or piece of evidence in a way that leaves unchanged our initial, very fixed view of the world and our sense of individual infallibility.
- '*Accommodation*' refers to the process by which human beings adapt their developing understandings and expectations to the realities and constraints of the social and physical world in order to arrive at better understandings or explanations. In this way, accommodation acts as a kind of counterbalance or complement to assimilation. A central part

of the learning of young children, for example, concerns the development of understandings that if certain actions are attempted (eating household objects, leaning forward into thin air, trying to turn a light on by hitting it, and so on) they will inevitably result in failure or pain (very often, the pain of parental chastisement!). Just as too much assimilation produces inflexible, self-centred learners, we might surmise that too much accommodation results in a very passive, uncertain learner afraid to make explorations or to take risks.

Piaget suggests that effective human learners achieve a certain balance of assimilation and accommodation in their interactions with the physical and social environment, through a process of 'equilibration' (Piaget 1975, pp. 30ff). To quote Douglas Barnes' succinct summary of how this works: 'By the simultaneous action of assimilation and accommodation [. . .] events are perceived as meaningful and at the same time generate changes in the interpretative procedures' (Barnes 1976, p. 22). An important point here is that assimilation and accommodation do not only enable us to make sense of the world, but that sense-making itself contributes, each time, to the way we think and perceive, and therefore to our capacity to make sense of *future* experience and events. In Barnes' words, 'These changes are *transformations* not additions' (ibid., emphasis added).

Piaget's suggestion that learning is an essentially active process of assimilations and accommodations, that does not depend on an adult such as a teacher to 'kick-start' it, lends obvious support to a range of activities and approaches associated with what has come to be known as 'child-centred', or 'student-centred' teaching: that is to say, teaching which begins with the learner's existing understandings and experience, helping them to build upon and develop these. It has also come to be associated with the kind of 'discovery learning' famously promoted in the Warnock Report (Warnock 1978). In terms of the implications for pedagogy of such a view of development, Piaget argues:

> in some cases, what is transmitted by instruction is well assimilated
> by the child because it represents an extension of some spontaneous
> instruction of [his or her] own. In such cases [the child's]
> development is accelerated, but in other cases the gifts of instruction
> are presented too soon or too late, in a manner that precludes
> assimilation because it does not fit in with the child's spontaneous
> constructions. Then the child's development is impeded, or even
> deflected into barrenness, as so often happens in the teaching of the
> exact sciences.
>
> (Piaget 1962)

The teacher's role here is quite clearly articulated as accurately identifying the child's current state of development and 'learning readiness', often basing this on what Piaget calls the child's 'spontaneous constructions' (i.e. those understandings that have come about through everyday experience), and then setting up appropriate learning activities whereby the child can actively engage with new, more complex thinking and concept development.

> This notion of the relationship between 'spontaneous constructions' and schoolbased learning is developed and problematised in Barnes' description of 'everyday' or 'action' knowledge, that is typically forged outside the formal learning context, and knowledge and understandings that are more formally developed in the school situation. Barnes emphasises the importance of students and their teachers making appropriate connections between this knowledge and the knowledge and understandings demanded in the school setting. Such a recognition includes an understanding on the teacher's part of the similarities and differences between the two kinds of knowledge, an ability to make connections between them, and an awareness of how to build on and develop action knowledge in the school setting.
>
> (Barnes 1976, pp. 29–31)

'Staged' development

The reference to '*stages*' leads us to a second feature of Piaget's overall theory that has left its imprint on much classroom activity that teachers nowadays take for granted, as well as on a great deal of subsequent developmental theory – including that of Vygotsky, whose work we shall consider shortly. This is the notion that children more or less 'naturally' move through a series of stages of learning development, in which they are able to handle progressively more complex concepts in progressively more complex ways.

Piaget defines three stages of development that all children can be expected to pass through at approximately the same point in their lives (Piaget and Inhelder 1969; Piaget 1971). These are:

- the *sensori-motor* period (from birth to about eighteen months);
- the *concrete operational* period (from about eighteen months to about eleven years);
- and the *formal operational* period, from about the age of eleven onwards.

The passage from stage to stage marks a fundamental and qualitative difference in the way children perceive the world, the way they process and respond to information, and the way they develop ideas and concepts: that is to say, the way they *learn*. In broad terms, the child is perceived in Piagetian theory as moving progressively and naturally (i.e. as part of an independent internal developmental process that we all experience regardless of where or how we live) from 'concrete', egocentric thinking which is very dependent on the physical proximity of the physical world, towards 'formal', abstract reasoning which takes place increasingly 'in the head'. This latter kind of thinking involves

- an increasing awareness of things happening beyond the immediate evidence of the senses (i.e. being able to conceptualise and think about things that cannot, at the time at which the thinking occurs, be seen, heard, touched, tasted or smelled);
- an increasing focus on the relations *between* things in the 'external' environment;
- an ability to develop and relate concepts internally, at a remove from the thing or event in which the concept is initially 'rooted'.

The chief differences between the three overarching stages or periods of development (see also Donaldson 1978, pp. 138–140) can be summarised as follows:

- During the *'sensori-motor'* period, which is divided by Piaget into a series of sub-stages, children move from an initial, profoundly egocentric situation of being 'unable to make any distinction between [themselves] and the rest of the world' (Donaldson 1978, p. 134) to a construction of the 'notion of a world of objects which are independent of [them] and of [their] actions' (ibid.). Understandings of the world during this stage of development remain very much limited to the child's visual and tactile contact with that world, even when the child has come to understand that things continue to exist when they are out of visual reach.
- The *'concrete operational'* period is also subdivided by Piaget, this time into two stages called the 'preoperational period' (lasting until about the age of seven) and the 'operational period' itself, taking the child up to approximately the age of eleven. During the concrete operational period, children begin to develop the ability to make associations between objects and events when some or all of these are physically absent. This provides for greater flexibility of thinking and reasoning, and enables the child better to understand transformations in the states of things. Children develop greater interests in explaining and understanding things during this period and are able to make *calculations* and arrive at *conclusions* through making comparisons and contrasts between objects and events.
- In the *'formal operational'* period, children develop, through an increasing 'internalisation', the capacity for logical, 'disembedded', decontextualised reasoning. In this stage, children no longer focus their thinking almost exclusively around 'things' and events, but around 'ideas'. They are able to reason logically on the basis of *premisses*, regardless of whether or not those premisses are 'true' or perceived to be so. We might say that in this stage they accept the principle of *hypothesising* and are able to use reasoning skills to arrive at conclusions. (For a more detailed

summary of this strand of Piaget's theory, see Donaldson 1978, pp. 134–140.)

> It is not difficult to make connections between Piaget's theory of 'staged' development and much that has become commonplace in a variety of education systems around the world. The very structure of formal education arrangements in the UK and elsewhere, with students being moved on to different schools at the ages of seven and eleven (coinciding with a hypothetical movement from the 'preoperational' to the 'concrete operational' and from the 'concrete operational' to the 'formal operational' periods) provides too close a match with Piaget's theory to be dismissed as coincidence, while much educational practice in the primary sector stills follows a 'physical-iconic-symbolic' template (Walkerdine 1982), that mirrors Piaget's notion of the development from concrete to formal thinking. It is common practice, for example, for teachers working with money in primary mathematics to begin by using real or cardboard money (physical), to move on to using *drawings* of money (iconic), and to end up using linguistic ('symbolic') representations of money: i.e. '£1' or 'fifty pence'.

The UK National Curriculum also mirrors Piaget's theory of *staged development*, both through its emphasis on definable levels of achievement and through its identification of 'key stages' which themselves parallel current arrangements for institutional transfer at age seven and eleven. In the light of this, the observation by Siegel and Brainerd that '[w]hen it comes to the study of children's intelligence, [Piaget's] theory dominates the landscape' (Siegel and Brainerd 1978, p. xi) appears as no exaggerated claim.

> Piaget's theory of development, we might say in conclusion, contributes to and supports one of the persistently dominant educational discourses of our time: that of the *linearity* of development. This discourse not only dominates school curricula, pedagogy and forms of assessment, but is becoming increasingly dominant in the field of initial teacher education, through such developments as the introduction of itemised 'standards' and 'competences' and the development of teacher profiles of competence.

Difficulties with Piagetian theory

Despite the congruence between much of Piaget's theory and much commonplace educational practice, Piaget has not been without his detractors. Piaget's notion of the child as 'active meaning-maker', for example, has come under oblique attack through criticisms – often from the political right – of some of the manifestations of child-centred, discovery-based teaching favoured in the 1960s and 1970s, which the theory appeared to support. Government pressure to return to more 'traditional', 'teacher-led', front-of-class styles of teaching might also be interpreted as implicit criticism of the 'active-meaning-maker' conception of the learner. The notion of 'pre-ordained' or biologically-determined stages of development has also come under attack (though not by central government) for a variety of reasons, of which the following are central:

- Because it is based on a universal model of development or maturation, the theory lacks the complexity to deal with *idiosyncratic* and *contingent* elements of teaching and learning – for example, the fact that there may be cultural variations in what are considered appropriate learning styles, or that there may be socio-economic or cultural factors supporting or impeding an individual's cognitive–academic development. This may lead to teachers too readily dismissing students who appear to fall behind in terms of 'normal progress' as cognitively deficient, rather than questioning *teaching* styles or curriculum content.
- Much of the theory is based on research carried out in contrived, experimental situations whose findings may not be as readily applicable to the 'real world' as Piaget seems to imply. (This issue will be further developed in Chapter 3, when we consider the role of *language* in teaching and learning.)
- Piaget has relatively little to say about *pedagogy*, seeming to imply that the teacher's prime function is to assess each student's developmental level and then provide them with appropriate learning materials. (This view of Piaget's theory, though not entirely without justification, does, however, need a degree of qualification – a point to which I shall return below.)

Criticisms of Piaget's experimental work, and questions about his subsequent theorising, have been raised by a number of commentators including Donaldson (1978), Langford (1979) and Smith (1996). They are also a prominent feature of Siegel and Brainerd's book *Alternatives to Piaget: Critical Essays on the Theory* (Siegel and Brainerd 1978). Two particular aspects of Piagetian theory that are interrogated in this collection of essays are first what is referred to as the '*performance–competence problem*' (Siegel and Brainerd p. xi), and second the issue of learning '*readiness*' (ibid., p. xiii).

The performance–competence and learning readiness issues

In relation to the performance–competence question, critics' concerns focus on the extent to which children's 'failures' in Piaget's tests can be interpreted as a sign of learning incompetence or simply as an unreasonable difficulty in the tests themselves, which may have taken too little account of their subjects' lives, language and experience and led to *untypically* poor performance. This proposed unreliability in the tests themselves opens the way to a fundamental questioning of the validity of Piaget's 'developmental stages', leading to a further questioning of how realistic it is to ascribe levels of learning readiness to students and to summon up corresponding curricular inputs.

That Piaget's artificial and overly difficult tests may have led him to over-simplify the learning process in his analyses is supported, argue Siegel and Brainerd, by the existence of 'major inconsistencies ... between what the theory says about the way intelligence develops and what the research actu-ally shows' (ibid., p. xi). Langford (1979) takes Siegel and Brainerd's concerns a stage further, suggesting that while Piaget is to be thanked for teaching us about the true nature of human learning, his work on developmental stages may have led to a Piagetian 'orthodoxy' in which teachers and curriculum planners 'may be presenting a limiting curriculum in the wrong way' (1979, pp. 1–2). Critics of the current UK National Curriculum, with its emphasis on levels of achievement measured against increasingly controlled teacher inputs, may well echo Langford's concerns. Some recent research suggests that teachers may also detect areas of mismatch between the way in which the National Curriculum is structured (according to notions of predetermined stages) and the kinds of 'Piagetian' learning it sometimes appears to espouse (active learning) (Halpin *et al.* 1999–2001).

Piaget and pedagogy

A third criticism levelled against Piaget, that his work offers teachers little in terms of pedagogy, is, as I have suggested, not without foundation but not entirely accurate either. To be sure, Piaget does prioritise the learner as active meaning-maker and does foreground in the teacher's work the role of assessor and provider. However, the notion of the teacher–provider does not imply an essentially 'transmissive' style of pedagogy, any more than it suggests a model of classroom practice in which students are allowed to embark by them-selves on some idealistic journey of discovery.

> Rather, the model implied by Piaget is one in which active learning is aided and abetted by sensitive and interactive teaching that takes full account of the child's existing knowledge and understandings of the world, using existing concepts as the basis on which to promote fuller and more complex understandings.

As Piaget puts this:

> I do not believe ... that new concepts, even at school, are always acquired through adult didactic intervention. This may occur, but

there is a much more productive form of instruction; the so-called
'active' schools endeavour to create situations that, while not
'spontaneous' in themselves, evoke spontaneous elaboration on the
part of the child, if one manages both to spark [his or her] interest
and to present the problem in such a way that it corresponds to the
structures [he or she] had already formed . . .

Piaget 1962 (See also Barnes 1976, pp. 79–80;
Donaldson 1978, pp. 140–141)

It is perhaps unfortunate that in the arena of public policy Piaget's notions of
'learning stages' are currently accorded rather more weight than his work on
'active learning'. It might be argued that a notion of universal stages of development far more rigid than Piaget ever intended (Piaget never intended, for
example, that the stages should be interpreted into 'incremental' or step-by-
step programmes of learning and instruction) has been responsible for the
reproduction of an inflexible and often inappropriate curriculum (see Langford
1979). Such a notion may also have contributed to the revised practice of
organising students into streamed or setted teaching groups on the basis of
spurious notions of intelligence, rather than seeking to understand the different
ways in which different students carry out their learning. (See Chapter 6 below
for further thoughts on different learning styles.)

If there is a more genuine difficulty with Piaget's theory, it is, perhaps, in
an unresolved tension between on the one hand accenting the creative, independent aspects of the individual child's learning (that is, presenting the student
as an active agent in the learning process), and on the other hand situating
the learner within a notion of universal development which *underplays* the
individualistic aspects of learning. As we shall see, this tension is partly overcome in the theories of Vygotsky and Bruner, who emphasise, respectively,
the social and cultural aspects of learning and teaching.

VYGOTSKY: LEARNING AND TEACHING AS ESSENTIALLY SOCIAL ACTIVITIES

In *Thought and Language* (1962), the influential Russian psychologist Lev
Vygotsky outlines a theory of learning and development that has much in
common with Piaget's theory but that differs from it in certain key aspects
and may be seen to move the theory forward.

Key elements of Vygotsky's theory that are common to Piaget's are :

- that learning is an active meaning-making process in which the learning
  process itself needs to be understood and prioritised;
- that learners move through age-related 'stages' in which learning
  undergoes qualitative changes; thus, children may learn in different
  ways from adults, including their adult teachers;
- that care needs to be taken to distinguish 'everyday' concepts from

what Vygotsky calls 'scientific' (deliberately taught) concepts, and to understand the interrelation of both kinds of concept development in the overall development of the child's cognition;

- that it is important to distinguish 'real' learning and concept development from 'rote' learning — described by Vygotsky as 'a parrotlike repetition of words by the child, simulating a knowledge of the corresponding concepts but actually covering up a vacuum'.

(Vygotsky 1962, p. 83).

> We might say in this respect that both Vygotsky and Piaget are concerned with what Barnes has defined as 'the central problem of teaching': that is, 'how to put adult knowledge at children's disposal so that it does not become a strait-jacket'. (Barnes 1976, p. 80)

There are, however, critical differences between Piaget's and Vygotsky's theories of development and learning, which are in part differences of *emphasis*. Centrally, whereas Piaget's emphasis is, from the start, on the 'internal', independent, 'psychological' development of the child's cognition, Vygotsky urges us throughout his writing to view learning and teaching as essentially *social* activities that take place *between* social actors in socially constructed situations. Piaget may see the child's early cognitive development as being rooted in active, personal explorations of the physical environment of things and of relationships between things, but Vygotsky is more inclined to perceive early development in terms of children actively exploring their *social* environment and being driven to learn by socially-rooted factors (such as the desire to please, to attract positive responses from adults, to participate in social networks and so on). Partly for this reason, Vygotsky places a great deal of emphasis on the relationship between thought and *language*, suggesting that language, like thought, begins as a social activity and that, from a very early age, thought and language become effectively inseparable from one another. To summarise this contingency in Vygotsky's own words:

- human learning presupposes a specific social nature and a process by which children grow into the intellectual life of those around them [and]
- [t]hought development is determined by language, i.e. by the linguistic tools of thought and by the sociocultural experience of the child. . . . The child's intellectual growth is contingent on [their developing expertise in] the social means of thought.

(Vygotsky 1978, p. 88; 1962, p. 51)

Vygotsky's theory of teaching and learning as essentially social activities has profound implications for classroom practice. In particular, it leads Vygotsky to the conclusion that the teacher's instructional input should not 'wait on' a child's internal developmental processes (as is implied, Vygotsky suggests, in Piaget's theory), but that it can actually *influence* a child's development, moving it along into areas in which it can handle increasingly complex ideas. Such a view places much more of an emphasis on *pedagogy*, accenting not just the 'when' and 'what' of education but also the '*how*'. By placing an emphasis on the importance of social processes and – in particular – the importance of *language* in the classroom situation, Vygotsky's work implicitly invites teachers to adopt strategies that are not only 'student centred' but that create spaces for students verbally to elaborate developing concepts, and that involve the teacher in a partnership model of teaching with the student. Such a model stands in clear opposition to arguments that advocate models of teacher 'transmission' and student 'reception'.

In practical terms, Vygotsky's theory suggests that school instruction should always be accompanied by opportunities for students to 'elaborate socially available skills and knowledge that they will come to internalise' (John-Steiner and Souberman 1978): that is to say, teacher *instruction* should always be accompanied by teacher–student and student-student *dialogue*. In this social context, the internal (and therefore 'invisible') 'developmental processes' set in motion by instruction are able to develop and flourish until the student 'possesses' them. When this happens, the processes are 'internalised' and (Vygotsky 1978, p. 90) 'become part of the child's *independent* developmental achievement'. In short, a kind of autonomy has been achieved, in which the student can bring acquired and developed mental functions to bear on the consideration of issues confronted both inside and outside the classroom, without further need (though this may sometimes remain desirable) of the physical presence of the teacher or other students.

Vygotsky's theory of the socially-rooted role of instruction and of its broad pedagogical implications leads him to introduce two additional concepts that are of particular interest to the classroom practitioner. The first is his notion of the 'zone of proximal development' ('ZPD'). The second is what might nowadays be called a theory of Language and Learning Across the Curriculum.

'Proximal development'

The 'Zone of Proximal Development' (Vygotsky 1962, 1978) describes the gap, in terms of 'mental age', between what a child can do unassisted and what that same child can achieve with the benefit of adult assistance. As such, it builds on the work of Dorothea McCarthy (1930), whose research suggested that children aged three to five could solve, with assistance, problems which five to seven year-olds were solving alone (Vygotsky 1978, p. 87).

Vygotsky's suggestion, based on his own experimental data, is that two children assessed – on the basis, it must be said, of the limited capabilities of standardised tests – as having 'mental ages' of, for example, eight might, on the evidence of similar tests, score mental ages of, say, nine and twelve when given appropriate active support by their teacher in completing the assessment

	student A	student B
(a) mental age of student: assisted on task	9	12
(b) mental age of student: working alone on task	8	8
ZPD (gap between a and b)	1	4

Figure 1.1 'Mental ages' and the 'ZPD'

activity. In this case (Figure 1.1), the children's 'zones of proximal development' would be measured as one and four respectively, and teachers' understandings of their current cognitive development, as well as their teaching strategies towards them, would be adjusted accordingly.

The whole concept of 'mental ages' is a contentious one, as Vygotsky's scepticism about their value seems to imply. His main point, however, is precisely that teachers need richer, more complex information on children's development than standardised tests can provide, and that the acquisition of this information depends upon the teacher working *with* (and also *conversing* with) the child. It also places an emphasis on *formative* assessment as opposed to the kinds of *summative* assessment still widely used in schools through, for example, public examination systems, SATs and the awarding of National Curriculum achievement 'levels' (see Lambert and Lines 2000).

Vygotsky's notion of ZPD, however, does not only have implications for testing and assessing students' development. Development is, argues Vygotsky, actually *created* by instruction, by virtue of which 'the only good kind of instruction is that which marches ahead of development and leads it' (1962, p. 104). According to this theory, pedagogy – in a phrase which carefully marks the break with Piaget's work – should be aimed 'not so much at the ripe as at the ripen*ing* functions' (ibid., emphasis added). To repeat a phrase which is returning to fashion both in the 'official' field of government pronouncements and the 'unofficial' field of school classrooms (Bernstein 1996), according to Vygotskyan theory 'Teachers do make a difference'.

Learning across the curriculum

The second concept introduced by Vygotsky on the subject of development and instruction concerns what he calls 'formal discipline'. Here, Vygotsky takes as his starting-point the criticisms of another developmental psychologist – Thorndike – of Herbartian theories of learning. One of Herbart's central claims had been that instruction in certain school subjects aids the child's development and performance in a range of apparently unrelated subjects: that is to say, it had proposed a particular theory of the 'transferability' of understandings and skills. Thorndike (1914) had rejected Herbart's theory, in favour of a more 'atomistic' model of school instruction in which, in Vygotsky's words, intellectual development is 'compartmentalised according to topics of instruction' (Vygotsky 1962, p. 102).

Vygotsky divides learning – and by implication teaching – into two broad kinds: on the one hand, 'narrowly specialised training in some skills such as typing involving habit formation and exercise' (the way in which some 'behaviourist' models might view all learning and teaching), and on the other hand 'the kind of instruction *given school children*, which activates large areas of consciousness' (1962, p. 97, emphasis added). It is this 'school instruction' – a distinction that has clearly blurred somewhat since the time of Vygotsky's original researches – that interests Vygotsky more and that leads him to conclude that 'instruction in a given subject influences the development of the higher functions far beyond the confines of that particular subject' (1962, p. 102). Vygotsky's elaboration of this (ibid.) is that 'the main psychic functions involved in studying various subjects are interdependent – their common bases are consciousness and deliberate mastery, the principal contributions of the school years'.

These notions of 'consciousness' and 'deliberation' are critical to Vygotskyan understandings of how learning itself develops and undergoes qualitative change: as such, they anticipate the later work of educationalists such as Margaret Donaldson (1978) and Valerie Walkerdine (1982) on the development in young people's thinking from 'concrete' to 'abstract', 'disembedded', 'decontextualised' thinking and reasoning, and indeed constitute an important link with Piaget's theories of the development of human intelligence from the 'sensori-motor' through the 'concrete operational' to the 'formal operational' (Piaget 1926). The 'conscious', 'deliberate' learner is one who is able to reflect on what they have learned, and indeed on the language through which their learning is taking place. They are also able to elaborate and discuss their learning with peers and with their teachers, are capable of making decisions and exercising choices in the pursuit of their learning, and can, to an extent, articulate preferences, beliefs and understandings that might previously have only existed in a 'common-sense', very partially apprehended way.

Practical implications of Vygotskyan theory

To summarise some of Vygotsky's central arguments on development and instruction, we might say that:

- children's cognitive development is achieved most effectively by elaborating ideas and understandings in discussion with their teachers and peers;

- children perform and develop better with help than without help, and ought to be given tasks that will test what is developing in them rather than what has already developed (the notion of stretching not just 'able' students, but those who may be perceived as under-achieving in comparison with any perceived developmental norms);
- children must develop 'conscious mastery' over what they have learned rather than merely being able to recite facts which may have little meaning for them (see also Edwards and Mercer's 1987 distinction between 'principled' and 'ritual' knowledge, returned to in Chapter 3 below);
- the development of such expertise is not subject-specific, and once acquired becomes a tool through which all learning is facilitated and enhanced.

If these are some of the chief tenets of Vygotsky's theory of the relation-ship between instruction and development, where do they lead us in terms of their implications for classroom practice? Some of these implications have already been touched on. They include:

- the importance of not waiting to teach something until the child is deemed able to 'absorb' it (this can apply to the use of reading-schemes in primary schools just as much as to the development of scientific concepts with older students);
- an opposition to the use and typically limited or misleading results of diagnostic tests that forbid any help being given to students by other students or by their teacher;
- an emphasis on the development of independent *processes of learning* rather than the memorising and regurgitating of facts or 'knowledge';
- the importance of perceiving learning, in all phases of schooling, from a genuinely cross-curricular perspective.

A fuller list might include considerations of:

- the importance of working towards a student–teacher relationship which invites and encourages dialogue rather than monologue;
- the importance of establishing forms of classroom organisation which enable and actively encourage collaborative learning and the facility for students to switch easily and naturally between discussion with peers and discussion with the teacher;
- mounting an active challenge to existing notions of intelligence and ability;
- giving full recognition to students' learning as an active – and inter-active – process, and to the changing, developing, provisional nature of a student's concepts and ideas;

- giving full and active recognition to the heuristic value of talking and writing.

All of this suggests a kind of teaching that creates (Bruner 1986) a 'forum' in the classroom, through which both students and teachers can have their say, and in which meanings are 'recreated' through processes of negotiation. It is a model that supports the notion that any effort on the part of the teacher to pass on concepts ready made to the student will result merely in 'empty verbalism' which 'simulates a knowledge of the corresponding concepts, but actually covers up a vacuum' (Vygotsky 1962, p. 83).

Vygotsky and the National Curriculum

Vygotskyan theory may not have contributed much *explicitly* to the content and organisation of the current UK National Curriculum, or to the rationale behind it. However, Vygotsky's theories are particularly important in the way in which the National Curriculum is *used*, in its twin functions as a curriculum plan and an assessment tool. Let us consider, for example, the following example, drawn from a practising teacher's own experience:

> Teacher A assesses student X as having achieved level 5 in a particular subject area, by comparing the student's performance against the descriptors of different levels of attainment (on a scale 1 to 8) provided in the relevant National Curriculum documentation. At a parents' evening organised by the school, teacher A informs student X's parents of the level that has been assigned to this student, explaining that this offers an indicator that their child's work and progress are currently 'average' for someone of their age. On receiving this news, student X's parents ask: 'But how do you know our child is not able to achieve at level 6, 7 or 8?'

The point here is that if Teacher A has not provided student X with *opportunities* to achieve at the higher levels, it will be difficult for the teacher to be sure that the student is incapable of achieving at those levels, and it would seem unfair to state that this was the case. *Is the judgement that student X is able to perform only at level 5 based, in this situation, on a pre-assessment of what the student is capable of achieving on their own?* If so, the danger is that the teacher's judgement that student X has 'achieved' this level of attainment might become a self-fulfilling prophecy that actually hinders the student's progress to more complex and demanding work. Effectively, teacher A will have awarded student X a level (amounting to no less than a 'grade') for their work purely on the basis of what the student had already achieved – a body of achievement which, of course, will have been dependent upon the work set by the teacher, which will in turn have been based upon the teacher's professional judgement as to what the student could currently cope with. The self-fulfilling prophecy then works as follows:

> 'I know that this student is achieving at level 5 from my level descriptors and because the student has successfully completed all the [level 5] work I have set them. I have not set them work that would demand a level of achievement above 5, because this would have been beyond them'.

> If teacher A were to adopt a *Vygotskyan* approach, rather than a 'learning readiness' one, student X might be actively and continuously encouraged to tackle problems and to attempt tasks, with the teacher's assistance, *beyond their current perceived level of achievement*: that is to say, the teacher's inputs would be aimed 'not so much at the ripe as at the ripening functions' (Vygotsky 1962). Such an approach might encourage the teacher to aim at the highest levels of attainment with their students, rather than those supposed to represent 'average' achievement, and to be able to provide a student 'grading' on a more informed basis.

	'Piagetian' perspective	*'Vygotskyan' perspective*
assessment	students assessed against norms; summative and diagnostic testing	individual assessments, student in consultation with teacher; emphasis on formative assessment
organisation	setting by ability levels	no clear reason to set
planning	establishment of whole-class targets with some individual targetting	individual target-setting
teaching	whole-class teaching, with individual tuition – not necessarily transmissive	individual and small-group work; whole-class teaching not excluded
resourcing	relatively inexpensive, depending on how model is put into practice	relatively costly

Figure 1.2 Possible pedagogic implications of 'Piagetian' and 'Vygotskyan' perspectives

We might say that whereas some forms of 'Piagetianism' lead the teacher towards a *summative* application of the National Curriculum levels, 'Vygotsky-anism' is more concerned with *working towards* levels. (For further examples of how 'Piagetian' and 'Vygotskyan' perspectives might lead different pedagogies, see Figure 1.2 above.)

JEROME BRUNER: THE *CULTURAL* CONTEXT OF TEACHING AND LEARNING

As has already been suggested, Vygotsky's work builds on Piaget's by emphasising the social rather than the purely psychological aspects of teaching and learning – an emphasis which, in turn, attaches far greater significance to matters of *pedagogy*. As with Piaget, however, Vygotsky's theory is not above criticism. One of the central difficulties is that Vygotsky appears to make too sharp a distinction between 'scientific' concepts (learned through deliberate instruction in school) and 'everyday' concepts (acquired outside the classroom setting and typically held in an 'unreflecting' way). Vygotsky seems to imply:

a)   that the development of 'scientific' concepts demands and represents a *qualitatively* different kind of learning and intelligence from 'everyday' concepts;
b)   that 'scientific' learning occurs only in classroom situations.

It is doubtful whether this latter suggestion has ever been true. However, in these days of home computers, home–school learning partnerships, homework pacts, and educational television, the dichotomy appears particularly improbable.

It could be argued that Vygotsky's very sharp division between school learning and teaching on the one hand and out-of-school learning and teaching on the other, in which the latter is rather devalued or overlooked, is one aspect of a larger problem with Vygotsky's theory in that it tends, as with Skinner and Piaget, to overlook, in its search for universal patterns of development, the more variable elements of teaching and learning and their cultural bases. In a theory which foregrounds the social, interactive elements of teaching and learning, this absence is particularly noticeable. What we might say of Vygotsky's theory is that for all its acknowledgement of the importance of the social context for learning and teaching, it is largely devoid of any overt political or 'ideological' dimension. It is in the light of this criticism that the work of Jerome Bruner becomes particularly important: for just as Vygotsky built on the work of Piaget to take some account of the *social* aspects of teaching and learning, so Jerome Bruner has built on the work of Vygotsky to suggest a much-needed *cultural* context for teaching and learning.

Jerome Bruner (1963, 1966, 1972, 1996) develops the ideas of Piaget and Vygotsky in at least three significant ways.

1)   First, he introduces us to the notion of 'spiralling' (see *The Process of Education*, 1963, and, for a useful summary, the Preface to *The Culture of Education*, 1996, pp. xi–xii).

   'Spiralling' describes the process by which the learner constantly returns to 'previous' learning and understandings in the light of *new* learning and new experience. Just as this new learning and experience compel us to reconsider and reconfigure previously held concepts and understandings, so those previously-held concepts and understandings help us to make sense of new experiences and conceptualisations as they occur.

   The notion of spiralling implies some degree of *provisionality* in learning. A concept such as love or magnetism or elephant, for example, may acquire a working meaning in the learner's mind at one point in time, but that meaning will be constantly revised as other learning occurs and as new contexts are presented. A child of five may well demonstrate 'knowledge' of what an elephant is – but this elephant is likely to be a very different animal from the one the same person knows ten or twenty years later.

   Spiralling denies the notion of a steady, incremental, step-by-step 'accumulation' of knowledge: it allows and encourages the learner to take steps backwards as well as forwards, and to revise understandings by revisiting them. Such a process will be instantly recognisable to most teachers, and offers both a more 'realistic' and a more dynamic model of the learning process than sometimes appears to be presented in the Piagetian model of development – although there are parallels between the notion of spiralling and Piaget's notion of reconstructing 'on a new plane what was achieved at the preceding level' (Donaldson 1978, p. 139). The notion that learners use new knowledge, understanding and experience to revisit and interrogate existing knowledge and cognitive structures as well as 'past' experience is now generally recognised among cognitive psychologists. As Cummins has recently observed in relation to this matter: 'there is general agreement [. . .] that we learn by integrating new input into our existing cognitive structures or schemata. Our prior experience provides the foundation for interpreting new information. No learner is a blank slate' (Cummins 1996, p. 75).

2)   Bruner's second major development, which may be seen as an authentic *departure* from the work of Piaget and Vygotsky rather than a continuation of it, is that he takes much more account of the role of the home and particularly of the mother/parent in a child's cognitive and linguistic development.

3)   This aspect of Bruner's work opens up a third development, involving considerations of the links and mismatches between the what and how of children's learning 'outside' the school environment and the what and how of their learning *inside* school (see also Tizard and Hughes 1984; Brice Heath 1983; Moore 1999a). It is in the development of this

last issue that Bruner begins to explore issues of *culture* and learning – an exploration that has made his work increasingly *political* as time has gone by.

It is in Bruner's most recent work that we see the issue of culture and education explored in its most directly political way. In *The Culture of Education* (1996), Bruner describes his work in terms of a theoretical journey – the same theoretical journey, it might be said, as that undertaken by large numbers of school-teachers during the same historical period. That journey started in the 1960s, when Bruner's work, like Piaget's and Vygotsky's before it, had been characterised by what Bruner calls a 'preoccupation' with the 'solo, intra-psychic processes of knowing and how *these* might be assisted by appropriate pedagogies' (Bruner 1996, p. xiii, emphasis added). It was only subsequently that his work became increasingly concerned with 'how *culture* affected the way in which children went about their school learning' – a concern arising, specifically, out of 'the discovery of the impact of poverty, racism and alien-ation on the mental life and growth of the child victims of those blights' (ibid.). This 'discovery' shifted Bruner's analyses of the learning process, already fundamentally social in its orientation, increasingly towards the contingent, idiosyncratic aspects of cognitive–linguistic development, helping teachers to understand that when children do badly at school the reasons might lie not in some kind of 'independent' development that can be characterised and analysed outside of any socio-cultural context, but rather in the social *condi-tions* in which the child lives and has grown up. Such a shift led Bruner to criticise Piaget's 'more self-contained, formalistic theories', suggesting that these 'had very little room for the *enabling role of culture* in mental development' (ibid., emphasis added).

Bruner's concern with issues of culture and poverty in education were already evident in the 1970s. In *Poverty and Childhood*, for example, he had argued: 'Persistent poverty over generations creates a culture of survival. Goals are short range, restricted. The outsider and the outside are suspect. One stays inside and gets what one can. Beating the system takes the place of using the system' (Bruner 1972, p. 160).

Such an understanding suggested for Bruner the need for a project – and a conviction on the part of the 'powerless' – which insists that 'their plight is *not* a visitation of fate but a remediable condition' (ibid., p. 161).

Bruner's suggestion that the socio-cultural context of education is as impor-tant to our understanding of how learning works as the more 'intrapsychical' theories of Jean Piaget suggest that teachers need to be as aware of different *ways* or *styles* of learning as of universal patterns of development. It is peda-gogically misleading, for example, as well as ethno-centric, for the teacher to assume that there is one standard way or set of ways in which learning takes place, or that learning styles are independent of broader cultural practices, or that ways of learning may be unaffected by ways of *living*.

This need to understand more about different learning styles is not confined, in Bruner's estimation, to teachers. For Bruner, the school-student, too, 'needs to be as aware of how [they go] about learning and thinking as [they are] about the subject matter [they are] studying' (Bruner 1996, p. 64). This 'metacognitive' aspect of learning, says Bruner, suggests the need for theories of development that are 'intersubjective' rather than 'objectivist'. *Objectivist* theories mark out a *separation* between the (teacher) theorist and the (student) 'subject' – as though the theorist is the 'complete', detached, all-knowing individual able to make some kind of 'pure', culture-free judgement about the subject, including judgements about their learning needs. *Intersubjective* theorists, by contrast, 'apply the same theories to themselves as they do to their clients' (1996, p. 64): that is to say, intersubjective theory is fundamentally *reflexive*, seeking to *use self-understanding* as a way of understanding the minds of others, and vice-versa.

> One major classroom implication of Bruner's argument for intersubjective theorising is that teachers should look carefully at their own practice, behaviour and perceptions when a student's learning appears to falter, rather than looking for the causes exclusively within the behaviour of the student. They should, moreover, bring their knowledge and understanding of themselves as learners to their understandings of how their students may be experiencing and managing their learning.

Bruner's growing emphasis on the cultural contexts of teaching and learning is an important one, which will be examined in greater depth in Chapter 4.

Development theory: the issue of student motivation

As has already been indicated, despite his more recent concern with issues of culture and poverty, much of Bruner's earlier work is more concerned with the culturally – though not socially – 'decontextualised' development of the individual. A significant part of that work concerns itself with issues of student *motivation* and on the implications of this for pedagogy (see, for instance, Bruner 1966, pp. 42–44).

As all practising teachers will recognise, one of the teacher's central tasks is to motivate students to want to learn where such motivation is lacking, and to ensure that existing motivation is not undermined or destroyed by the teaching itself (including, critically, the tasks and materials provided by the teacher). With regard to this, Bruner promotes a model of pedagogy in which the teacher is the *facilitator* of student *explorations* (Bruner 1966, p. 43). As an example of the kinds of issue confronted by the teacher in this role, Bruner suggests: 'A cut-and-dried routine task provokes little exploration; one that is too uncertain may arouse confusion and anxiety, with the effect of reducing exploration' (ibid.).

The issue of motivation cuts across most cognitive development theory. Thus, for Skinner the motivation to learn and to behave appropriately can be

inspired or encouraged by the existence of 'donated' *rewards:* rewards, that is, that emanate from 'outside' the individual learner (merit marks, special privileges, and so on). For Piaget, on the other hand, children are already internally and intrinsically motivated to learn, as part of their human identity: according to this view, the prime task for the teacher is not so much to motivate as to provide the child with what they need for appropriate learning and development to occur (though failure to accomplish this may result in the student becoming demotivated).

In contrasting Skinner and Piaget, it quickly becomes apparent that there are at least two kinds of motivation that we can talk about: that is to say (Scott Baumann *et al.* 1997) 'intrinsic' motivation, that exists 'already' within an individual or within an individual's response to and engagement with a given task, and 'extrinsic' motivation, that needs to be created from external stimuli or that is directed 'outwards' toward the achievement of some external reward. (We need to be careful, however, not to oversimplify these kinds of motivation, and in particular not to forget their cultural and social contexts.)

The notion of '*intrinsic*' motivation is sometimes used by teachers to describe the way in which the interest in a task lies 'within the task itself' (that is to say, a student may want to complete a particular assignment principally because it interests or excites them, rather than in order to achieve a high grade or to please their teacher or parents). It is also, however, very commonly used to refer to motivation that exists, already, 'within the child' (some students appear to be keen learners regardless of the task set, whereas others may seem to find every assignment tedious). Often, of course, both these kinds of 'intrinsic' motivation will be present together at the same time: a student who gets therapeutic pleasure from writing, for example, may find an 'intrinsic' *interest* in – and therefore respond positively to – most written assignments provided by the teacher.

In a further elaboration of these different kinds of motivation, Scott Baumann *et al.* (1997, p. 80) identify four main categories:

- intrinsic motivation, 'which arises from interest in the activity itself';
- social motivation, 'where the task or activity is [. . .] valued in the context of pleasing other people';
- achievement motivation, 'in which the person wishes to do well at the task in order to compete with others'
- instrumental motivation, 'where motivation is brought about by rewards and punishments which are extrinsic to the task'.

> In reality, children are likely to be motivated or demotivated in a variety of ways and in response to a variety of factors. Most teachers are therefore likely to attempt to ensure that their students are initially interested in a learning task or activity, and that they subsequently sustain an interest in it.

Ensuring that interest is sustained in an activity is likely to involve a combination of making the task interesting and relevant 'in itself' as well as explaining its relevance in relation to targets or goals such as achieving grades in public examinations or through National Curriculum assessments.

Teachers will be aware that sometimes a student finds a task boring or difficult in spite of the teacher's efforts to 'liven it up', but persists with it in the knowledge that it will help get them a good exam grade, which, in turn, will help them achieve some other goal like getting a particular job, going to university, or satisfying or pleasing another human being.

Few teachers would deny that the issue of motivation is an important and relevant one in relation to teaching and learning. However, it is not without its difficulties. One of these is that, as with other essentially psychological theories, it can lead teachers – and even governments – to dismiss individual students – or even whole 'groups' of students – on the basis of something that is intrinsically wrong in the students themselves: i.e. that they are 'unmotivated' rather than something that is wrong in society ('why and how are we producing unmotivated children?'). This is sometimes referred to as 'pathologising the individual' (Walkerdine 1982; Moore 1996).

More useful work on school achievement and underachievement needs to consider not just problems that may exist 'within the individual learner' but also the social and cultural contexts within which the individual's learning takes place. This involves taking into account such matters as

- self-image,
- personal expectations,
- the expectations of others,
- the school and classroom environment,
- the culturally-skewed nature of the school curriculum,
- the dominance in the teaching profession of white middle-class teachers, and so on.

It also needs to recognise what Pitt, Britzman and others have called the 'personal' in education. Britzman, for example, applying a psycho-analytical perspective to the observation and analysis of classroom practice and experience, suggests that learning can be a very painful and daunting experience in that rather than being perceived by the potential learner as an empowering opening-up of social, creative and intellectual doors it may also act as a reminder of what we do *not* know, regressing us to infant helplessness and causing us to 'clam up' (Britzman 1999). Elsewhere, Pitt, in an observation that compels us to be particularly careful in our pursuit of student-centred learning, argues that too great an emphasis on a student's personal experience, too sharp a focus on trying to 'bring out' the student in the classroom situation, can also become destructive and debilitating – not *empowering* the student but rendering them impotent (Pitt 1999).

If the concept of motivation is not without its problems, it does allow for the serious consideration of student *choice*. It might suggest, for example, that students may sometimes make deliberate decisions about whether or not to bother with a particular piece of work, an assignment, or even an entire course or courses, rather than just not being 'able' to do it or being 'lazy' or 'intrinsically unmotivated' or suffering from 'attention deficit disorder'. A student's failure to see a point or purpose in an assignment – or even in schooling altogether – can have many causes, including perceptions and experiences of schooling itself. This does not mean that we as teachers should wash our hands of such a student: we will always want to provide learning opportunities and encouragement for the student, whose own views of their future or understandings of the consequences of their refusals may be ill-judged. The point is that we need to understand *why* some students' motivation for school work is so lacking and, in doing this, to avoid lumping all unmotivated students together under the same cause-and-treatment umbrella.

The relevance of developmental theory for teachers

A knowledge of developmental theory is of little use if it merely gets quoted in support of policies based on other (e.g. financial) premises, or if it merely confirms existing practice. It becomes useful when it is used to support improved *practice* – either small-scale (e.g. the practice of individual teachers) or large-scale (e.g. developments in whole educational *systems*). Used in this way, the theory makes us think about educational practice and purposes, and invites us to challenge received educational wisdoms. It also, however, invites us to challenge the theory itself, as a way of developing our own theory and educational philosophy. Indeed, a refusal to do this contributes to much theory becoming 'canonical'. The notion of development by stages, for example, or of there being an effective distinction between language and thought, or of there being a qualitative difference between child and adult thinking are all examples of theories that have achieved 'commonsense' status. If we do not challenge these theories – even if we end up agreeing with them – we may become too easily trapped in them, allowing them to shape and frame the way in which we experience classroom 'reality' and construct our curricula and pedagogy.

The following questions, which relate both to the way in which education is typically structured in terms of primary and secondary education and to the National Curriculum's emphasis on 'levels of achievement', suggest an example of how existing educational theory might restrict the development of further educational theorising and of how such a danger might be avoided through teachers' *interrogations* of theory:

- Do we organise children's learning in terms of stages because independent research teaches us that this is right? Or do we construct the research paradigms and limitations – as well as our own practice – on the basis of practices and discourses that have nothing fundamentally to do with models of teaching and learning at all?

- Do children learn in a certain way 'naturally' – an understanding of which has led, over time, to the adoption of certain curricular and pedagogic practices? Or is it that the adoption of certain pedagogic and curricular practices has *constrained* children to learn in certain ways when there may be other, potentially more effective ways available to them?

Questions such as these need to be seriously addressed by classroom practitioners who want to develop and improve their understandings and practice. It is equally important, however, for the teacher to consider the existence and nature of different *styles* of learning, and not to seek to impose a universal blueprint. As this chapter has implied, there may be a number of possible patterns of development, all of which are worthy both of serious consideration and of serious doubt (see also the discussion of 'multiple intelligences' in Chapter 6 below). It seems to be the case, however, that it is the model of steady, linear, 'incremental' development that is regularly prioritised in current official educational discourses. When OFSTED inspectors visit schools, for example, they appear to expect to be able to perceive – and to report on – development or 'progression' in each student's learning *during the course of the lesson itself* (Moore and Edwards 2000), and not to be interested in the possibility that learning may proceed on occasions – or even at the level of generality – according to other possible models. These include models which acknowledge the possibility of initially slow development becoming increasingly accelerated, and models which suggest an erratic and hard-to-define progress, in which large steps forward may be followed by smaller steps back.

SUMMARY

This chapter has been based on a view that teachers need continually to revisit the questions: *What is education about? How does learning most effectively take place? What are my purposes in this particular lesson or set of lessons?* The chapter is underpinned by a belief that all teachers operate according to theories of learning, and that the more effectively we interrogate those theories, the more effective our practice is likely to be.

In particular, the chapter has elaborated the following general points:

- While some theories of learning tend to concentrate on the 'decontextualised' workings of the human mind, others – like those of Vygotsky and Bruner – take fuller account of the social and cultural contexts of learning. Given that schools are socially and culturally organised institutions, it is particularly important for teachers to be conversant with these theories.

● It is equally important for teachers to be familiar with a *range* of theories of learning and teaching, and to feel confident about selecting those aspects of the theories which they feel are particularly relevant to their practice. The wholesale acceptance or rejection of specific theories is not generally recommended.

● In considering the ways in which learning takes place, teachers also need to develop sophisticated understandings of students' motivation – or lack of motivation – for learning, and to incorporate such understandings into their classroom practice.

These general points have been supported by reference to four specific theorists: Skinner, Piaget, Vygotsky and Bruner. Of these key theorists, the following key points have been made:

● Many aspects of Skinner's theory have proved useful in the areas of pastoral work with school students and in some aspects of classroom management, in particular the rewarding of 'good' work and behaviour rather than the punishing of 'poor' work and behaviour. Skinner's work is generally overly behaviourist, however, and therefore proves less useful pedagogically or in enabling us to understand the complexities of the learning process.

● Piaget has made major contributions to our understandings of the learning process, in particular through his emphasis on human beings as *active meaning-makers* rather than passive 'recipients' of knowledge. This aspect of Piaget's work has become part of a commonsense wisdom that influences much of what we now take for granted as good classroom practice, including the importance of starting with students' experience and encouraging exploration and discovery. Piaget's other major contribution is the notion of 'staged development', which has influenced both pedagogy and curriculum, including the current UK National Curriculum. What is generally lacking in Piaget's work is an account of the complexities of actual learning and teaching in the formal classroom situation, including references to the social and cultural aspects of learning. As a result of this, Piaget has, arguably, little to say about pedagogy itself.

● In contrast to Piaget, Vygotsky has emphasised the social aspects of teaching and learning, describing learning, like language, as *fundamentally social in nature*. With its emphasis on the relationships between student and student and between student and teacher, Vygotsky's work has clearer implications for the actualities of classroom practice, as well as anticipating the value and importance of formative rather than summative assessment.

● Bruner's recent work builds on Vygotsky's, to consider not just the social but the cultural contexts of learning and teaching, including the impact of social conditions on the ways in which learning takes place or fails to take place in schools. Bruner emphasises the need for teachers to think about their own learning and development as well as their students', and to make constructive connections between the two.

SUGGESTED ACTIVITIES

1. Find and note down examples of the impact of (a) Skinner's, (b) Piaget's, (c) Vygotsky's and (d) Bruner's theories in each of the following areas:

    *   the National Curriculum in your subject or a related subject area;
    *   the pedagogic practice of other teachers at your school;
    *   your own pedagogic practice and educational philosophy;
    *   your school's policies and prospectus;
    *   your school's OFSTED report;
    *   any recent educational report or article in a national newspaper.

2. Produce two lists: one showing the aspects of your own theory of teaching and learning that you feel to be in line with or supported by national educational policy (including the National Curriculum and the present public examinations system); a second showing those aspects of your theory which you feel are not supported by public policy.

    To what extent is it possible or desirable to seek to put into practice theories of learning and teaching that are at odds with those promoted by central and/or local government?

SUGGESTED READING

In addition to the original texts of Piaget, Vygotsky and Bruner already cited in this chapter, the following texts are highly recommended:

Wood, D. (1998: second edition) *How Children Think and Learn.* Wood's classic text provides a clear and full account of some of the major theories of children's learning, including those of Piaget and Vygotsky, within an historical context of learning theory that dates back to Ancient Greece. The text is highly recommended for readers wishing to familiarise themselves more thoroughly with major theories of learning and development and their implications for classroom practice but who do not have the time to read original sources.

Barnes, D. (1976) *From Communication to Curriculum.* Though written some years ago, Barnes' book remains a key text for teachers and student teachers looking for support and inspiration in making connections between developmental theories and their own classroom practice. Barnes' book remains firmly rooted in classroom experiences that, despite the passing of the years, will still be familiar to teachers in all subject areas.

Bruner, J. (1996) *The Culture of Education.* Bruner's text offers a fascinating account of the author's own journey from an essentially psychological to a more cultural understanding of how learning works and its implications for pedagogy. This personal journey reflects a broader shift in educational theory away from an over-concern with 'internal' development towards a view of teaching and learning as essentially social and cultural in nature and as heavily dependent for success on the development and pursuit of appropriate pedagogies. The book also contains Bruner's theory of the importance of *reflexivity* in the teaching process, along with a useful summary of his important theory of 'spiralling'.

2 Teaching, Learning and Education

This chapter examines some of the often conflicting rationales for compulsory state education, and the different notions of teaching and learning that underpin them. The chapter considers not only the 'how' of teaching but also its 'what', drawing links between curriculum content, pedagogic styles and underlying notions of what education is – or should be – for. Readers are invited to consider the relationships between their preferred theories of teaching and learning and their own and central government's views as to the purposes of public education.

EDUCATION: PURPOSE AND PRACTICE

Educational aims and methods are inevitably value-led, concerned with the kind of society we wish to promote, and the kind of education best suited for that aim.

(Woods 1996, p. 14)

Why did such institutions [as schools] come to exist in the first place? What was, and is, their cultural significance?

(Doyle 1989, p. 2)

Orthodox curriculum theory derives its analysis of curriculum process from the teacher's objectives; [. . .] since the learner's understandings are the raison d'être of schooling, an adequate curriculum theory must utilize an interactive model of teaching and learning.

(Barnes 1976, p. 9)

The previous chapter considered some of the major theories of learning and teaching that we might expect to inform public education, and began to consider the extent to which those theories reflected central government policy on the one hand and practitioner wisdom on the other. There is another, equally important issue, however, that underpins issues of learning and development theory, and that is the issue of what *purpose* or *purposes* public education is intended to serve. If we are to make any sense of theories of teaching and learning as we endeavour to put them into practice, it is important to be clear about these purposes and the extent to which the educational purposes espoused by central government match or fail to match the educational purposes of classroom practitioners.

In this regard, there are some very large questions that teachers need to ask themselves:

1)   Why *was* the decision made to introduce compulsory formal education in the first place? What thinking went into the particular style and content of that education, and how, if at all, has that thinking changed over the years?
     To what extent are the 'official' purposes of education as revealed in government policy the same as teachers' 'unofficial' purposes (i.e. their own personal views as to what education should be for and about)?
2)   By what processes and practices do children learn most efficiently and effectively?
     Do different notions of what children *should* learn in school suggest different models of learning and different kinds of teaching?
3)   To what extent do the official purposes of education and the available theories of learning and teaching articulate with one another, and to what extent do they work oppositionally and dysfunctionally?

'Official' purposes of education

There has been no shortage over the years of official rationales for compulsory state education and the content of the curriculum. Every time a Government White Paper or Education Bill appears, it is sure to be prefaced by remarks about the broad purposes of education underpinning the precise measures and changes that are being recommended at any given point in time. While these purposes may vary from decade to decade or from country to country, a thorough reading of the documentation tells us that certain common purposes or rationales emerge time and time again. Figure 2.1, drawn from relatively recent UK government documentation, suggests what the chief of these purposes and rationales have been in recent years. The aims are mostly (with the exception, perhaps, of the last) laudable ones, to which the majority of teachers would readily subscribe. It is in the detail, however, that the difficulty occurs, and in particular:

- in the *cultural selections* (Lawton 1975) that constitute the school *curriculum*;
- in the typically 'hidden' motives behind those selections;
- in the constraints and prompts given to *pedagogy* by that curriculum.

Education:

- gives people more and better life and career opportunities

- helps people make therapeutic use of their leisure time

- develops peoples' knowledge and understanding of themselves and the world

- encourages people to work together in a spirit of tolerance and mutual kindness

- produces more fulfilled, 'rounded', law-abiding people

- gives youngsters a broader perspective on life and the world

- helps make the nation more competitive and prosperous

Figure 2.1 Official rationales for formal state education

(Sources include: 1943 Government White Paper on *Educational Reconstruction*; 1944 *Education Act*; 1992 Government White Paper *Choice and Diversity*.)

Although the official purposes of education as outlined above do not *necessarily* dictate the shape and nature of the curriculum itself, or the way in which teachers configure their practice, it is nevertheless true that embedded and implied within these purposes are certain dominant notions as to how the purposes might best be achieved: that is to say, some of these purposes 'suggest' a certain kind of curriculum, which in turn encourages teachers into certain pedagogical styles rather than others.

An example of how this looks in practice (reported in Moore and Edwards 2000), is the way in which public examinations that overemphasise the memorising of large numbers of facts (on the basis of a perceived purpose of providing students with 'knowledge' about the world) can push teachers away from encouraging their students to discuss *issues* towards much more tightly controlled reading and writing activities and to the promotion of 'teacher-centred', front-of-class pedagogies. Another often-quoted example is the way in which an official and insistent emphasis on students needing to develop, as a major priority, basic reading, writing and numeracy skills (with increasing Government prescription as to how such skills should be taught and learned), coupled with the persistence of a fragmented subject-based curriculum, can lead teachers to emphasise, in turn, the development of basic skills and the memorising of a very narrow range of 'validated knowledge', over the development of more sophisticated creative and reasoning skills or overactive engagement with the physical and social world (see Davies 1998; Kelly 1998).

Alongside the overarching rationales for having compulsory State education in the first place, there coexist many theories and views as to how learning most effectively takes place, such as those we have already considered in Chapter 1. As we have already seen, very complex and influential theories of learning have been developed in recent years by such educationalists as Skinner, Piaget, Vygotsky and Bruner. These do not always wholly accord with one another, and indeed in some cases there are major areas of disagreement. Teachers, however, draw selectively on these theories in their teaching, as do lecturers providing courses of initial and continuing teacher education. Though such theories may also be used, selectively, to inform government policy *implicitly*, there is evidence to suggest that they are surprisingly overlooked *explicitly*, both in official government policy related to educational purposes and in government-sponsored committees and working-parties aimed at improving *practice*.

> In the Plowden Report of 1967, there are just seven brief references to Piaget and none to Vygotsky; in the Bullock Report of 1975, there are no references to Piaget and just two to Vygotsky; and in the Warnock Report of 1978 there are no references at all to either of these major theorists. Such a situation may be seen as indicating that in terms of educational policy and development there remains something of a divide between what *education* is seen to be for and how effective *learning* is perceived to take place.

Mismatches between educational purpose and learning theory

If we accept that there are both broad *purposes* for state education (essentially to do with the development of social and basic learning skills and with the 'acquisition' of knowledge and understanding), as well as certain theories about how learning best takes place (and indeed, about what learning itself actually *is*), the question inevitably suggests itself:

> What happens if, in the teacher's practice, the manifest official purposes of education do not suggest or readily articulate with the teaching style suggested by the teacher's own philosophy and theory of learning?

The potential difficulty here is when there is a mismatch between the officially cited purposes of formal education, with its hidden implications for pedagogic style, and the models of learning development favoured by the teachers themselves, with their own implications for *curriculum* style. As we shall see, this becomes an even greater problem when we consider the possibility that, in addition to the 'official official' reasons given for state education, there may exist, in the shadows of these official rationales, a set of 'unofficial official' reasons that cannot, for political reasons, ever be made explicit within particular brands of democratic capitalism.

Elements of Purpose	Elements of Learning Theory
• to encourage co-operation	• learning social and collaborative
• to develop understanding	• learning demands oral and group work
• to develop basic skills	• interactive pedagogic style

a

• to encourage competition

• to acquire items of knowledge

• to acquire basic skills

• learning requires active/practical engagement with ideas

• learning characterised by problem-solving and risk-taking

b

• learning psychological and individual in character

• learners work best quietly and alone

• teacher transmits knowledge, understanding and skills to receptive students

Figure 2.2 Articulations between purpose and theory of education

Figure 2.2 suggests some of the difficulties that can occur for teachers when there are apparent areas of mismatch between what official policy instructs us or suggests we should do, and the models of learning and development we wish to put into practice (themselves embedded in our own views as to what education should be about). Any cited educational purpose above the line a–b articulates relatively easily with any corresponding theory or philosophy of teaching and learning above the line. The same applies for purposes and theories sited below the line. Difficulties occur when the line has to be 'crossed'. Thus, while it may be relatively easy for teachers to see how the 'social' educational need to promote co-operation articulates with a teaching style that favours group-work *as a means of developing learning and learning skills*, it may – to return to our previous example – be less easy to reconcile a teaching style that favours student *explorations* with an educational purpose more concerned with the 'acquisition' of a 'body of knowledge'.

One way of masking these potential divisions and mismatches within the official educational discourses is to describe education in terms of 'empowerment'. The notion of empowering students – especially those who have been historically disempowered – is a very powerful and popular one, that appears to prioritise an overriding purpose (the purpose of empower*ing*) above issues of teaching and learning *per se*. Politicians can thus argue, without much fear of contradiction, that basic literacy fundamentally *empowers* children, and that it must therefore be prioritised over other, less obviously empowering achievements that teachers might have in mind for their students. The question remains, however: To what extent can education really empower children, if the social system *within which it takes place* is fundamentally disempowering?

In reality, the situation is not nearly as straightforward as Figure 2.2 may appear to imply. In practice, teachers may find that some of the 'official' purposes of state education (or even some *elements* of particular purposes) match their own purposes and preferred styles while others do not, and that, even when there appears to be a strong element of mismatch, ways can often be found to make appropriate accommodations (Moore and Edwards 2000). Furthermore, although certain purposes may *suggest* certain practice, they do not necessarily *demand* such practice.

> It is quite possible, for example, that the demand for students to acquire basic skills can be accommodated within a classroom that emphasises the social, collaborative aspects of teaching and learning, and that encourages group work, oral work, exploratory work, problem-solving and risk-taking.

THE CONTENT–PROCESS DEBATE

Disjunctions between the implications of official educational agendas and the theoretical and philosophical views of practising teachers have spawned many of the central educational debates of the last hundred years. In particular, they are responsible for the confrontation between an often-repeated purpose of education, still embedded in many aspects of the National Curriculum and public examination syllabuses, that the priority for school-students is to acquire a certain 'body of knowledge' (an emphasis on curriculum over pedagogy and on content over process), and an alternative view, held very strongly by many teachers, that education should be much more about helping their students to develop learning *skills* through which they may not only 'acquire' knowledge but interrogate it independently: that is to say, more of a skills-based approach in which pedagogy is prioritised alongside curriculum and in which process – *how* children learn – is prioritised over content – *what* they learn.

Whereas the straightforward acquisition of a body of knowledge might suggest one form or set of forms of pedagogy, the development of learning *skills* might suggest another. It could be argued, for instance, that a *transmissive* teaching style, in which the teacher 'passes on information' to students orally or via worksheets and books, sits more comfortably with an educational purpose concerned principally with the memorising of information and the promotion of obedience, while a more student-centred ('progressive' or 'constructivist') approach is generally better suited to an educational purpose aimed at encouraging independence of thought and the challenging and interrogation of perceived wisdoms.

As Barnes has argued in relation to this matter:

> As the form of [classroom] communication changes, so will the
> form of what is learnt. One kind of communication will encourage
> the memorizing of details, another will encourage students to
> reason about the evidence, and a third will head them towards
> the imaginative reconstruction of a way of life. From the
> communication they will also learn what is expected of them
> as pupils. . . . They will find out how far they are expected to take
> part in the formulation of knowledge, or whether they are to act
> mainly as receivers.
>
> (Barnes 1976, p. 14. See also Freire 1972)

For Barnes and others, a clear distinction can be drawn between 'exploratory' teaching and learning and 'transmissive' teaching and learning. The latter is characterised by the teacher's handing down of formally approved knowledge ('cold' knowledge, as Barnes calls it) to their students, thereby maintaining barriers between 'school knowledge' and what the student already knows about the world from their out-of-school experience (referred to by Barnes as 'action knowledge'). *Exploratory* learning, by contrast, tends to break down such barriers by encouraging 'the learner's attempts at *understanding*' (Barnes 1986, pp. 79–80, my emphasis).

In exploratory teaching and learning, what is important is not just the selection of information to which the student is guided, but also the ways in which they are helped to interrogate, to make sense of, to challenge and to utilise that information for future purposes of their own choosing. The point about exploratory learning is not just that students should be 'enculturated' into certain knowledges, skills and practices in ways that may (for instance) fit them for the workplace, but that they should be enabled to leave school as active, willing and independent learners: a pedagogy which is more interested in the development of the student's *mind* than in covering a pre-set and very selective curriculum.

While Barnes does not suggest a straight choice for teachers between the exploratory and the transmissive modes of teaching and learning (most teachers today are likely to use both sets of techniques, depending on circumstances), he does suggest that the popularity or 'persistence' of the transmission approach is 'due partly to its capacity for maintaining discipline', which in turn relates to wider societal agendas and strategies for ensuring a compliant, manageable and (from the perspective of those who possess the most power and wealth) *useful* workforce (Barnes 1986, p. 85). That is to say, Barnes links a particular pedagogic style and curriculum content with a perhaps unspoken educational purpose: in this case, to 'control', 'select' and 'contain' the working population (Barnes 1986, p. 85). This is not an uncommon representation of state education, and one that educationalists continue to revisit. Paul Ernest, for example, criticises the current UK National Curriculum for *Mathematics* on the grounds that, in its current 'unique structure . . . for all students [it] serves social reproduction purposes rather than defensible educational purposes' (Ernest 1998, p. 25; see, too, Apple 1995).

By way of illustrating this point, Ernest offers the following comparison:

> An illuminating analogy is that between the National Curriculum structure and a fractional distillation device as used in chemistry or the petro-chemical industry. Fractional distillation ensures that different types of products are produced and tapped off at different heights in the distillation tower. Likewise, pupils at age 5 are fed into the National Curriculum structure, and tapped off at different heights from the framework. Low-grade products come out at levels 1-4, medium-grade products come out at levels 5-6, high-grade products come out at levels 7 or above.

Ernest's claim is that

> both social class and future career prospects of students correlate with these levels. Low gradings correspond to the semi-skilled, unskilled and unemployed. Medium gradings correspond to skilled blue and white collar workers. High level gradings correspond to managerial and professional occupations.
>
> (Ernest 1998, p. 25)

Like Barnes, Ernest suggests here that education, whatever teachers might want to *make of it*, is really *designed* not so much for the benefit of the individual student as for the reproduction of a compliant work-force in which some jobs – for reasons that have nothing to do with hard work or intrinsic value – will always be better paid than others. Such reproduction is ensured through the development of content-specific curricula rather than more open-ended forms of curriculum in which process is prioritised and individual strengths, weaknesses and needs are catered for.

PURPOSE, THEORY AND PEDAGOGIC ECLECTICISM

While most teachers will readily recognise the correlations between stated and unstated educational *purposes* on the one hand and particular *forms* and *styles* of teaching on the other, they will also recognise that this is a much more complex issue than may at first appear. One reason for this complexity is that there may well be discrepancies *within* each of the categories *'purposes of education'* and *'theory and practice of education'*. It is clearly the case, for instance, that different teachers – often working within the same school – espouse different views as to what constitutes the best educational practice (Moore and Edwards 2000), and that policy makers are by no means unanimous as to what the purposes of education are or should be (although, as has already been suggested, certain 'official' purposes do get repeated again and again down the years).

Another reason for the complexity is that in some respects there may be a clear *match* between purpose and practice in a school, while in other areas, in the same school and even with the same teacher's practice, there may be a manifest *mismatch*. This complexity is illustrated below in *Case Study 2.1*.

Case Study 2.1

- In one secondary school – School A – there exists a very close and very deliberate match between a whole-school programme aimed at promoting citizenship, and certain aspects of official documentation and policy related to this area of the curriculum and to the purposes of education more generally.

- The teachers' practice at this school, of encouraging lively classroom discussion in 'citizenship sessions', in which students are encouraged to explore feelings, attitudes and beliefs within an atmosphere of tolerance, pluralism and trust, accords well with notions of education as producing 'happy', 'rounded', 'balanced' children (DES 1992, p. 1) and of education for citizenship as being about producing 'an active and politically-literate citizenry convinced that they can influence government and community affairs at all levels' (QCA 1998, p. 9). Similarly, the school's English Department's policy, as part of its subject-specific citizenship work, of helping students achieve very specific kinds of literacy appropriate for selecting, reading and critiquing national newspapers matches *National Curriculum* requirements for the subject area (DFE 1995, pp. 19–21) as well as meeting official concerns about youngsters' understandings of national and international institutions and socio-political events (e.g. QCA 1998, pp. 15–16). In these cases, there appears to exist a workable match between the official perception of the purposes of *this aspect* of the school curriculum, of the teachers' perception of it, and of the pedagogic approach adopted in achieving those purposes.

- Such a harmony does not exist at all times and in every aspect of the curriculum, however, as it is experienced by students and teachers at this school. Geography teachers complain, for example, that the current examination syllabuses are too demanding and restrictive (in terms of the sheer amount of information that children are required to absorb and reproduce) for teachers and students to be able to dwell on what the teachers perceive as important *social* issues, or to explore interesting and educationally justifiable 'side-routes'. The school's English and D&T teachers, meanwhile, argue that in some important respects the National Curriculum works *against* what they believe to be the best educational practice – in the first case, by prescribing a canon of literary texts which severely limits opportunities for a fully pluralistic and fully critical approach to their subject area, and in the second by prohibiting opportunities for undertaking collaborative design projects
- Even in the citizenship sessions, all is not sweetness and light. Many teachers, for example, express deep concern about unproblematised 'guidance on moral values' (QCA 1998, p. 11) and, while they broadly support the notion of 'common citizenship' (ibid., p. 170), are far less enthusiastic about the idea of reproducing a 'national identity'.

(Moore and Edwards 2000).

Case Study 2.1 suggests that teachers' and schools' 'pedagogic identities' – i.e. how they perceive and present themselves and their professional practice – are constructed from a range of pressures, philosophies and discourses, and that they are typically situated within a range of discursive frameworks which may at times seem to pull them in different, perhaps even contradictory directions.

Recently, Basil Bernstein has considered precisely this set of issues in his discussion of the extent to which teachers' professional identities are currently constructed from a variety of educational *traditions* (Bernstein 1996, pp. 78–79; see also Halpin and Moore forthcoming). Bernstein begins by drawing a distinction between three broad categories of pedagogic identity, which he calls the 'retrospective' identity, the 'prospective' identity and the 'decentred' identity (Bernstein 1996, pp. 78–79).

- The *retrospective* pedagogic identity, prompted and supported by the policies and rhetoric of central government, involves schools and teachers drawing upon 'narratives of the past' to provide 'exemplars and criteria' for current practice: that is to say, it appeals directly to *existing* educational traditions – often, for no better reason than that they *are* traditions.

  In terms of curriculum content and construction, the retrospective pedagogic identity supports, uncritically, the division of school learning into areas of subject knowledge, and provides little or no support for radical changes of content within the individual curricula of discrete subject areas ('English', 'Maths', 'Art', 'Science' and so on). It may also be seen to support certain forms of classroom *practice*, such as tight teacher control over the introduction and elaboration of subject knowledge or curricularised skills.

- Bernstein's notion of the *prospective* identity is also prompted and supported by central government. Unlike the retrospective identity, however, the prospective identity links current practice and philosophy to certain (generally materialistic) understandings of the possible and likely *future* needs of society and the individual citizen: that is to say, it seeks to incorporate 'traditional values' into a 'modernising' turn.

  Unlike the retrospective identity, which seeks to 'stabilise' the past in an unfolding future, resisting any potentially threatening change, the prospective identity is characterised by its *selective recontextualisation* of certain features of past practice to defend or raise, through local practice, *economic* performance at the *national* level. Examples of the promotion of the prospective identity are to be found in repeated government emphases on the traditional 'basics' of education, and in the promotion of ICT and citizenship, within an otherwise unchanging curriculum structure, as a means of ensuring national economic competitiveness.

- The third identity proposed by Bernstein – the local or *decentred* identity – has two sub-varieties: the *instrumental identity*, in which the identity of the school and its teachers is geared mainly towards – and to a degree shaped by – the packaging and selling of the school *by the school* as a product in the local marketplace; and the *therapeutic* identity, which is forged by teachers' and schools' 'personal' and principled views as to what a good education should be about.

  The *instrumental* identity relates to such matters as the ways in which schools present themselves in prospectuses, through parents' evenings, through their school uniform and so forth, with a view to attracting parents and their children to the school.

  The *therapeutic* identity relates more to teachers' and schools' own views and practices on such matters as uniform, selection of students, student groupings and pedagogic styles, *regardless of the impact of such views and practices on student recruitment*.

Bernstein's theory invites questions as to the extent to which these varying types of identity – which are presented as not mutually exclusive and which may all be present in a school or a school classroom at any given point in time – are (a) constructively accommodated by schools and teachers or (b) lead to confusion, uncertainty and conflict (see, for example, Bernstein 1996, pp. 70 and 75; and Halpin, Moore *et al.* 1999–2001).

To return to 'School A' (*Case Study 2.1*) by way of example, this particular school maintains an essentially 'educational' or *principled* ('therapeutic') view that mixed-ability teaching is the most egalitarian and therefore the most acceptable way of organising students' learning.

At the same time, however, the school incorporates into its mixed-ability arrangements *elements* of setting and banding (including withdrawing certain students from some lessons for 'special attention'), partly in order to satisfy the demands of actual and potential parents who see their children as 'more able' and find mixed-ability teaching threatening or unacceptable.

The school may maintain its pro-mixed-ability stance in its own internal communications, but may modify this stance in its public voice – through, for example, its prospectus. Furthermore, while it may maintain a large measure of mixed-ability teaching on paper, much of that teaching might involve actual classroom practices in which students are rarely permitted to talk to one another, or are grouped according to notions of ability within the individual classroom, or are given very different kinds of work from one another under the banner of differentiation.

CURRICULUM AND CONTROL

Concerns about the extent to which the externally-fixed curriculum and imposed educational policies may impede the development of what teachers perceive as good educational practice are very real and cannot be ignored. Robert Hull, some years ago, provided the following shrewd insights into the way in which an externally-imposed curriculum – typically constructed around notions of 'possessed knowledge' rather than learning processes – can constrain and impede teachers, nudging them irresistibly in directions that are ultimately unhelpful for their students. Hull's particular interest is not just in the ways in which the externally-imposed curriculum might constrain teachers' *pedagogic* agendas, but in the ways in which the *language* of education (we might say, the language of *curriculum*) impedes teachers in any efforts to move beyond curricular constraints into areas that might offer opportunities for the development of learning skills and strategies *per se*. In such a situation, says Hull, 'concepts . . . come to be embodied in a kind of minimal grammar, a selection of language forms which is handled as if it were the concept itself' (Hull 1988, p. 49). The form of knowledge implicit in such a process Hull calls 'objectivistic', because (ibid.) 'it seems to define knowledge as an object and so equates knowing, and coming to know, with its possession; it effaces the crucial distinction between the learner's subjective experience of moving towards knowledge and the objectifying of a knowledge finally achieved'.

In Hull's interpretation, the constraints of the imposed curriculum and attendant forms of assessment often *trap* the teacher, not only in terms of what they do and say with their students but also, critically, in terms of how they pace their lessons. Echoing the fears of the geography teachers at School A, cited above, the emphasis on itemised knowledge rather than the development of learning skills sets up a possibility that 'the temporal rhythms that engage the pupil will not be those of [his or her] own learning but the imposed pace of the objectivistically defined "course", in which "knowledge" means a predefined set of items of content each with its own time-value' (Hull 1988, p. 131).

According to this analysis, the itemised curriculum, driven by a particular, knowledge- and culture-based understanding of what education should be *for* (essentially, the absorption of certain aspects or items of culture and cultural knowledge deemed, by the dominant culture, to have indispensable status) actually works *against* a theory of teaching and learning that, through its insistence on the development of independent and transferable learning skills, proposes a very different view of how classroom practice should look. In this view, what the curriculum achieves, in effect, is the blocking of particular forms of pedagogy ('student-centred', 'constructivist', 'experience-based', 'collaborative' and so forth), linked to particular sets of learning outcomes, by the imposition both of a certain number of items to be 'learned' and of a strict time-frame within which to learn them. Pedagogy which seeks to promote exploration and discovery is simply not allowed the time and space that is essential for its effective practice, and may even be pathologised as 'wasting time'.

THE SCHOOL CURRICULUM AND THE 'OUTSIDE WORLD'

In addition to the suggestion that there may be critical areas of match and mismatch between (a) the official purposes of education and the theories of learning by which teachers operate, and (b) the official purposes of education and the 'unofficial' purposes espoused by teachers, it is also often argued that there is a divide – perhaps a *growing* divide – between the skills and knowledge that young people are encouraged to develop and acquire *at school* and the skills and knowledge that are needed for individual and collective success in 'the world outside' (Blenkin *et al.* 1992; Kemmis *et al.* 1983; Apple 1980).

Such a possibility was mooted in 1971 by the educationalist Michael Young when, by way of his list of the 'organising principles' of the academic curriculum in UK schools, he commented on the extent to which 'most knowledge in a literate culture is fundamentally at odds with that of daily life and common experience' (Young 1971b, p. 38) – a comment which post-dates similar observations made by Goody and Watt in 1962 and by John Dewey in 1939, the latter of whom, on the basis of the manifest mess human beings appeared to be making of their lives, called into question the very principles upon which organised education was based and from which it had drawn its official rationale (see, for instance, Dewey 1939, p. 131).

More recently, criticisms of school curricula's 'out-of-touchness' have focused on issues of exclusivity/diversity and certainty/uncertainty: exclusivity and certainty, that is, in the curriculum, contrasted with a growing diversity and uncertainty in the way in which the world is generally experienced (Hargreaves 1994). Dan Davies has recently addressed both of these issues in critiquing the current UK National Curriculum for Science as 'Euro-centric, absolutist and monolithic, treating scientific knowledge as absolute and value-free' (Davies 1998, p. 46).

Criticisms like this, often made of national curricula for science and mathematics but also of humanities subjects such as English and geography (Moore 1998), often configure existing curricula as outmoded in their attempts to impose order and certainty on an essentially *uncertain* universe. With their dogged insistence on the achievement of right answers, tidy explanations and neat labels, such curricula are sometimes described in terms of a *modernist* project rooted in old-fashioned *Enlightenment* thinking (see Figure 2.4). An example of this kind of critique is offered by Hamilton, who describes the so-called modernist educational view as perceiving and seeking to represent the world as 'an ordered place', and of the 'elements of the world of knowledge as topologically invariant' (Hamilton 1993, p. 55). Elsewhere, Standish, in an oblique reference to the deficiencies of the school curriculum, suggests that '[m]odernism . . . assumes the . . . possibility of completeness' that is 'at odds both with human nature and with education' (Standish 1995, p. 133).

> The central point being made by Davies and some of these other commentators is that the subject-based curriculum, with its culture-specific selections of sanctioned skills and knowledge, is no longer sufficient – if it ever was – as an explainer and interpreter of the physical and social world. Nor does it necessarily provide students with the best *preparation* for working and social life.

In an alternative criticism of school curricula, James Cummins (1996) has focused on changing socio-economic conditions and relations of power in the wider world, focusing on the 'Euro-centric' and 'value-free' aspects of curriculum content and style referred to by Davies (1998). In what amounts, effectively, to an argument for the development of a post-colonial curriculum for a post-colonial world, Cummins critiques current curricula, still embedded in a colonial past, as being no longer appropriate either for the individual or for the 'competitiveness' of the nation state (DES 1992). For Cummins, nations whose school and wider social curricula persist in validating only a very narrow range of cultural expertise and of prioritising culture-specific itemisations of knowledge are in danger of financially and culturally collapsing in upon themselves, since: 'cultural diversity is the norm in both the domestic and international arenas. Around the world we see unprecedented population mobility and intercultural contact. [. . .] Educators concerned with preparing

students for life in the 21st century must educate them for global citizenship'
(Cummins 1996, p. 224). For Cummins, the reality of life outside schools is
that 'coercive relations of power' – that is to say, the racist, classist, sexist and
culturist practices embedded in a colonial past – have

> reached a point of diminishing returns, even for those socially
> advantaged groups whose interests they are intended to serve. The
> fiscal and social costs of maintaining the current structure of privilege
> and resource distribution far outstrip the costs that would be involved
> in shifting to more collaborative relations of power.
>
> (ibid., p. 222)

In terms of curriculum reform, Cummins argues, educators need to recognise
'[that] the economic and diplomatic realities of our independent global society
in the 21st century demand enormous critical literacy and problem-solving
abilities and the constant crossing of cultural and linguistic boundaries' (ibid.,
p. 220).

Cummins clearly sees both a political and a pragmatic set of arguments for
revising the content and style of school curricula to make them more relevant to a changing, post-colonial, ever-shrinking world, in which it is not
only ideologically right but also makes financial sense to treat people equally
and to enforce some sort of redistribution of wealth.

A not dissimilar point is made by Jerome Bruner who, having wisely pointed
out that 'schooling is only one small part of how a culture inducts the young
into its canonical ways', suggests that:

> schooling may even be at odds with a culture's other ways of
> inducting the young into the requirements of communal living. Our
> changing times are marked by deep conjectures about what schools
> should be expected to 'do' for those who choose to or are compelled
> to attend them – or for that matter, what school *can* do, given the
> force of other circumstances.
>
> (Bruner 1996, p. ix)

Bruner's observations lead him to ask:

> Should schools aim simply to reproduce the culture. [. . .] Or would
> schools, given the revolutionary changes through which we are
> living, do better to dedicate themselves to the equally risky, perhaps
> equally quixotic, ideal of preparing students to cope with the
> changing world in which they will be living?
>
> (ibid.)

What Bruner is really asking here is: should school curricula be 'retrospective', taking their content from 'the past' (that is to say, very limited selections from what has, in the views of some people, been most useful and successful and important in previous social and cultural practices), or should they rather be '*pro*spective', preparing students for – and helping them to shape – the future world in which they will be living: a world in which once-dominant cultural forms may rapidly find their authority eroded? To quote Robert Hughes, who clearly supports the latter view: 'In the world that is coming, if you can't navigate difference, you've had it' (Hughes 1993, p. 100).

> Bruner's point strikes at the heart of the issue of what formal education is fundamentally *for*. Is it, for example, to prepare students for an *existing* world – or, rather, some people's conception of an existing world (a project that might prioritise cultural reproduction and compliance)? Or is it to prepare them for a *changing* world, in whose transformations they might play an *active, contributory* part (a project that might prioritise critical literacy and critical citizenship)?

These issues will be returned to in Chapter 6, when we consider possible curricular and pedagogic alternatives to current dominant curricular forms. In this current chapter, however, it may prove more useful to look backwards rather than forwards, in order to develop a better understanding of where current curricular and pedagogic thinking and practice have come from if not from the theories of how students learn that we have already considered in Chapter 1.

EDUCATIONAL POLICY: THE NOTION OF THE 'UNOFFICIAL OFFICIAL' AGENDA

The work of commentators such as Cummins, Bruner and Davies invites us to ask the following key questions about the purposes of education:

- Where do the selections that comprise the current school curriculum originate?
- What perceived educational purpose(s) do they serve?
- Are those selections appropriate, either in terms of what we know about learning and development, or in terms of what skills will actually prove useful in the rapidly-changing world outside the school walls?

Such questions have been articulated by many educationalists, including Henry Giroux who suggests that the educational project for the next century should entail a serious debate that is not just about the 'management and economics of education', as is so often the case, but that addresses 'the most basic questions of purpose and meaning. What kind of society do we want? How do we educate students for a truly democratic society? What conditions do we need to provide teachers [. . .] and students for such an education to be meaningful and workable?' (Giroux 1992, p. 241).

At the heart of these commentators' observations are serious questions about the 'official' purposes of formal state education as indicated in central government papers and policies, and the extent to which there may lurk, behind those purposes, 'hidden' purposes (what we might call 'unofficial official' purposes), that may also be detected in government policies but that may be less fully articulated.

Central questions here are:

- Has public education really been about the development of the 'happy' 'rounded' individual in the happier, more successful society?
- Or has it, rather, been more about preserving the status quo – about equipping young people with the skills demanded of a socio-economic system that continues to privilege and to de-privilege its people, and that maintains the dominant social classes in their position of domination?
- *That is to say, has public education been, fundamentally, more about 'social engineering' than about 'personal and collective empowerment'?*

Just as Figure 2.1 drew on relatively recent government documentation to suggest some of the 'official official' purposes of education, so Figure 2.3, below, draws on earlier government documentation to suggest some possible elements of an enduring 'unofficial official' educational agenda. If such elements generally display, nowadays, a relatively low profile in public pronouncements, this may be because they are unlikely to have the same popular appeal as those more vociferously proclaimed 'official official' elements. Certainly, they are likely to be far less acceptable to many *teachers*, who are more likely (Bernstein 1996) to prioritise the 'therapeutic', self-improving aspects of education than the more utilitarian, economics-driven ones.

The possible contents of the 'unofficial official' agenda behind formal state education are, as has already been indicated, drawn from existing government documentation; in particular, they are drawn from some of the principal arguments put forward by politicians and educationalists – both in favour of and, interestingly, in opposition to – the introduction of universal state education, at a time when that introduction was still a matter for serious consideration and debate rather than a *fait accompli*.

In considering those arguments, we need to take account of two further matters: first, the extent to which 'unofficial official' rationales underpinning formal education *consciously and deliberately* seek to perpetuate economic and social divisions within society; and second, the extent to which apparently egalitarian, non-economics-driven rationales may contribute *less consciously* but nevertheless very significantly to the perpetuation of such divisions.

Education:

- ■ is designed to meet the changing needs of capitalism, to ensure that the rich stay rich

- ■ promotes and teaches certain kinds of 'morality' and 'values' aimed at preserving class structures and reducing profit-damaging crime

- ■ is designed to promote various forms of competition, including patriotism, to maintain the *status quo* and increase profit margins

- ■ seeks to compensate for the disintegration of organised religion and parental 'failings' by providing an alternative mechanism for social control

- ■ offers a convenient way of regulating the labour supply while at the same time freeing parents (including women) to go to work

- ■ ensures, through the coexistence of a private and a public sector, the organised division and regular supply of labour into owners/managers on the one hand and 'workers' on the other

---

Figure 2.3 Possible unofficial official rationales for formal state education

(Main sources: McLure 1986: *Educational Documents: England and Wales 1816 to the Present Day*; Selleck (ed.) (1968) *The New Education 1870–1914.*)

THE HISTORIC PURPOSES OF EDUCATION (1): ENLIGHTENMENT AND THE DEVELOPMENT OF THE INDIVIDUAL CITIZEN

If we begin with the original official arguments *in favour of* state education, we may find little evidence to support the view that there is a 'hidden' or 'unofficial official' agenda behind the introduction, perpetuation and style of formal, universal state education at all, most of these arguments being characterised by the same rhetoric as the more recent statements of education policy summarised in Figure 2.1.

For the Victorian poet, philosopher and would-be reformer Matthew Arnold, for example, the significant qualities of education were describable largely in terms of the *therapeutic* and the *social*: its central purpose was to soothe and ennoble the savage beast through the power of exposure to 'high culture' and 'reason', in order to produce happier individuals in a less strife-torn society (Arnold 1909, 1932). To borrow expressions from subsequent government documentation, public education was aimed at producing the 'happier child' enjoying the 'better start to life' and enriching 'the inheritance of the country whose citizens they are' (Government White Paper 1943). It was concerned with the 'spiritual, moral, mental and physical development of the community' (Education Act 1944) in which were produced 'rounded', 'balanced' and 'qualified' children with 'a respect for people and property', contributing to the nation's 'future work-force and the foundation for the economic development and competitiveness of this country' (DES White Paper 1992, pp. 1, 7).

Such claims for, and perceived purposes of, formal, organised education are often located within what is sometimes called the *Enlightenment* tradition (Carr 1995). This tradition – which itself began, in the eighteenth century, as anti-tradition and anti-authority – suggests that an improvement in the human condition – that is, the improvement of the lot of all human beings within a society – can be effected by the pursuit of reason and science on the one hand and the study and enjoyment of 'high culture' on the other. (Whether it is aimed at improving the lot of all individuals within the *world* is, as Davies [1998] implies, a matter about which the Enlightenment project is less clear.)

It is easy to see how such a view fits in with the superficially acceptable reasons for providing state education, and how it has shaped – and, arguably, continues to shape – the school curriculum. In Carr's view, Enlightenment ideals have prioritised 'knowledge over experience, certainty over contingency, and stability over change' (Carr 1995, p. 87). Within this world-view, the physical and social world are there to be *known*, to be described, to be under-stood: everything, ultimately, is knowable, and knowledge is freedom – freedom from ignorance and, ultimately, freedom from the chains of poverty and injustice. In terms of curriculum development, we might suggest that these ideals have led to such standard inclusions as compulsory religious worship, the identification and study of 'great literature', and a fragmented, itemised presentation of knowledge via the subject-based school curriculum (cf. Hamilton 1993, quoted above).

This, of course, is only one interpretation of – and one set of manifesta-tions of – Enlightenment thinking, and it would be rash to deny that, underpinning Enlightenment philosophy, were Enlightenment *ideals*, many of which were – and still are – based on humanitarian and egalitarian principles to which most practising teachers would readily subscribe. Figure 2.4, below, seeks, therefore, not to summarise Enlightenment thinking in terms of the educational context, but to isolate key aspects of Enlightenment thinking that may be viewed as having had the strongest impact on the development of state education in the United Kingdom and other 'developed' societies.

As has already been indicated, many commentators have observed that human activity in the twentieth century, in which science and technology have been utilised to create weapons of mass destruction (while the attempted development of 'reasoning societies' has failed to prevent acts of genocide, two world wars and the perpetuation and creation of the most appalling mass poverty), has rendered this particular brand of Enlightenment thinking some-what difficult to sustain, suggesting to many that the Enlightenment project itself needs either to be reconfigured or superseded. As Dewey famously observed at the time of the outbreak of the Second World War: 'it is no longer possible to hold the simple faith of the Enlightenment that assured

■ everything in the natural world is ultimately knowable,
categorisable, quantifiable and describable within the discourse of
universally applicable laws

■ the study of science, maths and technology will help human beings
to understand and ultimately to control nature (including our own,
with its unhappy tendency to violence and depression), and to
become – both individually and collectively – much happier and
more co-operative beings in a world made safer, fairer and more
comfortable for all

■ 'high culture' exists and is intrinsically superior to something called
'low culture' or 'popular culture' as well as having 'improving'
qualities for the consumer (that is to say, we can talk about 'right'
ways of doing things and 'wrong' ways of doing things, regardless
of outcome)

■ the study and appreciation of high culture, alongside the study of
science, maths and technology (involving learning to do the 'right'
things), will help produce larger numbers of better-behaved,
happier people

■ each individual has a relatively 'fixed', pre-social self that must be
worked upon (by parents and families, or, where they fail, by
educators) in order to ensure regularly 'good' and responsible
rather than regularly 'bad' and irresponsible behaviour

Figure 2.4 Key aspects of Enlightenment thinking in the development of state education

advance of science will produce free institutions by dispelling ignorance and
superstition – the sources of human servitude and the pillars of oppressive
government' (Dewey 1939, p. 131).

Dewey seems to suggest that while schools might have the potential to be
'cradles of democracy', the Enlightenment project itself – what we might call
its translation from high idealism into acts of social policy – has fallen into
the hands of those very same 'oppressors' whose power and influence it was
supposed to 'dispel' (see also Peters 1966; Giddens 1991). A critical question,
then, for teachers, is:

● What aspects of Enlightenment thinking and practice do we
want to preserve intact through school curricula and pedagogy,
and what aspects do we need to question, to reject, or to
expand upon?

Some current commentators believe that school curricula are still locked in
a narrow Enlightenment view of education, and that as a consequence governments have failed properly to address issues of curriculum development and

reform (Moore 1998). Such reform would lead to radical changes in the nature of schooling rather than what Bourdieu calls 'morphological' changes which affect 'nothing essential' (Bourdieu 1976, p. 115). An example of a 'morphological' change would be a change in the public examination system from end-of-course to continuous assessment. Such a change might favour individuals who had previously been discriminated against – because, for example, they were not strong at memorising, or because they were daunted by the atmosphere and semiotics of the examination hall – but the shift would only be marginal since the syllabus content and assessment criteria would still be loaded in favour of dominant social groups.

Cummins suggests that the sanctioning and development of *critical literacy* may provide one form of genuine educational change, arguing that:

> Genuine critical literacy threatens established systems of privilege and resource distribution because it reduces the potency of indoctrination and disinformation. Critical literacy enables us to read between the lines, to look skeptically at apparently benign and plausible surface structures, to analyze claims in relation to empirical data, and to question whose interests are served by particular forms of communication.
>
> (Cummins 1996, p. 219)

The 'apparently benign and plausible surface structures' that critical literacy seeks to critique are precisely those structures imposed by the Enlightenment-based curriculum – Cummins implying, like Davies, that even the more acceptable rationales for state education are underpinned by cultural bias in a curriculum that furthers the interests of the powerful over those of the systematically *dis*empowered (see also Chapter 4 below). A similar view may be seen as implicit in Jerome Bruner's observation that 'educational reform confined only to the schools and not to the society at large is doomed as essentially trivial' (Bruner 1972, p. 114).

THE HISTORIC PURPOSES OF STATE EDUCATION: (2) MEETING THE CHANGING NEEDS OF THE ECONOMY

If much of the Enlightenment educational project purported to be about the development of the self as a way of creating a more just, equitable and harmonious society, it was not without its more pragmatic side – a side which continues to be present in the Enlightenment discourse as it appears in more recent educational pronouncements and policies. It is there, for instance, in the DFE's White Paper *Choice and Diversity* (referred to earlier), in its talk of developing the 'future work-force and the foundation for the economic development and competitiveness of this country' (DES 1992, pp. 1, 7), and in another observation, which talks of the need for 'a respect for people and property' (p. 7). It is also evident in the earlier *Green Paper*, critiqued by Apple (1980, p. 11), which regrets the development of 'a wide gap between the world of education and the world of work' in which young people are 'not sufficiently aware of the importance of industry to our society, and . . . are not taught much about it'. Here, the *social* function of education, to produce the 'happier', more 'rounded' individual, is closely linked to a more obviously *financial* function, of increasing the nation's economic competitiveness and reducing costly crime. While such financial outcomes might well benefit all sections of the community, it could be argued that the *greatest* beneficiaries will be the 'haves' rather than the 'have nots', and that what we really need to foster in our schools is not competition and competitiveness but co-operation and a sense of social justice – not nationalism but *inter*nationalism (IPPR 1993, p. 180).

> While aspects of the Enlightenment project may be perceived as working, almost by accident, against the best interests of deprivileged sections of society it purports to help (consider, for example, the cultural bias that exists within education systems under the name of 'high culture', in which certain literary and artistic tastes are – somewhat 'irrationally' – elevated over others), we need to look at other official rationales for the introduction of universal state education – including initial *opposition* to it – to discover the more *deliberate* hidden agenda referred to above. Such a look reveals that this agenda seems to have had, from the outset, a very strong financial and social-reproductive spine, that had little concern for the welfare of the individual citizen other than the manner in which such welfare might impact on the broader financial health of the nation and, in so doing, ensure the healthy continuation of economic systems that would continue to reproduce social and economic inequalities.

As an illustration of this latter view, the following remarks, made by the schools inspector J.D. Morrell in 1858 on the criminal behaviour of the 'lower orders', suggest a far more cynical approach to the introduction of universal state education than that of Arnoldean humanists:

> If [the government] is obliged to watch them, to intimidate them, to repress them, often to imprison, prosecute and punish them [. . .] the idea naturally represents itself, whether in such a case it would not be wiser and better, as well as cheaper, to attempt some educational means of reformation, than to be ever engaged in a perpetually renewed struggle of force against force.
>
> (quoted in Selleck 1968, p. 8)

Here, a clear *economic* reason is given in favour of introducing formal state education: that is to say, at a time when the influence of another 'moralising' influence, the Church, is receding (itself an unanticipated by-product, it could be argued, of Enlightenment rationalism), education is perceived as a cost-effective way of reducing crime. What this view lacks – and what is included in the 'alternative' curricula argued by Cummins and others – is a suggestion that education might help to identify and remove the real *causes* of crime: causes such as poverty, inequality, and social injustice. Such an agenda might see education as militating for fundamental changes in society, rather than as in this case, merely reducing crime within an essentially unchanging and unequitable system. The education envisioned by Morrell might be aimed at producing 'happier' people, but at a people still fundamentally divided socially, economically and in terms of aspirations from one another.

The view that education is about making people happier, more socially useful and less expensive to 'run', without changing a social system in which land and money are distributed according to culture and birth rather than, say, to work-rates or personal attributes, is echoed in the following words of the President of the Board of Trade, H.A.L. Fisher, in August 1917, on introducing the 1917 Education Bill to Parliament:

> [T]he more reflecting members of our industrial army [. . .] do not want education only in order that they may become better technical workmen and [earn] higher wages. They do not want it in order that they may rise out of their own class, always a vulgar ambition. They want it because they know that in the treasures of the mind they can find an aid to good citizenship, a source of pure enjoyment and a refuge from the necessary hardships of a life spent in the midst of clanging machinery in the hideous cities of toil.
>
> (cited in McLure 1986, p. 174)

Here, the fundamental purpose of education – though dressed in Enlighten-ment terms – is perceived not as necessarily making more people better qualified for more advantageous jobs (the 'empowerment' discourse which is at the heart of much current educational policy-discourse) but as enabling people previously denied an education to *endure more easily* the 'necessary hard-ships' of life. The inscription of hardship here within the discourse of 'necessity' suggests a need not to *change* society but to encourage an *acceptance* in all social classes that what we have is the natural order of things: we might feel sorry for those at the bottom of the pile, but ultimately there is nothing we can do to change their status.

Views such as Fisher's were not new in the debate about the rationale for – and shape of – public education. In 1862, for example, Robert Lowe made the following pronouncement to Parliament on the issue of the purposes of bringing formal education to those to whom it had previously been denied: 'We do not profess to give these ['labouring class'] children an education that will raise them above their station and business in life . . . *but to give them an education that may fit them for that business'* (cited in Selleck 1968, p. 15, italics added).

Lowe's remarks suggest a further rationale for universal state education, and perhaps a more pressing one than the need to reduce crime – and that is to do with the 'business' of working-class families and the ways in which, as the industrial revolution developed, that business was undergoing fundamental change. Fifty years before Lowe's pronouncements, there may still have been a need, within the British economic system, for a workforce predominantly directed towards the mines, the mills and the factories. As the century progressed, however, while such workers were still in great demand, new kinds of workers with new kinds of skills were also being required in ever greater numbers: workers to undertake menial and servile work in shops and offices, for example, or within a service industry that was already beginning to expand and diversify in line with developments in technology. Such workers needed skills beyond those required of the mine, the mill or the factory floor: specifically, they needed certain levels of numeracy, literacy and what are still sometimes referred to as the 'social skills'. The only sensible way to repro-duce a work-force in which – to some at least – those skills were taught to appropriate levels was through formal, compulsory education.

Educating hitherto illiterate people to be literate is, of course, a potentially risky business, especially if those previously illiterate people have been and will continue to be economically and culturally disadvantaged. It is not surprising to discover, therefore, that official arguments in favour of state education were often linked to *caveats* and warnings: warnings, for instance, that if people became *too* literate they might rise up in opposition against their lot and effect the very kind of social revolution that a formal education system was intended to prevent. In this respect, Playfair, in 1870, was able to talk of '[a] lurking, though inexpressed fear, that the lower orders may be *too highly* educated [and that the State has done its duty] when it imparts the *rudiments* of knowledge' (cited in Selleck 1968, p. 15, emphases added); while more than half a century earlier Tory-led opposition to proposals for the establish-ment of parish schools, had been argued on the basis that 'instead of teaching [the labouring classes] subordination, [education] would render them factious and refractory' (cited by Simon 1974, p. 32, and Willinsky 1993, p. 68).

> The message behind such observations was clear: educate people to a certain degree that renders them compliant, but educate them beyond that degree at your peril. Make sure that the curriculum itself provides its new students with literacy and knowledge, but do not let it provide 'more-than-literacy' or develop powers of independent thought.

EDUCATION TODAY

At first sight the economic, *pragmatic* arguments for and about state education (it is needed to reduce costly crime, to meet the changing needs of the economy, it helps keep the country 'economically competitive') appear a far cry from the superficially more *principled* explanations (it is aimed at producing happier, more rounded individuals, better able to appreciate and enjoy 'culture', and so on) put forward by Victorian liberal humanists such as Matthew Arnold and subsequently reproduced by a series of government policy documents. However, it could be argued that both the pragmatic, utilitarian view and the Enlightenment view have a common root in wanting to preserve the *status quo:* i.e. not to encourage *challenge* of current social arrangements, institutions and attitudes with a view to working towards social change, but rather to *preserve* (or *con*serve) existing social arrangements, institutions and attitudes through encouraging people to accept them.

> We might also consider the possibility that these two educational agendas (the *utilitarian-pragmatic* and the *liberal-Enlightenment*) – however different on the surface – have had similar effects in determining the shape and content of the school curriculum. Either agenda, for instance, might suggest the development of a school curriculum that prioritises knowledge over process, the regurgitation of facts over cognitive explorations, personal and national competition over co-operation, uniformity over diversity, and quantification over qualification.

The tangible manifestations of such prioritisations are many. They might include:

- the itemisation, limitation and separation of sanctioned skills and knowledge into discrete subject areas;
- the streaming and setting of students according to reductivist notions of 'ability';
- the 'canonical', ethnocentric selection of texts and areas of knowledge within subject areas;
- an exclusive, inflexible view of what is or is not permissible work and behaviour;
- the persistence of quantitative, summative (in preference to qualitative, formative) assessment, leading to the grading of students and the publication of academic 'league tables'.

If we accept the implications in previous official discourses that compulsory state education was introduced in the first place for a number of reasons that included, centrally, a desire to produce a more appropriately-skilled work-force likely to commit fewer acts of theft and criminal damage, what questions do we need to ask about the *current* purposes of education?

One set of questions might run as follows:

- Have the utilitarian/economic/pragmatic rationales for state education and its specific form(s) been superseded by more 'acceptable' ones within what might be called a more humanitarian society, or have those rationales merely gone 'underground'? That is to say, is it just a case that politicians were more honest about their motives in the past than they are now, or have political agendas genuinely changed?
- What evidence can we find in the structures and contents of modern-day curricula, developments in the field of equality of opportunity, and favoured teaching styles to support or reject either of these possibilities? (What do we make, for instance, of the development of comprehensive education, or of school effectiveness programmes?)
- To what extent have the 'official needs' of education themselves moved on, as the industrial age is replaced by a post-industrial age of technology and by the further development of service industries?
- To what extent has the official educational agenda responded (for example, through curriculum and examination reform) to the fact that the UK is no longer, in the sense of occupying territories, a 'colonial nation'?

An additional question we might ask concerns the role of the dominant middle classes in fixing educational agendas and controlling educational change. Bernstein (1977) has argued, persuasively, that developments in education – be they departures from traditional practice or returns to previously questioned practice – tend to emanate from the middle classes and be particularly supportive of those classes' best interests at any given point in history. Thus, while at one point in time it might be perceived as being in the best interests of the middle classes to move towards de-streaming and continuous assessment, at another point it may be perceived as more advantageous to *return to* streaming and end-of-course examinations. Though such policy changes and developments might appear, on the surface, to have nothing to do with middle-class pressures and aspirations and everything to do with more 'objective' assessments of educational success and failure across the range of social groupings, these changes are perceived from this viewpoint as being influenced by *hidden* agendas that conceal their own existence and means of production.

In considering the questions listed above, we might well decide that education has indeed 'moved on' and that, for example, previously marginalised students are offered far greater opportunities nowadays to succeed and far greater, more informed help in doing so. On the other hand, we might equally come to the conclusion that all that has really happened is that, as public attitudes are more rigorously patrolled by humanist, humanitarian discourses, the pragmatic view – although still shaping much of what goes on in education

– has simply 'gone underground', while the more acceptable face of the Enlightenment view is allowed to voice itself ever more loudly. If that is the case, we may further ask ourselves if the aim of producing 'happier' more 'rounded' individuals is merely a rhetorical device, and, if *this* is the case, whether we should treat that device rhetorically ourselves (by de-privileging related aspects of our teaching) or whether we should adopt an oppositional stance to it.

Most teachers, of course, have their own views as to what constitutes a good education and those views certainly do prioritise the development of the 'whole person' rather than adopting a purely utilitarian stance. For teachers, the main challenge is in pursuing believed-in educational aims in believed-in educational ways, in situations in which they may sometimes feel supported by official discourses and policies and sometimes thwarted by them – a theme to which we shall return in Chapter 6 when considering possible future developments in education that we might wish to support or oppose. As has been argued elsewhere (Edwards *et al.* 1999, Moore and Edwards 2000), such difficulties have often led teachers towards a new kind of pragmatism, in which suspicious educational practices are sometimes carried out with reluctance and sometimes subverted, and in which spaces are found within the curriculum shaped by official agendas to pursue educational agendas which could themselves be classified as 'unofficial'.

SUMMARY

This chapter has considered the rationales for formal state education, and how these have impacted on commonsense notions of what the curriculum should look like and what constitutes good teaching. This has included a consideration of the development of formal education as part of the Enlightenment project, that may itself need re-evaluating in the light of current developments and needs.

The chapter has also considered some of the implications for teachers of matches and mismatches between central educational policy and the preferred learning styles and educational agendas of individual teachers and schools.

In particular, the following questions have been considered:

- To what extent do the official purposes of state education, and official views as to appropriate curricula and teaching styles, support or conflict with individual schools' and teachers' philosophies and theories of teaching and learning?
- Should school curricula emphasise 'process' or 'content' or both? What are the implications of such choices for curriculum content and for pedagogy? Should curriculum content ('This is what everyone should

know and be able to do') be prioritised over the development of effective learning skills, or *vice-versa*?

- How far do current school curricula meet or fail to meet the demands of a rapidly changing world? What might be missing or marginalised within existing curricula?
- To what extent does the school curriculum promote the development of happier, more rounded, more empowered individuals, and to what extent does it serve to perpetuate inequalities?

SUGGESTED ACTIVITIES

1. With reference to careful study of the National Curriculum for your own or a related curriculum area:

    - To what extent is the curriculum concerned with the acquisition of 'cold knowledge', and to what extent is it concerned with the development of language and learning skills or with building on 'action knowledge'?
    - Is the curriculum mainly 'retrospective' or mainly 'prospective'?
    - In what ways does the curriculum support the kinds of learning and the kinds of pedagogy you believe in, and to what extent does it act as an obstacle in this respect?
    - What additional skills and areas of knowledge might be required to make the curriculum appropriately suited to the modern world?
    - Are there any skills and areas of knowledge that might be appropriately deleted or downgraded in some way because they are now less relevant than they once might have been?

    (In approaching each question, draw evidence and examples from the relevant curriculum documentation.)

2. What aspects of Enlightenment thinking continue to characterise formal state education in your experience?
    (Try applying this question to curriculum, pedagogy and assessment.)

3. What aspects of the curriculum, formal assessment and your own teaching might be said to belong more to a colonial than a 'post-colonial' mindset? What, specifically, might be done in each of these areas of schooling to 'de-colonialize' formal education?

SUGGESTED READING

Apple, M. (1979) *Ideology and the Curriculum.* Apple's classic, 'deconstruc-tive' text suggests ways of interrogating taken-for-granted curriculum assumptions that root out underlying class and cultural bias, and suggests that formal systems of education, far from 'liberating' or 'empowering' students from all social and cultural backgrounds, tend rather to support and perpetuate existing class relations and relations of power. These ideas are further developed – and critiqued – in Apple's more recent work *Education and Power*, which emphasises the ways in which dominant interests and ideologies are *responded to* by teachers and students (Apple 1995).

Bernstein, B. (1996) *Pedagogy, Symbolic Control and Identity.* Like Apple, Bernstein renders taken-for-granted aspects of the school curriculum prob-lematic, suggesting that forms of educational provision officially based on notions of empowerment are really based on matters of economics and (by implication) the demands of national economies. Of particular interest is Bernstein's analysis of the ways in which 'official' economy-driven educa-tional practices collide with – or are incorporated within – the egalitarian-driven practices espoused by teachers.

DES (Department of Education and Science) (1992) Government White Paper: *Choice and Diversity: a New Framework for Schools.* Along with the more recent *Excellence in Schools* (DfEE 1997a), 'Choice and Diversity' is a useful example of the ways in which formal state education is conceived, pack-aged and promoted, and of the aspects of education that are currently prioritised within dominant, 'official' educational discourses.

McLure, J.S. (1986) *Educational Documents: England and Wales 1816 to the Present Day.* Along with Selleck's *The New Education 1870-1914* (R.J.W. Selleck, 1968), McLure's scholarly collection of educational documents provides invaluable insights into the original, publicly-stated purposes of formal state education, and the ways in which these have developed – or not developed – over the years.

3 Teaching, Learning and Language

This chapter focuses on the special role of language in teaching and learning, and on the relationship between language and thought. Language is examined both as a learning medium and as a teaching medium. Particular consideration is given to the importance of teachers' language in the promotion of learning, in its capacity to create appropriate working conditions, and in its ability to hinder or restrict learning. The role of students' own language in the learning process is considered, including the need for students to be able to operate effectively as speakers, listeners, readers and writers within – and beyond – a range of 'standard genres'. Histories and issues of language and learning across the curriculum are reviewed, as well as issues of 'mixed ability' teaching and of social class and dialect. Issues of language teaching itself are considered in the light of National Curricula and current debates about what constitutes linguistic competence. Readers are introduced to the concepts of functional, cultural and critical literacy, and of the roles and natures of these forms of literacy within the whole-school curriculum.

INTRODUCTION: LANGUAGE AND SOCIETY

It is hard to imagine human life without language; indeed, it is arguably language – or, more accurately, the capacity to produce symbolic systems and then to use those systems as means of communication – that gives us our 'humanness'. Without language, there would be no literature, no conversation, no diplomacy, no trade, no art, no Law, and no society as we know it.

Expertise in using and understanding language – whether spoken or written, whether internal or 'voiced' – is clearly important to anyone wishing to play a full, active, independent and co-operative part in society or even, for that matter, of living a life that is reasonably comfortable and happy. Language is, however, by its very nature, a two-faced phenomenon that is – as has been pointed out by numerous commentators (e.g. Lacan 1977, 1979; Foucault 1972) – as capable of enslaving, controlling and limiting us as it is of liberating us and expanding our possibilities and potential. Furthermore, language is a tool which, in addition to providing the means of arguing just causes, can be systematically used as a way of ensuring the cultural, social and economic dominance of certain self-privileging groups in societies at the expense of other, deliberately de-privileged groups – what Bourdieu and others have called 'cultural reproduction' (e.g. Bourdieu and Passeron 1977). It could be argued, with reference to this current book, that the National Curriculum for English, with its largely uncritical emphasis on 'standard English' and its insistence on the reading of certain literary texts in preference to others, represents one such way in which language – or certain forms and styles of language – is co-opted to the benefit of certain groups at the expense of others. As we shall see, other commentators (e.g. Kress 1982) have argued, in line with Foucault's hypothesis, that language *genres* – expertise in the replication of which we are always at such pains to teach our students – have themselves the capacity to restrict the ways in which we perceive and experience the world, as well as our expression, through language, of that perception and experience. That is to say, we may be said to perceive and experience the world through certain symbolic (centrally, linguistic) discourses that *pre-date* our entry into the social and physical world, and so our understandings of that world, and perhaps our sense of possibilities within it, are permanently and unavoidably filtered through those discourses.

Teachers, and particularly, in the current configuration of school curricula, first- and second-language teachers, plainly have a major responsibility for developing all their students' linguistic abilities. However, they must be careful not to let themselves restrict this development *just* to the acquisition of expertise in standard English and standard genres of writing and reading. Rather, they must constantly be alert for opportunities to extend and develop their students' linguistic skills in ways that will promote independent learning, personal development, *idiosyncratic* expression, and the opening of new cognitive/affective horizons, recognising that without such development the world as experienced by humans *through* language may quickly become a dull and stagnant place. At the same time, teachers need to be critically aware of their *own* use of language, regardless of the subject matter of their lessons, ensuring that their language opens up rather than restricts opportunities for learning through discussion, elaboration and debate.

THE IMPORTANCE OF TEACHERS' USE OF LANGUAGE IN THE CLASSROOM SITUATION

In Chapter 1 we considered Vygotsky's notion that all language and thought are, from a very early stage in the individual's development, effectively inseparable from one another and that, furthermore, all language-and-thought (we might say, all thought-in-language) is fundamentally social in form and function. Whether or not we accept Vygotsky's view, research leaves us in no doubt that the language used by students and teachers (and indeed by school textbooks) has a critical impact on the individual student's *learning*. Not only can complex ideas be shared through the use of appropriate language, but, equally, relatively straightforward ideas can be made difficult or obscured by the use of *in*appropriate language. Furthermore, language in the classroom can be used as a means of controlling and even limiting students' development, as well as of encouraging and facilitating it.

Just how important a teacher's language can be is neatly illustrated in Margaret Donaldson's critique of the findings of one of the experiments carried out by Jean Piaget to demonstrate children's progression from 'concrete' to 'formal' thinking (see Chapter 1 above). In this experiment, Piaget posed the following problem to children still deemed to be operating in the 'concrete operational' stage:

> *Edith is fairer than Susan. Edith is darker than Lily.*
> *Who is the darkest?*

Piaget reported that the children found this question either very difficult or impossible to answer, and attributed this difficulty to the fact that the children were still in the 'concrete operational' stage of cognitive development: that is to say, although they may have had no difficulty solving a similar question through arranging and rearranging three dolls (Donaldson 1978), they were unable to work out the right answer when given – and asked to use – words alone. As we have seen in Chapter 1, while the concrete thinker is able and concerned to manipulate *things*, the formal thinker is able to manipulate *'propositions'*.

Donaldson's critique of Piaget's interpretation of his experimental findings is based precisely on the fact that 'if it were a question of arranging three dolls in serial order, the task would be easy for [the children]' (Donaldson 1978, p. 139). Donaldson suggests, in fact, that the children taking part in Piaget's experiment may have already been able to operate in the kinds of ways associated with formal or abstract thinking, *as long as the question was put to them in a way that related to their familiar world and in a language that they understood*. In other words, the experiment itself may not have encouraged, invited or enabled them to show that they were able to reason in this way, and consequently the inferences drawn from the experiment may themselves be questionable. Put simply, the fact that the children may have benefited from the use of physical props to arrive at the right answer does not mean that they were incapable of 'hypothetical' thought.

Donaldson's implication that the difficulties experienced by the children in Piaget's experiment were linguistic-discursive rather than (as Piaget suggests) cognitive calls into serious question both Piaget's own analysis of his experimental findings and the experimental situation itself. Was there, for example, something fundamentally unhelpful about the way Piaget's question was put? Did the introduction of the names of people the children did not know act as an unhelpful diversion for them? Were they thrown by the unusual mixing of 'darker' and 'fairer' (a more familiar way of encountering such a question might have been along the lines: '*Lily is fairer than Edith. Edith is fairer than Susan. Who is the fairest?*')? Were they made uncomfortable by the 'test' situation itself? How would adults – presumed to be capable of abstract thought – fare when faced with the same question expressed in the same words? (How many, for instance, would also be thrown by the wording of the question? And how many would need to reach for a pen and paper to help them solve the question by making it more 'concrete'?)

Such questions raise serious doubts about whether Piaget's test was adequate for its aim. Did it, for instance, demonstrate the difference between concrete and formal thinking? Or did it merely demonstrate the difficulties that simple questions can produce when framed in unusual or inappropriate language?

This last point has very important implications for the classroom. In the past, several commentators have drawn attention to the teacher's use of language in the classroom and the difficulties that this can cause, both as it manifests itself in oral instructions and advice and as it presents itself in worksheets and other written materials (e.g. Barnes 1976, 1986; Hull 1988). Barnes, for example, has shown how difficulties in learning can occur when the teacher uses words in one, particular 'adult' way, which the students are used to using in quite other ways. Describing the practice of one teacher, who persists in using words within a strictly academic context as though they cannot exist in any other, Barnes argues that '[F]ar from helping [the students] to bridge the gulf between his frame of reference and theirs, the teacher's language acts as a barrier, of which he seems quite unaware' (Barnes 1986, p. 29).

Hull has also drawn attention to some teachers' reluctance to acknowledge the need to recognise potential differences of language usage between student and teacher and to ascertain what concepts – if any – students already have in relation to terms that are used 'academically'. Hull develops this point further, to suggest that when terms are used by the teacher as though everybody already knows 'what they mean', students become very reluctant to ask for clarification, for fear of appearing ignorant, stupid or inattentive. Thus, in a geography lesson: 'The working assumptions that "relief" and "Europe" were known terms made asking questions about them particularly difficult' (Hull 1988, p. 195).

Observations such as these take us back to issues related to students' 'out-of-school' knowledge – 'everyday' knowledge, 'action' knowledge, or whatever else we choose to call it – and to knowledge acquired in school through formal instruction, and of the urgent need for teachers to make visible and explicit connections between the two. That is to say, teachers need to build on students' existing understandings of the world. Inevitably, this means building on the *language* through which those understandings are explored and expressed. A failure to do so may result in students' learning being blocked through a sense of their own ignorance or a conviction of their own misunderstanding.

LANGUAGE AND CONTEXT: LESSONS FROM WORKING WITH BILINGUAL STUDENTS

The notion that teachers need to give appropriate recognition to their students' existing language skills, including the ways in which students may use certain words and phrases differently from the way they are likely to be used in the classroom, is an argument for taking full account of learning *contexts*.

The particular importance for teachers of being reflexive in relation to their own language use in the classroom has been highlighted in a good deal of work carried out by teachers and researchers in the area of working with bilingual students (see, for example, Krashen 1982; Levine 1983; Wright 1985). In a persuasive argument against withdrawing bilingual students from mainstream classes for 'decontextualised' language work to develop English language skills which can then be applied in more normal academic settings, Josie Levine, for example, has argued that it is a mistake to attempt to teach such students linguistic structures 'in isolation from the contexts in which they occur' (Levine 1983, p. 1). For Levine, bilingual students, regardless of how much expertise they may possess in the main language of instruction, can only develop their language skills in normal classroom situations, surrounded by the normal language flows experienced by all other students, as they are happening and as they relate to specific classroom events. (To be taught the vocabulary likely to be used in a science experiment on reactivity, for instance, and only subsequently to be involved in such an experiment is considered in this model to be less effective – in terms of developing scientific understanding *or* language repertoire – than learning the appropriate vocabulary and structures whilst engaged in the meaningful activity of the experiment itself. In the latter case, involvement in the experiment and the recollection of it will help 'fix' the new vocabulary and structures and give them a logical place within the student's overall language repertoire.)

The issue of teaching language itself as a new language is one that most teachers are likely to find themselves only peripherally involved in if at all. (See, however, 'Language Across the Curriculum', pp. 74–75 below.) There is another aspect of the language-in-context argument, though, which is of more immediate relevance to all classroom teachers. For Levine, the point of teaching bilingual students in normal 'mainstream' classrooms is not just to provide them with opportunities through which to develop their English language skills in normal, meaningful contexts: it also recognises the importance of what we might call a 'second context' for the development of language and learning, comprising the student's existing cognitive and linguistic skills. Thus, in a passage that echoes the arguments of Douglas Barnes outlined in Chapter 1 above (Barnes 1976), Levine argues that: '[i]t makes both human and pedagogic sense to use the natural features of pupils' lives to build an educational context out of what they already have access to and out of what they already know and can do' (Levine 1983, p. 192; see also Wiles 1985a, p. 20, and 1985b).

Levine is particularly concerned that the recognition of the full context in which teaching and learning take place – *including* the student's existing cognitive–linguistic skills – should help teachers avoid the practice of providing their students with work that demands cognitive levels *below* those which the student has already achieved (see also Moore 1999a).

The following example, drawn from Moore 1995, illustrates how such an approach might work in practice. Although the example is of a teacher working with a *bilingual* student who has very little English, the applicability of the example and its related issues to the teaching of monolingual students should be immediately apparent.

Case Study 3.1

Teacher A has a student in her Year 8 mathematics classroom who has just arrived in England and has virtually no spoken or written English. The student has, however, been to school in her native Bangladesh, and the school's enquiries have revealed that the student has enjoyed her mathematics classes there.

The teacher wants to develop the student's thinking at a level appropriate to her chronological age, but lacks the means to be able to communicate her wishes through a common language and at a linguistic level she would normally adopt with students of this age.

A central question for the teacher is: Does she provide the student with work below *her cognitive level, on the grounds that she cannot explain more sophisticated tasks to the student through the use of appropriate language? Or can she seek other ways round the problem, that will enable the student to demonstrate and work at her actual cognitive (rather than her second-language) level of competence?*

In this particular case, the mathematics teacher uses a programme with her class that enables students, sometimes working individually and sometimes in groups, to focus on mathematical concepts that they find particularly tricky or that she feels they are ready to tackle on the basis of their previous work. Her pedagogic approach is essentially 'student-centred', giving students a considerable degree of responsibility for determining the specific *direction* (and, to a lesser extent, the pace) of their own learning. The teacher has seen the bilingual student – who is quite new to the class, having only arrived in the UK three weeks previously – showing a particular interest in an exercise involving squares that another bilingual student in the classroom has been working on. She decides to begin by giving her new student a related exercise, partly in order to involve the student in active learning and partly to assess her current cognitive level and needs. The task selected is to identify the number of squares in a grid – shown as Figure 3.1 below. This activity suggests another, related purpose to the teacher, which is: to get the student familiar with the English word 'square' – and other relevant vocabulary –

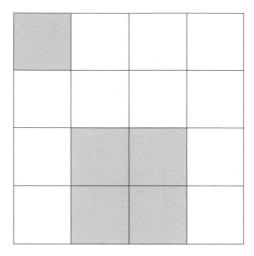

Figure 3.1 The 'How many squares?' problem

through an activity that's fairly interesting, that she can do, and that isn't going to insult her intelligence.

Sitting down with her student at the start of this activity, the teacher explains the task as well as she can:

T: (slowly and clearly) This is about squares. Squares. (Prints the word 'square'.) Squares. . . . (Draws a series of different-sized squares for the student, each time repeating the word 'square' until the student responds by saying 'squares' herself.)

S: Squares.

T: Good. That's right. Squares. Squares. (T. runs her pencil round a series of squares in the diagram – one of the smallest, the largest, and one intermediate – each time repeating, with the student, 'square'.) Squares. OK. Good. Now. . . . How many squares? How many?

S: (Looks puzzled)

T: (Returns to the three squares she has indicated, holding up fingers each time) One square. . . . Two squares. . . . Three squares. . . . How many? (Exaggeratedly shrugs her shoulders.) How many squares? One? . . . Two? . . . Three? . . . (T. uses fingers to demonstrate, continuing to shrug after each question.) Four? Five?

S: (Smiles)

T: (Also smiling) You count them. Write down how many. (Turns to a student in the next seat, who speaks the same first language.) Rafi, you've done this exercise before, haven't you. Will you help her? If she doesn't understand, tell her what she has to do.

In this study, the teacher uses two strategies to help her to help her student:

1)   the use of 'non-linguistic' or visual clues, such as gesture and drawing;
2)   the use of the student's strongest language, through encouraging her to talk in that language to another student who speaks the same first language but is more fluent in English.

Both of these linguistic strategies are set within a contextualising strategy of trying to match the cognitive input provided by the teacher with the cognitive developmental level of the student. That the strategies are successful on this occasion is suggested by the fact that the student goes on successfully to complete the task, only consulting Rafi when she needs to know what she has to do with her answer ('twenty-six') and how to write that answer down in English numerals.

Happy that her student can cope with the activity set, the teacher next gives her a similar task involving triangles, then spends some time with her going through the English numbers 1–1000, giving the student a list of these numbers and getting her to write down beside each number the equivalent number in her own strongest language. Deciding on the basis of her performance so far that the student is able to tackle more complex tasks, the teacher now gives her the exercise on ratio and proportion (an example from which appears as Figure 3.2), which she also completes successfully.

What this short case study underlines is the need for teachers to learn to adapt their own language to suit their audiences if they want effective and appropriate *learning* to ensue. Those audiences may comprise particular year groups (sixth-form students, for example, may represent a very different audience linguistically from students who have just arrived in secondary school) or particular individuals within the same year group (as in this study). *It is also important that the teacher recognises that, just as their own language can facilitate or hinder comprehension, so a student's own language can express or mask an understanding of concepts – a point we shall return to when we look at the work of Derek Edwards and Neil Mercer, below.*

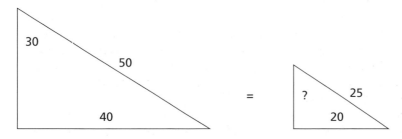

Figure 3.2 Ratio and proportion exercise

TEACHER LANGUAGE AND CLASSROOM CONTROL

In addition to understanding how the teacher's language operates in terms of facilitating or hindering students' cognitive development *per se*, teachers must also be aware of the extent to which their language controls the flow of what we might call 'curricular input': that is, the amounts and types of information with which students are provided at various times and the extent to which students are allowed or encouraged to explore and interrogate such information.

Sometimes, of course, teachers quite appropriately use language as a means of introducing or maintaining order in the classroom in order for effective learning to be able to take place. Several commentators, however (e.g. Barnes and Hull, whose work we have already considered), have expressed concern about the ways in which the teacher's language (and the language of *textbooks*) can — almost invisibly to the teacher and their students — control curricular input to such an extent that it may be seen to hinder the students' 'natural' cognitive development: *that is to say, there may be a danger that teaching can have the opposite effect of its intended purpose, and actually hinder or restrict learning that might otherwise take place.*

The way in which this occurs has been described elsewhere as 'language rationing' (Moore 1999a) — a process by which the teacher and/or textbook or work-scheme carefully limits the kinds of language — and therefore the cognitive development — permitted in the classroom, feeding in 'new language' as they deem appropriate and fending off any attempts by their students to introduce new language or new concepts and understandings themselves.

Relating this kind of linguistic control to the development and control of students' *cognition*, Edwards and Mercer (1987) refer to two distinct kinds of classroom understanding and expression, which they call 'principled' knowledge and 'ritual' knowledge. 'Ritual' knowledge describes a student's knowledge of classroom *procedures*, including a practical understanding of classroom *rituals*. It includes the notion that if students can give teachers the 'right answers' on cue, accurately read their teachers' intentions, do precisely and 'demonstrably' what their teachers want them to do and so forth, they can, to an extent, be perceived as successful students even though they might not have grasped certain fundamental concepts which they would be able subsequently to develop independently of the classroom situation. (There is a parallel here with Vygotsky's distinction, referred to in Chapter 1, between true concept development and 'rote' learning — described by Vygotsky as 'a parrotlike repetition of words by the child, simulating a knowledge of the corresponding concepts but actually covering up a vacuum' [Vygotsky 1962, p. 83]).

'Principled' knowledge, in contrast to 'ritual' knowledge, implies that the student *has* grasped a fundamental concept and that their cognitive development has progressed in some way. For principled knowledge to occur, Edwards and Mercer argue, certain other conditions must apply: for example, students must be allowed genuinely to experiment, to explore and to debate, both with the teacher, with one another and on their own.

One of Edwards' and Mercer's central arguments is that teachers may some-times overtly adopt – and believe themselves that they are practising – a policy aimed at developing principled knowledge, while at the same actually pursuing, perhaps unwittingly, strategies that promote ritual knowledge. In so doing, they may actually be presenting barriers to cognitive–linguistic development that might otherwise have taken place. Some of these strategies – described as 'making knowledge significant and joint', 'cued elicitation' and 'the use of reconstruction, presupposition and paraphrase' – will be familiar to most teachers, and are summarised below.

'Marking knowledge as significant and joint'

'Marking knowledge as significant and joint' (Edwards and Mercer 1987, pp. 134–142) describes the various processes by which teachers manage and control the curricular content of a lesson while at the same time creating an illusion that their students are 'discovering' it for themselves. Essentially, this involves the teacher's using a series of signifying devices that validate certain items or areas of knowledge and understanding above others and that simultaneously imply that such items are already in the 'joint owner-ship' of the class. This includes the validation of specific manifestations of such knowledge and understanding, such as individual students' volunteered answers and observations.

In Edwards' and Mercer's account, this marking is achieved through a variety of sub-strategies such as the invention and repetition of formulaic phrases which students can repeat parrot-like on cue, or the conducting by the teacher of 'speech in unison', whereby the whole class reiterates a phrase or formula together. A formulaic phrase picked out by Edwards and Mercer from their observations of young students working with pendulums is 'the shorter the string, the faster the swing' – the repetition of which phrase may be said to substitute for a principled understanding of what is actu-ally happening, and which may even be invoked to contradict the evidence of the students' own experiences of the physical world.

The use of formulaic phrases and speech-in-unison are related by Edwards and Mercer to a particular pedagogic device of 'validation', in which the teacher, either through words ('That's *right*' in response to one student's contribution, as opposed to a perfunctory 'uh-huh' in response to another's) or through gestures (writing up one student's contribution on the board but not another's) suggests the acceptability of one answer over others, even though alternative contributions may be allowed to be 'aired'.

Cued elicitation

A particular sub-strategy for marking knowledge as significant and joint relates to the way in which the teacher may invite and control students' oral contributions in whole-class 'discussions'. Essentially, 'cued elicitations' are discourses of the 'teacher initiates–student responds–teacher provides feedback' variety described by Sinclair and Coulthard (Sinclair and Coulthard 1975; see also Stubbs 1976, pp. 108–111). In this particular variation, 'the teacher asks questions while simultaneously providing heavy clues to the information required' (Edwards and Mercer 1987). Such clues may be provided through the teacher's choice of wording, intonation, pausing, gesturing and so on. In the following example of such a discourse (Moore 1995), a teacher of young bilingual students invites the class to contribute an answer while making it quite clear that there is only one 'right' answer:

T: (holding up a piece of card) This is a square. What colour is it? It's. . . . (Points to the word 'green' in a list of names of colours on the board.)

Ss: (in unison) Green!

T: Good! That's right. Now, then. . . . (Holds up another piece of card, which is blue.) Here is another square. Is *it* green? (shakes head)

Ss: (in unison) No!

The use of reconstruction, presupposition and paraphrase

A further cluster of linguistic controlling devices relate to the ways in which teachers may

● paraphrase what students have said, giving it a particular gloss;
● reconstruct what they decide took place in the lesson when 'recapping later';
● 'forestall disagreement, and shape the direction of the discourse and the interpretation put upon experience' through 'presupposing certain things as known or understood'.

(Edwards and Mercer 1987, p. 146)

To illustrate how presupposition works in practice, Edwards and Mercer quote two teacher-questions to two different groups of students:

(1)   'What are you finding? Any results at all?'
(2)   'Now is it the shorter string which is going faster, or the longer?'

The first question, Edwards and Mercer argue, is open-ended, allowing for the possibility of the students' discovering nothing whatsoever in the experiment. The second, however, *presupposes* that something very specific will be happening – that one pendulum will be swinging faster than another, for example, and that this will be related to the length of string – and posits the question on the basis of that presupposition. We might say that this latter question is something of a *leading* question, aimed more at achieving the required answer than at finding out what the students have learned.

The various strategies described by Edwards and Mercer enable the teacher to adhere, without too much fear of being deflected, to a preplanned course of action, covering an externally-designed and externally-monitored syllabus while making it appear that the students are 'discovering' the syllabus for themselves and working at their own pace and direction. (Readers might find it useful and interesting to compare and contrast this teaching methodology with the 'error-free' learning promoted by Skinner and described in Chapter 1 above.) 'Classroom discipline', necessary for the pre-planned programme to be completed in the allocated time, is also achieved in this way, through the very shape and nature of teacher-controlled discourses and organisation. Thus, when the teacher introduces the notion of 'turn-taking' in relation to different groups of students being given tasks with different sets of apparatus and feeding back their findings to the class as a whole, this may *appear* to have its basis in some scientific or pedagogical principle, but may equally, in reality, be 'oriented to the organisation of the lesson in terms of its physical props [e.g. pendulums] and behavioural activity' (Edwards and Mercer 1987, p. 117).

There is, of course, a price to be paid for this illusion, and it is the students who must pay it. In their account of the operations of cued elicitation, Edwards and Mercer argue:

> The best interpretation that we can make of the pedagogic function of cued elicitation is that it embodies an actual educational process in which the students are neither being drawn out of themselves, in the e-ducare sense, nor simply being taught directly in the 'transmission' sense. Rather, they are being inculcated into what becomes for them a shared discourse with the teacher (discourse in the broadest sense, including concepts and terminology as well as dialogue).
>
> (Edwards and Mercer 1987, p. 143.
> See also Walkerdine 1982)

Although the use of the linguistic teaching strategies described by Edwards and Mercer are not without some value, it is clearly important that they need to be *seen* as strategies to be used *selectively*, rather than being allowed to become discursive *habits* whose sole function is that of controlling the pace and content of the lesson.

In common with the ideas of Barnes and Hull, outlined in Chapter 1, Edwards' and Mercer's work underlines the importance of teachers' taking very careful stock of the language they use in the classroom (see, too, Kyriacou 1986), recognising that their words have the potential to restrict and control students' learning as well as to open up a sense of possibility, and indeed that their words have the power to promote or to preclude the kinds of *social relationships* needed for effective learning to take place (Capel *et al.* 1995, p. 83).

> While the control of learning may not always be a bad thing when there is a syllabus to cover (although we may, of course, take issue with the existence and nature of the syllabus itself!), teachers do need to be wary of exercising so much control that students are, effectively, underachieving. In particular, they may need to *monitor* their own verbal inputs (spoken and written) to lessons, to ensure that they do not overdominate linguistically in the classroom.

LANGUAGE ACROSS THE CURRICULUM

To make such statements as *language plays a central part in learning, and the teacher's use of language is critically important,* or *we learn through speaking, listening and writing, and the way in which we are encouraged to speak and listen and write affects the nature and quality of our learning* may, today, sound like common sense. However, the importance of language in the learning process has not always been recognised as fully as it is today. In some of the more 'traditional', teacher-led classrooms of the past, for example, the assumption was that in order to develop cognitively students needed merely to listen to what their teachers told them and to read the texts that were placed in front of them. If effective learning did not ensue, this was thought likely to be because of some deficiency in the student.

For today's understanding of the importance of language in learning – and the perceived need for schools as a whole to develop policies and strategies on language and language-use – teachers in the UK owe much to the Bullock Report, *A Language For Life*, published in 1975. One of the central suggestions of the Bullock Report was that, precisely because all learning takes place through the medium of language, it is the responsibility of *all* teachers, regardless of their subject specialism, to help develop their students' language skills in appropriate ways. This involves an awareness and understanding on teachers' parts of the nature and importance of speaking, listening, reading and writing in the learning context.

Through its assertion that 'all teachers are teachers of language', the Bullock Report effectively challenged the notions that language development could be divorced from cognitive or affective development, and, in the field of secondary education, that language development was the concern solely of the English Department while that of other subject areas was 'curriculum content'. It also helped draw a necessary distinction between the subject 'English', which has its own particular curriculum content (for example, the study and enjoyment of literature, and the development of creative and personal writing skills) and 'language', which teachers and students use in all teaching and learning activities.

Following the publication of the Bullock Report, many schools developed their own policies for *Language Across the Curriculum*. Such policies took many forms. At some schools, different subject areas took it upon themselves to focus on specific areas of language development, including the development of styles and uses of language peculiar to the subject area. At other schools, teachers concentrated on developing students' language skills through cross-curricular initiatives involving language-focused collaborations between departments. Yet other schools attempted to compile inventories of students' language needs and to focus on identified aspects of language in a cross-curricular way on a year-by-year basis. As might be expected, these initiatives met with varying degrees of success. Some policies undoubtedly got no further than the policy document: that is, they became statements of intent rather than descriptions of actual practice (Torbe 1976). At many schools, however, language across the curriculum policies undoubtedly helped change entrenched attitudes towards language and learning for the immediate benefit of large numbers of students.

As will already be apparent, one of the key underpinnings of the promotion of language development across the curriculum was a particular view of the way in which learning itself takes place and of the relationship between language and thought. This underpinning is expressed in the following words of Mike Torbe on the topic of 'talking', in the NATE publication *Language Across the Curriculum: Guidelines for Schools*:

> Talking includes a wide variety of kinds of talk. The range extends from the formal public lecture to an unknown audience . . . through business meetings, planning meetings, interviews, gossip, casual chat, to intimate sharings . . . Talk . . . includes . . . the formal or prepared occasion, such as the lecture, or the teacher addressing the whole class, where the language is often pre-planned. But it also includes the kind of talk which happens when a group of people are sharing experiences, solving problems, exploring new ideas, and so on. Talk of this kind is often hesitant, inexplicit and discursive, but is essential . . . to learning. We would therefore make a distinction between talk which is a more spontaneous activity which grows and changes its direction according to different purposes, and talk which is more formally ordered, planned and organized.
>
> (Torbe 1976, p. 7)

Readers will be immediately aware of the similarities between Torbe's words and the theories of development of Piaget and Vygotsky and the practical criticisms of Barnes and Hull outlined in the two previous chapters. The notion of language 'varieties' (Torbe 1976, p. 8), which become incorporated into a person's 'language repertoire', will be of particular relevance when we consider issues of education and *culture* in the next chapter.

Students' language: the importance of speaking, listening, reading and writing in the learning context

The notion of 'language repertoires' referred to by Torbe and others includes the suggestion that for effective learning to take place students need to be taught how to speak, listen, read and write in a variety of ways and in a variety of contexts. As has been pointed out already, this may sound obvious: however, the principle has not always been translated into classroom practice, especially where the development of speaking and listening skills is concerned. The 'traditional' curriculum, indeed – or, rather, the way in which it has been traditionally 'delivered' – has emphasised writing over reading and reading over speaking, and assumed that, as long as students are quiet and looking in the right direction, listening is not something that needs to be actively taught (Moore 1998).

The construction of the current post-Bullock UK National Curriculum for English shows how far the official and unofficial teaching agendas have moved away from the promotion of such practice – a shift in line with other developments away from an overemphasis on whole-class, teacher-led pedagogies towards a greater emphasis on student-centred, interactive models of teaching and learning. Thus, speaking and listening skills are accorded as much priority in the new National Curriculum documentation for English as are reading and writing skills, while reading itself is seen as a much more complex and creative activity than the mere decoding of information or analysis of literary devices (DFE 1995).

There is no room here to explore in any depth how the various language skills can operate together, how they can promote general learning as well as language development, or how teachers might co-operate to encourage expertise in speaking, listening, reading and writing. The following pointers, however, are offered as starting-points for readers' own investigations.

SPEAKING AND LISTENING ACROSS THE CURRICULUM

The importance of speaking and listening in the learning process has already been acknowledged in Chapter 1 – in particular, with reference to Vygotsky's reminder that learning and teaching are fundamentally social activities. The encouragement and management of students' oral interactions with one another is an extremely important aspect of the teacher's work, but one that is also fraught with difficulties – to such an extent that many teachers are often very wary of allowing it to occur as often as it should. Not only do students talking among themselves generate a great deal of noise, which may often be construed as a loss of classroom discipline, but the teacher will also be concerned that students do not take the wrong kind of advantage of such activity to discuss matters that are of little or no relevance to the topic in hand, or do not sit back and take an 'easy ride' while other students in the group do all the talking. *As every teacher knows, the monitoring and management of oral work in the classroom can be very demanding of both time and energy. It is also axiomatic, however, that oral work has to be encouraged if students are to continue to be active and independent learners.*

Useful guidelines on the management of small-group discussions and activities are provided in the National Curriculum Council's/National Oracy Project's booklet *Teaching, Talking and Learning in KS3* (NCC/NOP 1991). These guidelines are in turn based on a learning model devised by Reid, Forrestal and Cook in their book *Small Group Learning in the Classroom* (1989). The guidelines offer a staged structure for teachers and students, to ensure that group discussions are constructive, focused and controlled while at the same time ensuring opportunities for students to explore, reflect and elaborate.

The five stages are:

- *engagement* – designed to activate students' interest in the topic and 'give them a stake in the activity';
- *exploration* – involving 'giving students time and a structure to enable them to make sense of the [provided] information for themselves';
- *transformation* – during which students are helped to 'focus their thinking', to sort their ideas into some kind of pattern;
- *presentation* – involving the sharing of ideas with one another, including with the class as a whole;
- *reflection* – when students review what they have said and done, make decisions, and 'select ideas for further study'.

Oral work can be organised in a number of ways that help both students and teacher (Reid *et al.* 1989). At all times, however, the teacher needs to ask:

- *When* is it best to organise learning in small groups? (and when not?)
- *How* can learning be maximised?
- *How* does the teacher know how long activities should or will take, and when to intervene or bring matters to a close?
- *What* will be done if students do not talk about the topic in hand?
- *How* can students be helped to listen to and value each other's contributions?

The encouragement and development of listening skills is particularly important here, and too often overlooked. If students are aware that they will not be asked to summarise or respond to other students' observations, they may do no more than remain silent while other students are talking, simply waiting for another space in the conversation to fill with their own ideas. These ideas might not relate to anything else that has been said and might have been quite untouched by the discussion.

> A major challenge for teachers is to find ways of encouraging students not only to listen to the views and understandings of others but to use those views and understandings to check, to question, to challenge and even to confirm their own existing views and understandings.

READING ACROSS THE CURRICULUM

Between 1978 and 1982, a Schools Council Project *Reading in the Secondary School* carried out an extensive investigation into the nature and uses of reading across the secondary curriculum. Its main findings, which have subsequently been reproduced in a number of smaller investigations, can be summarised as follows:

- A relatively small proportion of students' time in lessons was spent reading. Furthermore, this reading was frequently fragmented into short bursts, approximately half occurring in bursts of less than fifteen seconds in any one minute. This pattern was accounted for by activities such as:

  * reading questions from textbooks or worksheets prior to writing answers;
  * copying from books or the board;
  * 'skimming' texts in search of answers to literal questions.

  This kind of reading was demanded by teachers partly on the premiss that it made subjects more 'accessible' to 'weaker students' – a view which, as has already been suggested, is itself highly questionable.

> Clearly, school subjects will differ in the emphasis they place on learning from written texts. However, if generally there is very little continuous and 'engaged' reading going on across the curriculum it seems bound to limit students' opportunities to *develop* their reading, including their ability to profit from it. For this reason, many schools encourage all subject departments to find opportunities to build continuous reading activities into their subject syllabuses and curricula.

- Many of the texts which students were required to read were too difficult for many of them to manage. This was a particular problem with students transferring from primary to secondary schools at age eleven. Students were also often asked to read different *types* of text in the primary and secondary phases of education, typically concentrating more on stories and 'topic books' in primary schools but using subject-specific textbooks much more in secondary schools.

Some secondary-school teachers have subsequently attempted to simplify some of the texts they use with their students. This can be very time-consuming, however, and more difficult than it might at first glance appear. Furthermore, simplified texts will be less likely to help students become familiar with the range of vocabulary appropriate to their learning. Other options for teachers include developing collaborative and group reading activities, enabling students to support one another's reading, and helping students to understand how to use their new textbooks.

- While most students were relatively competent at 'literal' comprehension, they found it much more difficult to *learn* from their reading by 'reading between the lines' and comparing what they were reading with what they already knew.

An illustration of this can be provided in a consideration of the text: 'Mrs Robinson gazed with mixed feelings of joy and sorrow at the old house.' 'Literal' questions might be 'What did Mrs Robinson gaze at with mixed feelings?' or 'What words were used to describe Mrs Robinson's feelings as she gazed at the old house?' – to which the answers, relatively easily arrived at, might be 'the old house' and 'joy and sorrow'. A more challenging question, such as 'What do you think the writer means by "mixed feelings of joy and sorrow"?' or 'Why would Mrs Robinson feel this way?' or 'Describe a time when you have had mixed feelings about something' would prove far more challenging for the student, and more likely to develop both their understanding of the text and their ability to express that understanding to others.

The Schools Council Project concluded that the most effective way of improving comprehension and helping students to learn from their reading (as well as to enjoy it!) was to provide them with opportunities to improve their ability and willingness to *reflect* on what they read. Among the strategies suggested in order to achieve this purpose was the use of DARTs (Directed Activities Related to Texts) – a range of collaborative group reading tasks designed to enable students to focus on the structure and meaning of different types of text encountered in school. (DARTs include *sequencing* exercises, in which students are given a text that has been cut up and has to be put back together in a logical or imaginative way; *prediction* exercises, in which the endings of texts are removed and students have to suggest what might happen next; and *cloze* passages, in which students have to fill in missing words that have been blanked out of the text by the teacher.)

> Readers might wish to consider students' reading habits in their present school. Are the Schools Council Project's concerns about reading still valid? Or is there an extent to which teachers have been able to respond to the difficulties and bring about a change in reading habits? To what extent does the current National Curriculum itself promote or limit students' opportunities for continuous reading?

WRITING ACROSS THE CURRICULUM

The *Bullock Report* (1975), to which reference has already been made, and, more recently, the *National Writing Project* (1985–89) have offered a view of students' writing which values it as a means of *developing and promoting learning* rather than as something which just happens 'after the learning has taken place' in order to provide a record for public examinations or for the teacher to mark. Margaret Wallen, in the National Writing Project's book *Writing and Learning* (1989), sums this up by suggesting that 'What is needed . . . is a range of writing activities which are truly effective in encouraging learning because they demand the reorganisation of knowledge by learners themselves, and allow both teachers and learners to make the learning process as visible as it can be' (Wallen 1989, p. 91).

> The notion of writing making learning itself 'visible' is as important as the notion of writing helping to organise and develop thoughts, offering the teacher an excellent opportunity of diagnosing each student's current capabilities and planning future pedagogy accordingly.

Wallen summarises the strategies developed by teachers who took part in the National Writing Project – drawn from all curriculum areas – as follows:

- strategies which enable students to initiate their own writing and become actively involved in their own learning by using their existing knowledge as a starting-point;
- strategies which help students to develop their awareness of what is involved in writing and hence to develop greater control over their own writing;
- writing activities which encourage students to rework knowledge for themselves and so promote learning in a direct way.

(for specific strategies, see Wallen 1989, pp. 92–95).

Such advice offers an interesting point of comparison with the recent development of 'writing frames' (Lewis and Wray 1994, 1998), which are often aimed not so much at giving students 'ownership' of their writing or promoting its heuristic value, as at encouraging students to develop their writing skills through organising their thoughts in very specific, 'generic' ways (see 'Genre, register and extending language repertoires', below).

> As with the issue of reading, and with reference to what has already been said in Chapters 1 and 2 about matches and conflicts between public policy and effective learning, a useful exercise is to consider whether the current National Curriculum in the UK promotes or obstructs the kinds of writing activity suggested by the National Writing Project.

Genre, register and extending language repertoires

The *Bullock Report* not only suggested the need for teachers to address their own language use: it also recognised that school students themselves need to be encouraged to use language in a wide variety of situations and in a wide range of styles. While part of this involved encouraging students to develop skills in reading, speaking, listening and writing, another part related to the different *kinds* of language that students might need to use *within* their speaking and writing skills. The language that might be expected of them in writing up a science experiment, for example, might be significantly different from the language they might be expected to use in writing a story, which in turn might be different from the language they would be expected to use in presenting an argument (see also Flower 1966).

Much of this is a matter of *convention* or *genre*. There may well be certain concepts, expressed in certain subject-specific vocabulary, that students will need to develop if they are to succeed in science, just as, it could be argued, the development of a wide vocabulary might help a student to write more effective poetry or short stories. However, it does not necessarily follow that science can only be learned or that poems and stories can only be written using *certain kinds of linguistic constructions*. Furthermore, it has been argued (Kress 1982) that formal, 'generic' language styles can actually hinder active, creative, exploratory *thinking* by making the student *servile* to the linguistic forms in and through which learning takes place.

The issue of genre is a tricky one, in much the same sort of way as is the issue of standard English that we shall consider shortly. Given the nature of the current school curriculum and related assessment criteria, it is clearly important for school-students to be able to recognise and work in a variety of genres if they are to succeed academically, and it is incumbent upon teachers working within the constraints of that curriculum to ensure that their students develop these 'generic' skills (Lewis and Wray 1994, 1998). Thus, teachers working within the humanities may need to teach their students how to structure a written *argument* along the lines 'introduction, two paragraphs for, two paragraphs against, conclusion', and how to deliberately remove the 'I' in favour of a more 'dispassionate' voice, in addition to helping them explore and develop the *ideas* contained within the essay. On the other hand, it is equally important for teachers to keep sight of the fact that genres are *cultural constructs* (Kress 1983, Moore 1999a) and that there may be other, equally valid linguistic formats and styles in which to complete written tasks. (For instance, there may be other perfectly good ways of presenting an argument than that outlined in the above example.) This cultural factor, to which we shall return in the next chapter, is particularly important when teachers are working with bilingual or bidialectal students. For such students, there may be critical mismatches between the genres favoured by the mainstream education system and the genres favoured by the communities within which they principally live (Moore 1999a). Such mismatches, which are rather less likely to occur in the case of monolingual, standard-English speakers, may result in students being told that their verbal expression is 'wrong' when in fact it may simply be *different*. In this case, the deficiency may be the school's for failing to recognise the difference for what it is. Kress, who has written at some length on the issue of genre in education, suggests that although it is important for students to develop expertise in the range of standard school ways of expression, this does not mean that the genres themselves have an intrinsic superiority or 'correctness'. Kress describes generic mismatches in the following terms:

> Access to writing is not equally available to all members of a society.
> [. . .] Social dialects differ in their proximity to the standard defined
> and encoded in the written language. [. . .] For certain social groups –
> the professional classes, for instance – the structure of the spoken
> form of their dialects is very strongly influenced by the structures of
> writing. For some children the syntax of writing will be more familiar
> than for others, to whom it may be totally unfamiliar. Hence in a
> group of children some may start with a knowledge which others
> have yet to acquire.
>
> (Kress 1983, p. 33)

In Kress's account, differences in language style between students and schools easily become miscategorised in terms of error:

> [T]hese are transgressions against style, and as such we may consider
> corrections of this kind as paradigm cases of the notion of error
> arising out of conventionality. Its function lies in coercing the one
> who is corrected into adherence to convention. In essence the
> question is one of etiquette and manners, like opening your egg at
> the blunt or pointed end. There is, of course, no reason why the
> teacher should not point out what the 'best manners' are, as parents
> ought not to be stopped from teaching their children to balance peas
> on the back of a fork. Indeed, the teacher can hardly do other than
> encourage [expertise in] conventions, such as spelling. Where a young

school-leaver's chances of getting and keeping a job may depend on
his or her [expertise in] such skills, teachers may give quite inordinate
attention to such otherwise trivial abilities.

(Kress 1982, p. 188–89)

Kress's suggestion that expertise in recognising and replicating certain formal
or 'standard' linguistic and representational genres needs to be learned by
students, but that ignorance of a genre is more likely to be a matter of experience than 'ability', has very important implications both for assessment and
for pedagogy. In particular, it encourages us away from a 'student deficit' view
of academic language performance towards one which recognises
cultural–linguistic bias in schools and schooling and challenges the teacher
rather than the student to make good the problem. For Kress, students who
lack out-of-school expertise in certain 'favoured' linguistic forms and styles do
not need to 'replace' or 'correct' existing linguistic forms and styles in which
they *may* have recognised expertise outside the school setting: rather, they
need to *add* expertise in the favoured academic genres to genres in which
they already have expertise, building in the process on their existing generic
skills. In this way, they will not be deceived by classroom language into
believing that they are stupid because they do not understand, but will come
to recognise that school language itself is an arbitrary barrier which they can,
with the teacher's help, overcome. This is what is meant by the expression
'*extending one's language repertoire*'.

Kress's ideas have been fleshed out by other linguists, who have supported
their observations with close reference to empirical research carried out in
working-class communities. Such writers include Brice Heath, Tizard and
Hughes, and William Labov, whose work we shall turn to below.

Standard and non-standard English: the 'linguistic deficit' debate

Just as school students are expected to be able to operate in 'standard genres'
(for example, to write a story according to certain pre-set criteria, to present
an argument in a certain formulaic way, or to write up a science experiment in a particular visual and linguistic style), so they are expected to operate
using 'standard English'. The ability to use standard English is, it is quite
rightly argued, a major factor in enabling students to pass public examinations
and in giving them access to better-paid, more prestigious jobs on leaving
school. It could be argued, of course, that this is only true because we live
in essentially ethnocentric societies which are intolerant of linguistic difference
(including 'deviations' in terms of accent and dialect); however, as long as
such a situation remains, the empowerment discourse can be invoked in support of developing students' standard English skills as part and parcel of school
curricula. Certainly, such an argument continues to be pushed with increasing
insistence, both in public pronouncements on 'standards' and through National

Curriculum documentation (see, for instance, the England and Wales National Curriculum for English, 1995, with its repeated references to standard English [DFE 1995]). Clearly, the understanding is that schools should not only help students to learn by paying attention to language *in the learning situation*: they are also required to develop students' 'standard' language skills *in themselves*.

In this regard, the presence of large numbers of non-standard English speakers in many of our schools has presented something of a difficulty for teachers. In the past (Moore 1998, 1999a) it was normal practice to treat non-standard *dialects* of English as simply 'gone wrong' versions of something called standard English, which itself was typically misdescribed as 'correct' or 'proper' English. In such an interpretation, the teacher's job was clear: the corrupted, 'grammatically incorrect' versions of English used by large numbers of students had to be corrected; effectively, it had to be eliminated and replaced with 'correct' English. (A parallel in bilingual education is the 'subtractive' model of language development, whereby bilingual students are thought to need to shed their first language if they are ever to develop full fluency in a second.) This notion of the correctness of standard English and the incorrectness of non-standard English has been supported in the development of the National Curriculum for England and Wales. *English in the National Curriculum*, for example, (DFE 1995) suggests that 'standard English is distinguished from other forms of English by its vocabulary, and *by rules and conventions of grammar, spelling and punctuation*', and that 'the grammatical features that distinguish standard English include how pronouns, adverbs and adjectives *should be* used and how negatives, questions and verb tenses *should be* formed' (DFE 1995, p. 3, emphases added).

The view that only standard English was correct often resulted in non-standard dialects being perceived as 'lazy' or 'slovenly': consequently, the students who *used* them were themselves perceived as lazy or slovenly, and thus not much could be expected of them academically. As with the genre issue, a *deficit* view of the development of such students was invoked.

This deficit view did not *always* imply laziness on the part of the student, of course. Indeed, a more liberal, if equally misguided, view, suggested that we should feel sorry for such students: that they came from impoverished cultures that simply lacked the linguistic richness and variety of the more educated classes. This view suggested that such students could – and should – be helped into a world of proper language that would lighten their lives – though of course they would have to leave behind their local, inhibiting cultures in the process. Famously, an acrimonious debate on this very subject erupted in the UK in the 1960s, when Basil Bernstein wrote about 'restricted' and 'elaborated' linguistic 'codes' (Bernstein 1971a) – the former describing working-class language, which was seen as very heavily dependent on current and concrete contexts, the latter describing middle-class language, which was seen as having the capacity for more abstract, decontextualised reasoning. Although Bernstein suggested that it was the language rather than the users of language that had – or that lacked – the full capacity for abstract thinking, his view was nevertheless seen as a deficit model, that pathologised working-class learners rather than the linguistically biased educational system in which (according to other commentators) they were taught, and it invoked a particularly bitter response from a colleague of Bernstein's, Harold Rosen (1972). Rosen argued that so-called working-class language was in no way inferior to the standard English favoured in schools, and that it was dangerous, as well as mistaken, to suggest that it was.

Rosen's argument was further developed by the American linguist William Labov, who undertook empirical research into the language patterns of young, black, working-class Americans. Labov's work (e.g. Labov 1972) led him to draw two very important conclusions:

1) Non-standard English dialects are just as rule-bound and as regular as standard English. It is not that they do not follow grammatical rules: they simply follow grammatical rules which are *different from* those used in standard English (see, too, Stubbs 1976, p. 33). The implication here is that speakers of non-standard dialects are not lazy or slovenly users of language. Furthermore, they possess all the basic language skills they will need if they are to develop expertise in and use standard English. That is to say, they cannot be accused of lacking linguistic ability.

2) In many ways and situations, non-standard dialects of English are more vibrant, more flexible and, ultimately, more effective than standard English. As Labov expresses this:

> *Our work in the speech community makes it painfully obvious that in many ways working-class speakers are more effective narrators, reasoners and debaters than many middle-class speakers who temporize, qualify, and lose their argument in a mass of irrelevant detail.*
>
> (Labov 1972, pp. 192–93)

In the UK, Labov's arguments against the innate superiority of standard English have been supported by socio-historical accounts of the development of standard English as a prominent social dialect (e.g. Trudgill 1983; Perera 1987; Perera 1984, pp. 211–214; Stubbs 1976). Opposing the patently erroneous notion that standard English is some kind of primordial English of which all other Englishes are corruptions, such commentators have shown how standard English itself started as a regional dialect of English and became a dominant social dialect as the result of geographical accident. As such, it is no better, no more varied and certainly no more or less 'grammatical' than any other variety of English. Nor should dialects be perceived as mutually exclusive: that is, anyone should be capable of operating in more than one dialect, in the same way that bilinguals are perfectly capable of operating equally proficiently in two or more different *languages*.

The work of educationalists like Labov, Stubbs and Trudgill is highly significant for all teachers – especially if we accept the Bullock Report's suggestion that all teachers are teachers of language. The notion that we should 'replace and correct' non-standard English use, for example – which previously proved counterproductive, often resulting in 'linguistic self hatred' in the student (Trudgill 1983; Coard 1971) – does not hold up if we accept that non-standard dialects are different rather than wrong, and if we believe that the skills used in the practice of non-standard dialects can be utilised (or 'transferred') in the practice of standard English. Rather, teachers might seek to replace the 'subtractive' model of language development with an 'additive' one in which – as with the development of genres – students are encouraged not to abandon non-standard forms but to add so-called standard ones to them. They might also consider ways of showing 'standard' speakers how their own language might be enriched by the addition of non-standard forms and constructs, and perhaps even to militate as best they can for a change of culture that no longer judges a person's worth on the basis of the way they speak or write.

FUNCTIONAL, CULTURAL AND CRITICAL LITERACY

We cannot leave the question of language and learning without a consideration, however brief, of the concept of literacy which underpins so much of the school curriculum and the ways in which our students are taught.

It can have escaped no one's attention that central governments in the UK and elsewhere continue to voice concerns about standards of literacy and the need for all students to develop 'basic skills'. As was suggested in Chapter 2, these concerns are typically expressed within the discourse of 'empowerment' – and, we might add, of 'not letting our children down'. We also saw in Chapter 2 how the desire to promote literacy was at the heart of the initial drive towards free public education for all in the UK, how this desire had both pragmatic and humanitarian roots, and how some policy-makers feared that sharp increases in the number of literate citizens might lead to civil unrest.

It could be argued that the current UK government's concerns about basic literacy for all are part of an ongoing drive for universal literacy that dates back to the very inception of State education. Without wishing to undermine what seems a perfectly laudable and decent objective, it could also be argued, however, that these concerns are, essentially, for the development of a very basic, narrow kind of literacy that might provide young people with some measure of *limited* empowerment but that will do very little to change the essentially disempowering society in which they may feel they live.

A major part of the problem here is that 'literacy' is often interpreted as meaning 'being able to read and write' – that is, being able to decode the printed into the spoken (and the 'thought') word, and to encode the spoken (or thought) word into the written word. This, however, is a definition of basic or – as some commentators have preferred to call it – *functional* literacy. In his article *Culture or Canon? Critical Pedagogy and the Politics of Literacy*, McLaren (1988) describes not one but *three* kinds of literacy: *functional* literacy, *cultural* literacy and *critical* literacy. His argument is that students need to develop expertise in all three of these literacies if true empowerment is to ensue, but that typically the first two of these literacies are developed in school curricula *at the expense of* the third (see also Fairclough 1989).

- *Functional literacy* is defined by McLaren as basic decoding and encoding skills: what is often meant when the term 'literacy' is used by policy-makers and practitioners.
- *Cultural literacy*, on the other hand, involves 'educating students to be . . . the bearers of certain meanings, values and views': that is to say, the kind of literacy required (for example) in genre replication, or in accepting the importance of certain items and forms of knowledge over others. Cultural literacy is what 'enables' a student to write what is perceived by the teacher as a good story, a well-presented argument, a good drawing, and so forth.
- *Critical literacy* is fundamentally different from these other two literacies, in that it is concerned with the development of independent analytical and deconstructive skills. In McLaren's words, it is concerned with involving students and their teachers in 'decoding the ideological dimensions of texts, institutions, social practices, and cultural forms . . . in order to reveal their selective interests' (McLaren 1988, p. 213). Its central purpose is 'to create a citizenry critical enough to both analyse and challenge the oppressive characteristics of the larger society so that a more just, equitable, and democratic society can be created' (ibid., pp. 213–14).

> We might say that whereas functional and cultural literacy seek to help the student to succeed within an unchanged society, critical literacy has in mind a different educational agenda, which is aimed at changing society itself in ways that will help everyone to succeed. If cultural literacy provides students with the ability to replicate genres, to develop ritual knowledge, to recite sanctioned facts, critical literacy shows them how to understand those genres, that knowledge, those facts for what they are: that is to say, the preferences and *selections* of privileged classes, presented as though they had some universal, intrinsic value.

The kind of activity that teachers might undertake with their students in the development of critical literacy skills is hinted at by Kress, whose work on genre we considered earlier:

> If the teacher were to focus on questions of convention, to make them and the degree of choice which exists in each instance a subject of discussion (none in morphology, next to none in syntax, some in tense, more in the choice of words, and much in aesthetic matters such as repetition), then the child would gain an important insight

not only into the nature, function and uses of language, but also into the nature of social behaviour and its foundations in more or less rigid rules and conventions.

(Kress 1983, pp. 188–89)

Other teachers might wish to take critical literacy a lot further than this, engaging with their students in more obviously political, anti-coercive discussions and activities. What all critical literacy activity tries to accomplish, however, is to help school students to develop expertise in critically interrogating the messages they receive and the wide range of texts with which they engage, in order that they may be better placed to take an active, critical part in the development and improvement of democratic societies. A major part of this activity involves helping students to understand how language itself operates for and against their best interests, both in the educational setting and beyond.

SUMMARY

This chapter has considered the centrality of language to effective teaching and learning, suggesting that language has the power to control, to limit and to confuse as well as to empower, to liberate and to illuminate. Particular emphasis has been given to the following points:

- For effective learning to take place, the teacher's use of language in the classroom is as important as the language that is used by the students themselves.
- Teachers need to recognise, build on and make use of their students' existing and developing language skills in supporting their academic and creative endeavours.
- There is a continued need for schools to develop policies for language across the curriculum, and for these to be appropriately implemented. In particular, students need to learn how to use a wide variety of language forms in a wide variety of learning and social contexts.
- Notions of linguistic 'correctness' need to be replaced by teachers and policymakers by notions of linguistic variety and by the appropriate development of students' linguistic *repertoires.*
- To become fully empowered, students need to be not only basically or 'functionally' literate, but also to be culturally and critically literate. Critical literacy empowers students to 'read' how society operates, and in particular to discover the biases and power relations that lie behind social and cultural transactions.

SUGGESTED ACTIVITIES

1.   Through observation and self-evaluations, assess the extent to which the teacher initiates/student responds/teacher provides feedback model of classroom interaction can be described as the norm in today's classrooms.

    Can you identify any practices which ensure that this model does not overdominate?

    Are there any ways in which the National Curriculum in your subject area supports or challenges these patterns of teacher–student interaction?

2.   In what ways can writing be used to *develop ideas* in your subject area (rather than merely express what is already known by the student)?

3.   Find and critique examples of

    (a)   your own language
    (b)   language in textbooks or worksheets you have used that you feel, with the benefit of hindsight, may have hindered rather than helped your students' understanding of lesson content or of instructions you have given. How, precisely, might these difficulties be overcome in future lessons?

4.   Discuss, with colleagues, ways in which work with bilingual students might be made more effective in your subject area through specific attention to the students' existing cognitive–linguistic skills (i.e. their existing grasp – in whatever language – of concepts and communication skills).

SUGGESTED READING

Barnes, D. (1986) 'Language in the Secondary Classroom' in Barnes, D., Britton, J. and Torbe, M. (1986) *Language, the Learner and the School* (3rd edition) pp. 9–88. Through reference to everyday classroom experiences and activities, Barnes shows how teachers' language can – deliberately or unwittingly – serve to limit the development and expectations of some students, and how it can perpetuate social inequalities. A particular interest in this thirty-year-old text lies in considerations of the extent to which language-use, and an awareness of the importance of language-use, in the classroom has or has not developed in the intervening period.

Bullock, A. *et al.* (1975) *A Language For Life*, Chapters 9–12. This watershed text formally recognised the centrality of language to the learning process, as well as introducing the now commonplace – though still often misunderstood and overlooked – notion of language across the curriculum. Though its language is annoyingly sexist, and though many of its ideas have subsequently become commonplace, the Bullock Report remains an interesting and important historical document that sets out much of the educational agenda for the last quarter of the century and that serves as a benchmark against which to measure subsequent developments and progress in the area of language and learning.

Cummins, J. (1984) *Bilingualism and Special Education: Issues in Assessment and Pedagogy.* Read in conjunction with Cummins' more recent book *Negotiating Identities: Education for Empowerment in a Diverse Society, Bilingualism and Special Education* offers a useful presentation of many of the major language issues regarding the teaching and learning of bilingual students, and provides a persuasive argument for the potential cognitive benefits of being bilingual. Particularly useful is Cummins' illustration of the way in which an imperfect understanding of language development on the teacher's part can lead to bilingual students being dismissed as cognitively or linguistically deficient.

Edwards, D. and Mercer, N. (1987) *Common Knowledge: The Development of Understanding in the Classroom.* Edwards' and Mercer's research-based account of school learning focuses on the ways in which the teacher's language can control and limit as well as facilitate and extend students' learning, and of the ways in which students can learn to succeed academically by providing the 'right' answers in the right form, often at the expense of genuine understanding.

Stubbs, M. (1976) *Language, Schools and Classrooms.* Stubbs' book still provides one of the most embracing, easily-digestible accounts of the ways in which teacher and student language impact upon learning in school classrooms.

4 Teaching, Learning and Culture

This chapter explores the cultural aspects of teaching and learning, with particular reference to culturally mixed classrooms. Using some of the ideas of Pierre Bourdieu, the chapter considers the positioning of the teacher as learning-facilitator and, simultaneously, bearer of dominant cultural ideologies, and of the practical tensions associated with this duality. In exploring these issues, the chapter considers cultural variables in preferred learning styles, as well as in curriculum content. Readers are encouraged to take full account of cultural variables in the classroom, through processes of reflection and reflexivity.

SOCIAL ENGINEERING AND MERITOCRACY

We have already considered, in Chapter 2, the suggestion that education may be as much about social engineering as about personal empowerment. Such a suggestion implies that school-students are subjected to different forms of education, allied to different teacher expectations, according to the socio-economic class from which they come. An adequate supply of managers, for example (mainly drawn from the middle classes), is ensured, along with an adequate supply of labourers, clerks, shopworkers and so on (drawn mainly from the working and 'lower middle' classes). Such a view contests the notion of a curriculum fixed by its internal 'rightness' (in Matthew Arnold's words [1909, pp. 10–11] the 'best that is known and thought in the world'), arguing that the curriculum at any given point in its history reflects the views and interests of particular social groups – often at the expense of the views and interests of others. As Raymond Williams puts this point of view: '[education systems] claim that they are transmitting "knowledge" or "culture" in an absolute, universally derived sense, though it is obvious that different systems, at different times and in different countries, transmit radically different selective versions of both' (Williams 1981, p. 186; see also Apple 1995).

This chapter aims to explore these possibilities further, giving particular consideration to the ways in which culture may be used in education systems as a way of disguising, perpetuating and legitimising institutional bias and inequality (essentially, unacceptable forms of 'differentiation'), and of presenting a particular 'reality' in which some students are configured and perceived as simply more or less clever, motivated, or hard working than others. Such a reality is often configured in terms of 'merit' (i.e. school-students succeed or fail on 'merit' rather than, for instance, because of the nature of schooling itself, or the socio-economic conditions in which they live) – a notion which may sound preferable to rewarding *privilege*, and which appears on the surface to support many people's notions of the comprehensive ideal, but which itself may disguise institutional bias and undesirable educational practices.

The dangers inherent in such a view have been famously described by Michael Young, who coined the term *meritocracy* in 1958. In Young's analysis (Young 1958), meritocracy leads to the early identification and special treatment of children identified as 'more able', and is linked to educational practice that emphasises quantification, test scores and qualifications as ways of assessing and rewarding such ability. It is easy to see how, within such a system, notions like 'intelligence' may serve to disguise cultural bias, precisely because intelligence itself is described and perceived as 'culture-free' or something which exists 'in itself', rather than as a socio-cultural construct. Within the discourse of intelligence and ability, notions of deficit and advantage inherent within the individual student may be held responsible for lesser or greater achievement rather than, say, matches and mismatches between the cultural preferences and preferred learning styles of the student and the school.

Several commentators have described the ways in which cultural bias in the curriculum not only 'disguises itself' but also operates to present a false picture of 'able' (often, middle-class) and 'less able' (typically working-class) students, which itself can be used as a justification for unequal distributions of jobs and pay. Michael Apple (1979) has described in some detail the ways in which the school curriculum may be regarded as biased in its arbitrary selections of what skills and knowledge should and should not be included – a view elaborated in the work of Pierre Bourdieu, whose theory we shall consider in more detail a little later. As we have seen in the previous chapter, commentators such as Kress (1982), Brice Heath (1983) and Labov (1972) have drawn attention to class and ethnic differences in favoured styles of spoken and written language (as well as in favoured *topics* of conversation and debate, favoured literary and non-literary texts, and so on), and to the implications for working-class and ethnic-minority students entering school systems which favour and validate cultural forms and preferences that are more familiar in dominant middle-class communities. Tizard and Hughes have also described class- and culture-based differences in what is deemed acceptable *non-academic* behaviour – including some forms of linguistic behaviour – suggesting that, again, students from middle-class homes are far more likely to find a close match between what is expected and valued at home and what is expected and valued at school than are students from working-class homes (Tizard and Hughes 1984).

What each of the above commentators has in common is, first, a view that the kinds of behaviour, areas of knowledge and skill, and forms of expression promoted within formal educational systems are essentially 'arbitrary'. This does not mean that they were selected *randomly* (they are, rather, depicted as being selected – consciously or unconsciously – precisely *because* they reflect and promote middle-class over working-class, and ethnic-majority over ethnic-minority interests), but that, beyond a certain functional level, they have no *intrinsic* justification for their inclusion at the expense of other kinds of behaviour, areas of knowledge and skill or forms of expression. As has been argued in the previous chapter, standard English may be a very useful and important dialect for students to acquire and develop, but that does not imply that it is *inherently superior* to other dialects of English: indeed, it could be argued that a huge part of the potential usefulness of standard English would disappear if we developed more culturally and linguistically tolerant *societies*.

The second thing that unites these commentators is a recognition – more or less explicit – that the arbitrary nature of school curricula (and we could extend this argument to considerations of particular styles of *pedagogy*) is rendered *invisible* through its manner of presentation: that is to say (Moore 1998), the curriculum is typically presented as a rational, unbiased selection of skills and knowledge, made against a background of universal, a-cultural – rather than local, culture-specific – criteria. The texts recommended for study in the *English* curriculum, for example, may be *presented* as having an intrinsic, unarguable worth. However, a more accurate explanation of their recommendation may be that they comprise a collection of the works that are best loved by an essentially middle-class readership and that do most to celebrate and promulgate middle-class tastes and values. Similarly, the practice of promoting 'factual knowledge' in history or geography over an understanding of the ways in which human beings live, work and behave together, may be *presented* as crucial 'basic knowledge', but in reality it may promote a very limited and limiting view of people and the world that specifically shies away from potentially subversive questions about such matters as the interrelationships between poverty and wealth.

The 'God-given' way in which school curricula are typically presented – chiefly, through examination syllabuses and assessment criteria, and through related textbooks and schemes of work – is likely to reduce the possibility of students who are minoritised by those curricula *being aware of* their inherent cultural bias, any more than favoured students are likely to be. Thus, rather than understanding the school curriculum in terms of its offering middle-class students a clear *advantage* academically, such minoritised students may be led to perceive *themselves* as intellectually or academically deficient and to underperform accordingly: that is to say, if the cultural bias in the curriculum is not made sufficiently clear to the students it marginalises, those students may remain unaware of the bias, and may interpret the regular achievement of relatively low grades as evidence of their own innate inability (see also Moore 1999a). In a curriculum that values and treats standard English not simply as a useful social tool but as a form of communication that is superior to other forms, for example, the non-standard speaker may well be led to believe that they are incapable of performing correctly something which, for many of their classmates, appears to be performed with the greatest of ease. The fact that these same classmates would find it equally difficult to operate in non-standard dialects is not allowed, in the current configuration of the curriculum, to become an issue.

If the above analysis is accepted, even in part, then there are clear implications for teachers in terms both of their *expectations* of 'cultural minority' students (students, that is, who are minoritised by virtue of ethnicity, class or gender) and of their *assessments* of such students. There are also, however, as we shall see, implications for *planning* and *teaching*. A particular issue here is that of 'differentiation', which we shall consider later in this chapter, and in particular a need to ensure that differentiation does not confine itself to facile and misleading notions of 'able' and 'less able' students. Before turning to these more practical matters, it will be useful, by way of contextualisation, to review some of the theory related to cultural bias in education.

PIERRE BOURDIEU: THE THEORY OF HABITUS AND FIELD

One of the most thorough and well-argued cases relating to cultural bias in school curricula is presented by the French sociologist and anthropologist Pierre Bourdieu. Although Bourdieu's theory may seem dated in some respects – notably, in its rather 'deterministic' leanings – it nevertheless offers a useful starting-point for discussing this crucial set of issues. In order fully to appreciate Bourdieu's theory of cultural bias, however, it is necessary first to understand a little of his theory of 'habitus' and 'field'.

Building on Dewey's understandings of habits and 'habitudes' (Dewey 1932, pp. 92–94), 'habitus' is the word used by Bourdieu to define a person's socially acquired yet – to the person in whom it resides – generally *invisible* 'disposition' (Bourdieu 1977). It is (Bourdieu 1971) 'the system of modes of perception, of thinking, of appreciation and of action' that human beings carry with them into the full range of social milieus (for example, the school in which they operate as a student or as a teacher) and the full set of circumstances (for example, the social circumstance in which vastly different financial rewards accrue for the same hours of work) within which they move and operate. These very real, often readily quantifiable social milieus and circumstances are described by Bourdieu as 'fields'. In Bourdieu's representation, the individual habitus can, at least in theory, contribute to *changes* in fields, but it also affects the ways in which the individual perceives and understands those fields. In particular, the habitus is likely to affect the individual's notions of what, for them, is *achievable* within any given field, thus setting very clear parameters for the individual in terms of personal ambition and expectations (Bourdieu 1990b, pp. 20, 59).

To understand how the habitus operates, two further things need to be understood, the first concerning the precise relationship between the habitus and the field, the second concerning the nature of the habitus itself. Although the habitus may have some impact upon the field, Bourdieu's suggestion is that the field itself is what originally shapes and creates the habitus: that is to say, the habitus is essentially a subjective internalisation of the 'objective' conditions within which the individual operates: in a sense, we *become* what pre-existing social conditions and attitudes *make us*. This is what Bourdieu means in his following description of the concept of field: 'I define field as a network, or configuration, of objective relations between positions objectively defined, in their existence and in the determinations they impose upon their occupants, agents or institutions, by their present and potential situation' (Wacquant 1989, p. 39. See also Bourdieu 1977; Jenkins 1992, p. 84; Young 1971a, pp. 10–11).

As will be seen from the above quotation, field is concerned both with culture and with privilege (and lack of it). Fields are, as Jenkins puts it, 'social arena[s] within which struggles or manoeuvres take place over specific resources or stakes and access to them' (Jenkins 1992, p. 84; see also Apple 1995). If we consider education systems – or even individual schools – in terms of *field*, questions we might ask are:

- What kinds of struggle and manoeuvre take place here?
- What parties are involved in these struggles and manoeuvres?
- What resources are at stake?
- Who does and doesn't have access to them?
- What are the relations of power within which these struggles and manoeuvres take place? In particular, who has power and who does not? And what different *kinds* and *degrees* of power are in operation?

To help answer these questions, a further point about the nature of fields needs to be clarified. This is that although, in Bourdieu's configuration, there may be many different *kinds* of field, with significant differences between them, there are also essential similarities or homologies between them. Every field, for example, has, by definition, 'its dominant and its dominated, its struggle for usurpation or exclusion, its mechanisms of reproduction' (Wacquant 1989, p. 41). To put this another way, we might say that fields are, willy-nilly, characterised by:

- inequalities;
- (unequal) competition;
- power relations;
- strictures and constraints;
- preferentialism and subordination.

This *homology* arises partly from the fact that every 'local' field (what we might term every 'sub-field') draws its essential characteristics from 'parent fields' or, as Bourdieu prefers it, 'fields of power' (ibid.). The 'field of power' is (Jenkins 1992, p. 86) 'the dominant or pre-eminent field of any society; it is the source of the hierarchical power relations which structure all other fields'. The field of power may be viewed as the overarching system of socio-economic relations within which all other fields – such as that of the education system or the individual school – and all other agents exist and operate.

If the habitus arises out of, is shaped by and reflects the fields in which it operates, and if those fields themselves are mechanisms by which power relations are established and confirmed and through which cultures are validated and degraded, why, we may ask, do individuals and groups of individuals who are actively and deliberately 'dominated' and 'excluded' not rise up more effectively or regularly against their situation, seeking to change the nature of the fields in order to improve their own personal situations and prospects? Bourdieu suggests that this is partly because the fields are so tightly structured and controlled by the dominant classes that resistance is at best piecemeal and at worst futile. There is another issue at stake, however, in Bourdieu's analysis, which leads us back to the question of the nature of the habitus itself. This issue concerns the relative scarcity of another form of resistance: that is to say, a resistance that questions the very value of the resources or stakes for which the dominated struggle – often without hope – for possession.

Why is it, for example, that working-class and ethnic-minority students and their parents do not question the particular middle-class selections of knowledge and skills that constitute the school curriculum and with regard to which their own abilities will be measured through public examination systems that validate and promote those middle-class selections?

From a 'Bourdieusian' perspective, the answer to this question is twofold. First, the dominated, excluded, marginalised members of society do not necessarily know or understand that they are dominated, excluded or marginalised in the particular, often very *subtle* ways they are – or, if they do recognise it, they may themselves impute social inequalities and their own underachievement to the 'natural order of things'. Second, what is at stake within the given field – in the school setting, for instance, the conferment of academic or creative success through the possession and demonstration of particular areas and kinds of knowledge and skills – may be seen not in terms of its 'mode of production' (Marx 1977; Eagleton 1983), but as *intrinsically legitimate* or superior. As Jenkins (1992, p. 85) puts this: 'The existence of a field presupposes and, in its functioning, creates a belief on the part of participants in the legitimacy and value of the capital which is at stake in the field.'

If we again focus on the school setting and relate this view to the observations previously made in this chapter and the last, this particular configuration suggests that marginalised students from working-class or ethnic minority backgrounds do not necessarily view (for example) the selection of literary texts on an English syllabus as being based on cultural *preference* (the cultural preference of the educated middle class), but rather on matters of intrinsic *quality*. Thus, they may, as a corollary, view literary texts favoured by and within their own 'home cultures' as inferior and not *worthy* of wider study – a view which, in turn, may lead to cultural self-deprecation and low self-expectation.

The way in which the arbitrary selections that comprise the school curriculum are disguised in a manner that renders them obvious, universal, 'natural', and – in particular – based upon notions of relative importance and merit, is paralleled, in Bourdieu's theory, by a corresponding *self*-deception, whereby the dominated individual's lack of choice and opportunity – caused by the conditions that prevail in the field itself – is either not seen at all by the individual or is misrecognised in terms of their own deficiency.

In its most extreme configuration, Bourdieu's theory of habitus and field appears very deterministic, offering little hope – or help – to the student or teacher who wishes to challenge cultural bias in school curricula and examination syllabuses. Other configurations, however, are less pessimistic. Bourdieu has suggested, for example, that the habitus, despite being typically hidden away from us and therefore to all intents and purposes invisible and unalterable, *can* be changed by *changed circumstances*, and that consequently one's ambitions and *expectations* may change with it. He has also – in a phrase that is potentially of great significance for classroom teachers – suggested that the habitus can be *controlled* by the 'awakening of consciousness and socio-analysis' (Bourdieu 1990a, p. 116): that is to say, by direct 'political' analysis, with one's students, of how societies are structured and individuals come to be structured, privileged, coerced and controlled within them. Some commentators (e.g. Apple 1980; MacDonald 1980) have taken issue with the deterministic leanings of Bourdieu's theory, arguing that ideologies and cultures are not only *reproduced* in schools: they are also *produced* there. Such an elaboration of Bourdieu's view prioritises an investigation of the nature of *consent*, without which, it is argued, cultural reproduction could not successfully occur. It includes, inevitably, considerations of the extent to which culturally minoritised families may actively *choose* to 'buy into' aspects of dominant cultures and ideologies, in order to further their own social and financial interests.

CULTURAL CAPITAL, SYMBOLIC VIOLENCE AND PEDAGOGIC ACTION

'[T]here is, diffused within a social space, a cultural capital,
transmitted by inheritance and invested in order to be cultivated.'
(Bourdieu 1971, p. 201)

As we have seen, one of the key characteristics of Bourdieu's notion of habitus is its 'invisibility', and one of the key characteristics of field is its illusion of 'naturalness': that is to say, its appearance not as a socio-historical construct initiated and underpinned by unequal social and power relations, but as simply 'the way things are'.

Nowhere, for Bourdieu, is this invisibility and this illusion of naturalness more evident than in the field of education, and in particular in the cultural bias upon which, he argues, formal education is founded: an education which, in terms of its content and modes of delivery, is presented not as biased at all but as neutral and even altruistic and egalitarian in nature, and which is often perceived by students and their parents in the same way. Bourdieu has written at length in this regard about what he calls 'symbolic violence': that is to say, the assertion, chiefly *through* educational systems, of one set of arbitrary cultural forms and preferences by the powerful people who 'own' and practise them, above other sets which they perceive – and encourage *their* owners to perceive – as inferior forms (see, for example, Bourdieu and Passeron 1977, p. 5). The selection of forms, practices, beliefs, items of knowledge and so forth that make up the content of the school curriculum may be perceived as arbitrary precisely because it is culture-specific and not because it is intrinsically or universally more valid or more 'right' than a selection that might be based on other cultural forms, practices and preferences. On the other hand, the selection is presented to students and their parents – and typically experienced by students and their parents – precisely as if it *were* intrinsically superior or right: a sleight of hand achieved principally through the development of formal, 'independently assessed' examinations and tests of students' expertise in these cultural arbitraries. As other commentators have put it, merit is thus distributed, through acts of symbolic violence in the educational setting, 'with reference to an absolute index of intrinsic worth' (Jenks 1993, p. 13), in that 'excellence and scholastic achievement are defined in terms of [an] arbitrary cultural paradigm' (Jenkins 1992, p. 112).

According to this view of education – which, as we shall see, has clear and highly significant implications for teachers, not least in the area of student assessment – students whose 'home cultures' most closely match those cultures validated within the educational system (let us call them 'good-match students') will enter that system already in possession of what Bernstein and others call 'cultural capital' which can, as it were, *accumulate* in the form of positive reports, high teacher expectations, constructive and laudatory marking, examination success, monitorial privileges, and so forth. (In an alternative account of this accumulation, Thompson directs us to a distinction between '*cultural* capital', which 'includes knowledge, skills and . . . educational qualifications', and '*symbolic* capital', which refers to 'accumulated praise, prestige and recognition' [Thompson 1990, p. 148]).

Students whose 'home cultures' provide less of a match with 'school culture' may, by contrast, have little or no formally-recognised cultural capital to begin with, and may need to work harder than 'good-match' students if they are to achieve any. Effectively, these students will find themselves assessed from the outset not in relation to their expertise in their own favoured cultural forms and practices, but in relation to their expertise in those of other groups of people, with quite different cultural orientations and experience. Furthermore, the habitus with which 'good-match students' enter the system may not only persuade them of the value of a 'good education' and of the inherent rightness and fairness of the education system: it might also predispose them to *succeed* within the system, in that their *expectation* is that they can – and probably *will* – succeed within it. When they find themselves confronted with familiar-looking tasks that they can achieve fairly easily, and see other students struggling with the same (to those students, *un*familiar) tasks, their view that they are particularly gifted rather than particularly privileged may be given a boost which will help translate that expectation of success into success itself. The habitus of those other students we have mentioned, meanwhile, may already dispose them to fail within the system, even though they, too, may believe that a 'good education' is important and that the education system is fair and just. In this particular understanding of cultural bias within education systems – bias which *systematically* ensures cultural reproduction and, consequently, the preservation of a hierarchical *status quo* – it is the school's and therefore the teacher's function to perpetuate the myth of 'naturalness': to ensure, that is, that students continue to misrecognise the curriculum as both natural and neutral. It is important, also, that students continue to perceive schools as possessing 'relative autonomy' – that is to say, of there being no direct, causal link between the school curriculum and powerful interests in society. If such a link were perceived by students, the curriculum would be seen by those same students for what, in Bourdieu's view, it really is. By consequence, the education system itself would be undermined and, along with it, the existing power relations and structures of the larger society. As Jenkins puts this: 'Pedagogic work legitimates its product by producing legitimate consumers of that product' (Jenkins 1992, p. 107).

If we accept the view that school curricula – and, we might add, school pedagogies – are culturally biased and systematically operate in the interests of small numbers of students to the detriment of large numbers of others, we might feel the need to ask the following questions:

- What, if anything, can teachers themselves do about this bias – i.e. to what extent can they act, to use Giroux's phrase, as 'transformative intellectuals' (Giroux 1988)?
- In particular, to what extent can teachers oppose curricula in actual classroom situations and/or seek to promote equality and justice through changing students' opinions or through 'making visible' to them the extent and manner of formalised oppression and the objective relations within which such oppression occurs?

Bourdieu raises these difficult issues himself through his considerations of *pedagogic action* (what teachers do – and can do) and *pedagogic authority* (the way in which teachers are presented and perceived as curriculum legitimisers), seeming to conclude, somewhat pessimistically, that teachers, as representatives of the 'arbitrary power' that imposes curriculum content and style, are in no position realistically to challenge the system *with their students* or to be taken seriously by students in any overt attempts to do so. To use Bourdieu's terminology, Pedagogic Action (PA) is inseparable from Pedagogic Authority

(PAu), which stands as the 'social condition of its exercise' (Bourdieu and Passeron 1977, pp. 11–12). In this view, the teacher who seeks to come clean by exposing the culturally-biased system to their students – by helping them to understand, for example, through direct teaching, the biased and unfair nature of the curriculum – is ultimately doomed to failure, since to do so would involve stepping outside the teacher's authoritative role, and indeed outside the whole legitimising process that produces and supports that role (Bourdieu and Passeron 1977, p. 12). Once you are working as an active agent within the system, it seems – as one supporting the system through one's social position – you can do nothing to change that system from within.

Case Study 4.1: Cultural capital and symbolic violence in the classroom

The following case study, reported in greater depth elsewhere (see, for instance, Moore 1999a), illustrates what cultural capital and symbolic violence can look like in actual classroom situations. The study involves the production and assessment of a written text carried out in a secondary-phase English lesson; however, it would be just as easy to provide an example from other subject areas and from the primary or tertiary phases of education.

   The study concerns a fourteen-year-old Bangladesh-origin student called Abdul, who at the time of the study has been living in the UK for eighteen months and who had virtually no written or spoken English on his arrival. Abdul's English teacher has set the class a project for their public examination folders, of writing a love story. After quickly producing a first draft, to which his teacher has made copious surface-error corrections in red pen, Abdul presents the following 'first chapter' of his story for his teacher's further consideration:

Love Story

   Once upon a time I saw a girl and I asked her, 'Where are you going?'
   She said 'I'm just going somewhere. What are you asking for? Do you want to know for some special reason?'
   I said 'No. I was just asking where you are going, I'm sorry. I hope you don't mind.'
   She said 'That's okay.'
   Afterwards, I saw her on the bus. I was sitting at the front and she was at the back. After about five minutes, two boys got on. They sat at the back near the girl and one of them said to her 'Hello. Where are you going?'
   She was scared, and the boys tried to do something bad to her.
   I went over and asked her, 'Are these boys troubling you?'

She said, 'Yes. can you help me, please?'
I took her and we got off the bus.
Then I said, ' Can you get home all right?'
She said, 'No, I can't go home. I'm too scared.'
I said 'O.K. I'll take you.'
After half an hour, she said, 'I want to say something.'
I said, 'What is it?'
'How do I tell you? I can't tell you.'
I said, 'Go on. Tell me what it is.'
Then she said, 'I love you.'
Then I said, 'I love you too.'
Another day she and I went to the park. I said to her, 'Do you have any brothers?'
She said, 'Yes. I have one brother.'
I said, 'How old is he?'
She said, 'He's fifteen or sixteen. I'm not sure.'
Then I said, 'Have you got a sister?'
She said, 'No I haven't.'
Then she asked me, 'Do you have any brothers or sisters?'
I said, 'Yes. I have one brother and three sisters.'
She said, 'How old are they?'
I said, 'My brother is twenty-five years old and one of my sisters is twenty. Another sister is twenty-one years old, and the other one is eighteen.'
Then she said, 'Are they married?'
Then I said, 'Yes, two are married and one is not married.'
Then she said 'What about your brother?'
I said, 'My brother is married. He had two daughters and one son. Now he's only got two daughters because his son died.'
She said, 'Oh'.
I said, 'Have you got a father?'
She said, 'Yes, I have.'
We went home. Now we go out every day.

End of part one.

It is in Abdul's teacher's response (below) to this second draft that symbolic violence and the full implications of cultural capital show themselves like the tip of an iceberg. The response also shows, however, how easy it is to 'miss' the manifestations of cultural capital and symbolic violence, when they are caught in the shadow of the much more immediately visible problem of ineffective teaching:

> T: (reading through Abdul's revised draft with him) *'After half an hour she said, "I want to say something." I said, "What is it?" "How do I tell you? I can't tell you." I said, "Go on, tell me what it is." Then she said, "I love you." Then I said, "I love you too." ' Yes ... I'm a little worried about this bit. Would she say 'I love you', just like that? It seems a bit sudden. ... Would they really say that? Maybe they should say it another time, when they've got to know each other better? What do you think about that?*
>
> A: (shrugs)
>
> [. . .]
>
> T: *All this stuff about relations. ... This isn't really necessary, is it. ... For the reader. ... What do you think?*
>
> A: (silence)
>
> T: *I mean, I think you could really cut a lot of this out, couldn't you. Cut most of this out.* (Puts lines in the margin against this section.) *Just put here* (writing in the margin): *'We talked about our families. She said she had a brother. I told her my brother was married. ...' You see, that's the other thing ... I don't know ... I mean, do people talk that way? In real life? Do they talk about how old their brothers and sisters are?*
>
> A: *Yes, Sir.*
>
> [. . .]
>
> T: *And this here: you suddenly say, 'Now he's only got two daughters because his son died.' And she* (T smiles). *... She just says 'Oh'.*
>
> A: (smiles with T)
>
> T: *I mean, don't you think. ... Do you think they'd just talk about it like that, as if it didn't matter?*
>
> A: (silence)
>
> T: *Would they say that?*
>
> A: *Yes.*

When teachers and student teachers are shown this dialogue, their tendency is to treat it as an example of 'bad teaching' (Moore 1999a). They suggest, quite rightly, that – like the teacher's wholesale red-ink corrections of the student's first draft – these subsequent suggestions appropriate the student's work and critically restrict opportunities for the student's independent development as a writer. There is more going on here, however, than mere 'overmarking'. *What that overmarking is inextricably linked to in this case is a denial that there may be alternative ways of experiencing life and telling stories than those legitimised by the teacher, the school, the National Curriculum and the Public Examinations Board.*

To put this another way, we might say that underpinning the teacher's suggested corrections is an unquestioned assumption that there is only one way or set of ways for people to talk to one another, and only one way or set of ways of telling a story: in both cases, the ways favoured and promulgated by privileged cultural groups in British society. Within the realms of this particular field of etiquette (see also Chapter 3 above), you do not formally discuss relatives with a potential lover on your first meeting – either in real-life situations or in fictional ones – and if someone in the family dies, you are not so cold-hearted as to talk about it as if it were just another aspect of living. These are the ways, the conventions, the discourses that the teacher has been brought up with and successfully initiated into, and in the heat of the classroom situation there is no question in his mind that these are the right ways, the right conventions, the right discourses. The possibility of *multiple realities*, leading to linguistic diversity in the broadest sense that embraces genre, perception and form, remains *invisible* in the pedagogic act, as does the possibility – we might say, the likelihood – that this student has previously learned, and even been praised for his expertise in replicating, ways of telling stories that do *not* conform to the culture-specific criteria enshrined in the English National Curriculum or public-examination system. Such ways might (for example) give a very low priority to such matters as 'convincing dialogue', 'well-rounded characters', 'social realism', and all the other criteria against which Abdul's story is likely to be judged for examination purposes in the UK, but a relatively high priority to quite different socio-literary formulae, including the need to establish relationships through such rituals as exchanging familial details.

> For the teacher's purposes on this occasion, the student's previous learning experiences and expertise in the replication of cultural–linguistic forms might as well not exist: the teacher's task has too readily been configured not as a matter of extending an already rich and varied language repertoire to embrace new forms and styles, but as introducing quasi-universal 'correct-ness' into a consciousness that has been previously 'empty' in this department. In short, Abdul's *alternative* way of telling a story has been perceived as a *deficient* way by his teacher, and the teacher's pedagogy is fashioned accordingly. Not only that, but Abdul's personal *experience*, his own lived reality that shapes the *content* of his story has also been treated as if it were invalid or mistaken.

To return to Bourdieu's analytical framework, we might say that what Abdul 'lacks' (a lack, of course, projected upon him rather than residing within him) is not some kind of innate 'ability' or 'motivation', but rather a certain kind of *cultural capital* which is legitimised and recognised within the school, the educational system and the larger society. The student *has* cultural capital, of course: for example, he has expertise in the particular storytelling skills favoured within the school system in his native Bangladesh and within the local Bangladeshi community in the UK. Such capital, however, proves to be not transferable. When he arrives in the UK education system, there is, as it were, no exchange rate: he cannot 'cash in' his existing capital; nor indeed is it recognised as having any worth by and within that system. In order to achieve cultural capital in his new school, Abdul must work very hard to discover which particular cultural forms and practices are validated by the institution – in this case, for example, not only that stories should be written in a certain way but that any dialogue they contain should, *despite* his teacher's affirmations that they should be 'true to life', also conform to certain patterns which may be different from the patterns that are most familiar in his own everyday experience of life. In doing this, he will have to make decisions about how to reposition his own currently *preferred* cultural forms and practices, including the possibility of abandoning some of these altogether.

If the issue of *cultural capital* manifests itself in the way in which Abdul's story is *assessed*, it is in this latter set of considerations that we see *symbolic violence* at work. In considering symbolic violence, it is important to make a distinction between, on the one hand, the symbolic violence of the teacher and, on the other, a larger, institutional and systemic symbolic violence that operates through such mechanisms as national curricula and public examination syllabuses.

The teacher's own use of symbolic violence is manifested principally in the assertion that there are 'right' and 'wrong' ways of doing things, that these are neither negotiable nor culture-specific, and that there is no need to enter into any dialogue with the student as to why certain stylistic, representational alterations are being promoted. Such violence is particularly apparent in the above Case Study, in the teacher's rejection of the student's confirmation that – for example – people *would*, in real life, talk to each other in the ways replicated in his story. The teacher, however, does not construct the National Curriculum, or the public examination criteria by which Abdul's work will be judged and as a result of which Abdul's cultural capital will be cashed in – in the form of an examination grade – for academic currency that will, in turn, act as cultural capital opening doors to a university place or to a prestigious and financially rewarding job. In essence, the teacher's perceived job in this case is to ensure, as far as he is able, that the student does as well in the (symbolically violent) public *examination* as can possibly be engineered. If this means that debates with the student about relativism or cultural pluralism have to be shelved, it is a price that the teacher feels obliged, on behalf of both parties, to pay (Moore 1999a).

We can say that if the immediate manifestation of symbolic violence appears in the teacher's words to the student in the assessment process, the greater, almost 'hidden' violence lies in the examination criteria that specifically and uncompromisingly marginalise the student's home culture – in this case, by insisting that his preferred manner of storytelling is inadmissible.

> The implication of this is that if teachers seriously want to challenge symbolic
> violence, they need to look outwards to the deeper structures within which

their practice is located, as well as inwards to their own practice within the classroom situation. In particular, they may wish to develop ways of challenging as fundamentally culturist, classist or racist the very criteria by which their students are assessed.

Culture and differentiation: the multicultured classroom

The notion that people may – both individually and collectively – act to bring about societal *change*, including change within the education system itself, is supported by Bourdieu's suggestion that the habitus can be modified and controlled by the 'awakening of consciousness and socioanalysis'. The implication here is that rather than waiting on changes in the larger society – changes in the 'superstructure' – to occur before real change can take place at the 'local level' (e.g. in schools and classrooms), it is precisely *through* local action that teachers can help promote those larger societal changes that in turn will effect changes in education globally. If teachers encourage their students to be more tolerant and pluralistic in their outlook, for example, or to understand how bias operates within societies, those same students may, in turn, upon leaving school, join an ever-growing band of informed and empowered citizens whose collective alternative voice it will become increasingly difficult for policy-makers to ignore.

Experience suggests that there are, indeed, many ways in which teachers can, with some degree of success, operate in anti-culturist ways in the school classroom that may challenge some of the coercive practices and views that students might otherwise take for granted. Some of these ways concern manifest *institutional validations* of minoritised cultures, such as the introduction of public notices and welcoming signs in a range of languages and registers (not just minority *languages*, but – less commonly – minority *dialects*). Others may involve the use or development of text books and other teaching materials designed to undermine the myth of linguistic and cultural 'rightness' or to counteract stereotyping related to gender, ethnicity or class. (The English Centre's *The Languages Book* [Raleigh 1981] and the ILEA's *Language and Power* [1990] are two examples of such materials still widely used in secondary-school classrooms. For an account of the way in which school textbooks can often have the *opposite* effect – of representing, unchallenged, the 'existing order', see G. MacDonald 1976.) Others may involve teachers adopting *individual* strategies to validate students' favoured cultural forms in the classroom, such as encouraging and wall-displaying student texts written and presented in 'unconventional' ways, or ensuring that when students themselves introduce 'alternative' viewpoints or express themselves in 'non-standard' ways these are not rejected or marginalised as wrong.

> This does not mean, of course, that teachers do not have a responsibility to encourage their students to succeed academically by teaching them the standard curriculum and showing them how to express their knowledge and understanding in standard ways. It does, however, mean that teachers need to allow non-standard ways to flourish alongside standard ones and that when students do express themselves in non-standard ways, as Abdul did in the example quoted above, their non-standard approaches are not treated – or seen to be treated – as if they were signs of intellectual or creative deficiency. This may involve a change of *mindset* on the teacher's part, so that when a student appears to do or say something 'wrong', the teacher's first question becomes: *Could this student be operating here within an 'alternative' set of cultural practices?*

An example of the kinds of ways in which both assessment and pedagogy might be affected by such a change of mindset is offered by a practising teacher, Ann Taber, who spent a good deal of time working with Asian-origin students in the 1970s, and whose fascinating and helpful accounts of that work deserve a wider audience than they have had.

Taber (1978; 1981) identifies a range of areas in which what is accepted as good and normal within one culture – let us say, within the privileged culture of a particular institution – may be considered strange and even bad within another culture (for example, a marginalised culture in a particular institution) – and *vice versa*. Taber not only questions the Western European's unquestioning acceptance of certain norms of representation as 'correct' and 'real', but strives herself to attain a cultural 'distancing', that enables her to appreciate qualities in her students' work that might otherwise remain hidden. In the process, this distancing also makes visible to her the normally *invisible* processes and preconceptions by which the marginalisation of such students' cultures is typically established and perpetuated.

In the following passage, Taber describes how, after initially judging her students' skills to be deficient in that they seemed unable to represent objects three-dimensionally, she came to readjust her assessment after considering the possibility that, for purely cultural reasons, her students might not be *trying* to represent objects three-dimensionally:

> One needs to think more carefully about what is taken to be a 'realistic' representation of a three-dimensional world. Our standard method of drawing objects from a fixed point of observation (more or less the procedure of photography) produces a picture that totally distorts certain aspects of reality [. . . .] I began to realise that I was judging [my students'] work by the standards of a procedure that they had not attempted to use. Their drawings had an element of truth and power that projective representation cannot achieve as it involves technical problems that mar visual clarity [. . . .] The projective

method is only a 'realistic' style when defined by current 'Western' ideas.

(Taber 1981, pp. 61–2)

Elsewhere, Taber describes how the same approach altered her assessment of how her Asian-origin students used colour:

> The question frequently asked by them [students from 'other' cultural traditions], 'What colour shall I use?', caused me great perplexity. My rather lame replies, such as 'you will have to decide for yourself', simply covered up my inability to understand exactly why they were asking such questions[. . . .] It occurred to me that in the art with which they were familiar there might be a scheme of colours and they might feel that this was the case with all art work [. . . .] the colours in religious art are not selected for reasons of visual aesthetics but are dictated by the choice of subject matter, and so are symbolic like a logogram or hieroglyph. An awareness of the iconic meaning of colour may help the art teacher to understand some students' attitudes towards the use of paint [. . . .] When seen in this light, the question 'What colour shall I use?' no longer implied to me a naive lack of understanding that selection of colour was an important part of the student's work [. . .] but had to be regarded as a serious intellectual enquiry. I felt that a satisfactory answer to the question would have to give the student some insight into the 'western' philosophy of art compared with his own.
>
> (Taber 1978, p. 2)

Taber's words serve as a very useful reminder to teachers not only of the need for *differentiation* in classroom practice (Figure 4.1) but of what the word differentiation actually means – or should mean. Differentiation is generally regarded as a planned process of classroom interventions, designed to maximise every student's potential and to take account of every student's individual needs at any given point in time (McGregor and Moore 1999). This is an adequate summary as far as it goes. However, questions remain such as:

- Who decides what a student's needs are?
- How do we *know* what a student needs?
- Are students' needs solely curriculum-referenced (e.g. this student needs to know more about such-and-such for their exam; this student needs more work on their spelling, etc.) – or do they include questions about personal and cognitive–linguistic *development* (e.g. what does this student need in order to progress and develop as an independent, proactive learner)?

For Taber, differentiation is clearly a matter of understanding the different cultures and different cognitive–academic 'starting-points' of the various

---

Differentiation by outcome
The teacher sets the same task for all students but anticipates variable outcomes. Example: all students are asked to write a story within a particular genre or on a particular theme. The task is equally demanding for all students, giving everyone an opportunity to produce what is, currently, their best work. The teacher's assessments of each student's work will reflect the different levels of expertise within the class, in relation to the set activity.

Differentiation by response
The teacher varies their response to students' work according to their knowledge of each student's previous performance. Example: student A produces a one-page piece of ill-prepared writing, having previously handed in lengthy, detailed stories. The teacher responds less positively than to student B who, having previously only been able to manage half a side, hands in one side of detailed, stimulating writing.

Differentiation by task
The teacher sets different tasks for different students, according to notions of their current expertise, understanding or knowledge.

Differentiation by stimulus
A form of differentiation that also caters for different preferred learning styles: for example, some students prefer watching or listening; some prefer reading; some prefer finding out 'for themselves': the teacher prepares a variety of stimuli on the same theme, *directed* to specific students.

Figure 4.1 Modes of differentiation

students within the classroom. Only in this way can the students' various needs and strengths be recognised and understood, and only in this way can appropriate, constructive assessments of students' work and subsequent pedagogies be constructed.

We might say that Taber's approach suggests a move on the teacher's part away from perceiving the *classroom* as *multicultural* to perceiving its *students* as *multicultured*. The term multicultured (Moore 1999a) is a potentially useful one for teachers, since it acts as a permanent reminder that we are *all* 'cultured people', many of us living our lives within – and exhibiting in our produce and behaviour the skills, preferences and etiquettes of – a number of different metacultures. To talk of some people as 'cultured' and others as 'uncultured' is, of course, an absurdity: it has often served, however, to imply an inherent superiority of some cultures over others, by way of suggesting that those 'other cultures' are simply not cultures at all.

The particular interpretation of differentiation in the multicultural context implied by Taber is a much subtler and more constructive variation of

'Differentiation by Response' (Figure 4.1, above). It finds support in the work of Capel *et al.* (1995), who remind us that this particular understanding of differentiation ought not to be confined – as it too often appears to be – to bilingual students, but should be applied to all students from marginalised cultures, including, centrally, students from ethnic and class minority backgrounds. Like Dunn (1987, p. 3), who suggests that '[s]*tudents from different cultures have different learning styles*', Capel *et al.* show a particular concern for the ways in which cultural variables impact not only upon *curriculum content* but also upon the modes by which learning is carried out – a concern which immediately calls into question 'universal' theories of learning and development, including some of those that have already been reviewed in Chapter 1 of this book. (See also Gardner 1993, on the theory of 'multiple intelligence', explored further in Chapter 6 below).

Capel *et al.* begin with the assertion that: 'Providing the same educational opportunities for all is not a guarantee that all pupils can take advantage of them. Equal opportunities policies must go beyond "provision" to consider "access", whereby pupils are enabled to take advantage of the curriculum' (Capel, Leask and Turner 1995, p. 120).

Setting all students in the class the same written or representational assignment, as in the case of Abdul or of Ann Taber's students, does not equate with equality of opportunity. Students need also to be helped by the teacher to ensure that they have understood the task and can find an appropriate and feasible way into it. For that to occur, the teacher needs to be aware – in general terms, at least – of the student's cognitive–affective and cultural background, and in particular to appreciate that students do not all come to school with the same cultural preferences and skills, that there may be different ways of learning that suit different students in the class, and that students may possess an abundance of knowledge and skills that are never usually made use of or welcomed into the classroom if they are not explicitly referred to in the school curriculum. As Capel *et al.* put this in their advice to student teachers:

> each pupil brings to school unique knowledge, skills and attitudes formed by interaction with parents and peers, through their everyday experience of the world, and through the media. [. . .] Many pupils have skills of which the school is not aware. [. . .] All pupils bring a *view* based on the acceptance of particular cultural values.
>
> [. . .]
>
> Such diversity of background is found in your classrooms; planning for differentiation has to take account of differences in culture, expectation, knowledge and experience. [. . .] It is the teacher's job to make the curriculum interesting, relevant and cognitively digestible.
>
> (ibid., p. 122)

The danger, as we have seen in the case of Abdul, is when teachers do not plan for differentiation in this way, but rather overlook the student's cultural background as if it did not exist. As Capel *et al.* conclude: 'Teacher expectations have a significant effect on pupils' self-esteem, motivation and achievement and it is easy for teachers to make damaging assumptions about pupils from backgrounds different [from] their own' (ibid., p. 248).

In translating some of these ideas into broad strategies for classroom practice, James Cummins has usefully suggested a '4-phase instructional framework'. Although this framework is designed for teachers of bilingual students, it is relevant to work with all students who may be seen as culturally marginalised within the larger society and the educational system. Within this framework, teachers are urged to:

- activate prior knowledge/build background knowledge;
- present cognitively engaging input with appropriate contextual supports;
- encourage active language use to connect input with students' prior experience and with thematically-related content;
- assess student learning in order to provide feedback that will build language awareness and efficient learning strategies.

(Cummins 1996, p. 75)

This instructional framework is structured by Cummins around four basic components geared to giving students 'access to the power of language and accelerate their academic growth'. These components are:

- active communication of meaning;
- cognitive challenge;
- contextual support;
- building student self-esteem.

(ibid., p. 74)

Such an approach not only prioritises the importance of teachers' 'getting at' their students' existing skills and knowledge in order to provide teaching that is neither patronising nor unrelated to previous experience; it also emphasises, as in Capel *et al.*, the importance to the individual's learning *of the way in which they perceive themself, both as a student and as a human being.*

MULTICULTURALISM AND ANTI-RACISM

Lucas and Katz describe in the following terms classrooms which are genuinely 'multilingual': that is to say, classrooms in which there are not just a range of different 'first languages' spoken by the students but in which those languages are validated and used alongside the main language(s) of instruction:

> In practice [. . .] the classrooms were multilingual environments in which students' native languages served a multitude of purposes and

functions. They gave students access to academic content, to classroom activities, and to their own knowledge and experience; gave teachers a way to show their respect and value for students' languages and cultures; acted as a medium for social interaction and establishment of rapport; fostered family involvement; and fostered students' development of, knowledge of, and pride in their native languages and cultures.

(Lucas and Katz 1994, p. 545)

What Lucas and Katz are describing here is, essentially, a classroom environment which might be said to be *culturally or symbolically inclusive* (Moore 1999a). Certainly, the students will all still be expected to sit public examinations which are likely to prioritise the cultural preferences, skills and knowledge of the 'majority culture'. However, the teachers have devised ways of saying to their students that their 'heritage' languages and cultures are both valid and welcomed in the classroom. Such teachers will want to help their students develop the 'additional' cultural skills and knowledge – and of course an enjoyment in the cultural forms and practices – that will be needed for success in the public examination system: however, this will not be at the expense of existing cultural forms and practices – including existing languages – already owned by the students.

The adoption of pedagogic practice such as this inevitably takes full account of the nature of culturism itself in schools, classrooms and educational systems, *and the way this may be experienced by minoritised students*. Henry Giroux has described culturist practice as involving the subordination of marginalised cultural practices and their 'replacement' by dominant ones in a way that seeks to consign minoritised groups' struggle 'to master-narratives that suggest that the oppressed need to be remade in the image of a dominant white culture' (Giroux 1992, p. 116). This particular power relationship, underpinned by an unquestioning belief in the superiority of white, Western, middle-class values, skills and practices, continues to dominate in many institutions, where in recent times it has been encouraged and accentuated by the refugee status of large numbers of multicultured students. In this relationship, the dominant social groups and their 'representatives' set themselves up as *benefactors*, hoping to discover in their victim-students not merely progress but gratitude.

As Giroux, providing a particularly illuminating description of the way in which hegemony operates at the local and personal level has argued: 'Multiculturalism is generally about Otherness, but it is written in ways in which the dominating aspects of white culture are not called into question [. . .] [T]he norm of whiteness [becomes] an ethnic category that secures its dominance by appearing to be invisible' (Giroux 1992, p. 117).

Even in the 'multicultural' classroom, multicultured students may experience exclusion through the kind of 'double invisibilisation' described by Giroux: on the one hand, their existing cultural experiences and expertise are rendered invisible by a refusal to allow them to penetrate a curriculum which is resistant to genuine change (Moore 1998); at the same time, that curriculum

is presented – or perhaps we should say, is made to appear to 'present itself'
– as a handed-down item received equally by all members of society regardless of who they are or what positions of power they occupy. That is to say,
those who have *manufactured* the curriculum hide all evidence of their part in
its construction: they become innocent bystanders who just happen to be
handily placed to help initiate others into its emancipatory wonders.

CULTURE AND IDENTITY

Giroux's account takes us very firmly into the area of culture and *identity*, and
a concern that we all should have as teachers about the extent to which dominant cultures, especially when these are institutionalised as in schools and school
curricula, can impose themselves on other cultures in ways which fix or alter
– not necessarily for the good – the ways in which people perceive themselves and the social and physical world.

   One response to this situation, where it is perceived and apprehended by
marginalised students, is that such students choose simply to 'opt out' of the
system altogether. Paul Willis has famously described how this may operate
with respect to white working-class male students (1977), and more recently
Fordham has demonstrated a familiar phenomenon amongst black students,
who may become very critical of other black students' academic success as
examples of 'acting white' and 'selling out' (Fordham 1990, p. 259). Fordham
describes how, in school settings, many black adolescents 'consciously and
unconsciously sense that they have to give up aspects of their identities and
of their indigenous cultural system in order to achieve success as defined in
dominant-group terms'. For many such students, argues Fordham, 'the cost
of school success is too high': that is to say, they are unprepared to sacrifice
their favoured cultural forms and practices in order to achieve academic success,
since to do so would be to accept an unwanted change of *identity* and to risk
rejection by their peers (Fordham, 1990, p. 259: see also Ogbu 1992; Cummins
1996, p. 145). Such students may find that their deliberate and conscious *resistance* to dominant white cultural practices, however, results in severe restrictions
to their upward mobility, 'often culminating in students dropping out of school
prematurely'.

   A failure to take full and serious account of issues of identity – which are
clearly far more complex than may at first appear – may be held responsible
for many of the moves towards 'multicultural education' being reduced to the
mere tacking on of multicultural 'aspects' to an essentially unchanging, monocultural curriculum and pedagogy, in a way that accentuates and perpetuates
culturist practices rather than fundamentally challenging them. Some forms of
multicultural education have thus been dismissed as the 'Divali and steel-
band' model: that is to say, assemblies may be held in recognition of Divali,
and groups of African Caribbean students may be encouraged to form
steel-bands to perform at parents' evenings; however, the preferred languages
of the students in question, and some of their preferred practices and areas of

expertise that are less easily incorporated into the school's overall ethos and identity may be effectively banned from the classroom as well as from a curriculum within which they will, ultimately, be assessed in terms of their ability and achievement.

> As Gillborn and Gipps have argued (1996), schools and teachers must guard against becoming complacent about multiculturalism in education, constantly revisiting the issue to explore exactly how much has been achieved in this area and how much more needs to be achieved. This may lead school and education authorities to seek to supplement or replace multicultural policies with anti-racist ones, which not only take on a more overtly political aspect within the school and the school classroom, but also seek to critique aspects of institutional culturism that may exist in national curricula or public examination criteria.

MULTICULTURALISM AND THE TEACHER

As has already been suggested, the 'pedagogic authority' residing in the teacher does not necessarily exclude the possibility of effective teacher action in the area of anti-culturist practice, part of which inevitably involves a personal challenging of the constitution of the school curriculum and of the criteria by which students are assessed; that is to say, a radical questioning of the received *purposes* of education. Observers like Ann Taber provide us with supportive examples of how classroom teachers can take positive steps in this direction within current curriculum arrangements and constraints, through casting aside their own cultural assumptions about good and proper practice and daring to envisage alternative ways of seeing and doing that are not configured as wrong but rather as *rendered* invalid by formal educational systems and processes.

The challenge that teachers can mount to culturist practice, wherever they find it, to an extent is bound to be local and variable. Teachers alone cannot be expected to undo biased examination systems and national curricula 'overnight' (although they might choose to consider whether or not such an undertaking is totally out of the question in the longer term). Furthermore, as long as those larger systems exist teachers will always be constrained to work within them, in the knowledge that to do otherwise would be to risk putting their students at an even greater disadvantage. Even when teacher action is confined to the classroom itself, the invasive presence of externally-fixed curricula and assessment criteria, not to mention the absorption of such curricula and criteria into the workings, structures and policies of the individual school, sets clear limits on what can realistically be achieved.

Teachers can, however, make an achievable beginning by introducing and sustaining a small number of 'safeguards' into their regular practice, along the lines of those suggested by Taber. These might include:

- recognising that all students are different and that their ways of perceiving and of learning are also different;
- asking, when a student does or produces something that is not what was required or expected: 'Could this be a cultural issue?'
- understanding that the selections that comprise the school curriculum are *only* selections, and that other selections might be equally valid – that the curriculum itself is not 'God-given' and will doubtless undergo many changes and transformations in the millennia that lie ahead;
- refusing to allow terms such as 'ability' and 'intelligence' to become fossilised and unquestioned – understanding that all students are able and intelligent, and that if they are seen to be failing academically at school there are likely to be many contributory factors that have nothing at all to do with innate 'ability'.

Teachers in culturally mixed classrooms cannot be expected to know and understand intimately the 'home cultures' of all the students in their classrooms. They can, however, avoid making easy assumptions about those cultures or refusing to acknowledge that they exist at all. It should be remembered that Taber's challenging of her own assessment of her students, and of her pedagogy with them, arose, initially, not from an intimate knowledge of those students' cultural heritages, but, rather, from a recognition of her *lack* of knowledge. It was that recognition that enabled her to challenge the basis on which her previous assessments and pedagogy had been based.

Taber's ability to identify her own culturist stance through a process of making her familiar, taken-for-granted cultural preferences *strange* remind us that cultural bias is likely to manifest itself in many different ways and forms in the school classroom, and that these may not be at all obvious to us unless and until we *make* them obvious. Although this chapter has focused on cultural bias as it relates to bilingual and bidialectal students, teachers still have to ask themselves serious questions about other forms of bias that may manifest themselves both in the school curriculum and in their own taken-for-granted pedagogies.

One manifestation of bias that we have not considered in this chapter is that of *gender bias*, as it affects both female and male students. Currently, there is a great deal of public concern over the apparent underachievement of many male school-students in the UK, with the suggestion that this may, at least in part, be related to curricular elements that boys find irrelevant or unappealing. For many years, however, researchers have raised important questions about the ways in which school curricula and pedagogies militate culturally against the interests of *female* students. Spender, for example (Spender 1980, 1982), has described the ways in which, in the official language of education, girls are effectively rendered 'invisible' through such practices as repeatedly referring to students and teachers as 'he' (see also Torbe 1986, pp. 147–8; Weiner 1985; Ord and Quigley 1985, pp. 116–117), as well as through male-oriented selections of knowledge and facts, over-referencing to male scientists and historical figures, and so forth. More recently, Paechter (1998) has suggested that girls' education *continues* to be subordinated to boys', calling into question our daily assumptions of 'normality' and offering her analysis as a way into exploring the situations of other subordinated groups, *including* children from lower socio-economic groups, ethnic minorities, and those with special needs.

Paechter's work in particular reminds us that the study and understanding of how one social group is culturally marginalised within educational settings and systems can be useful in developing parallel understandings of the situations of other marginalised groups. It also implies the importance for school-students themselves in experiencing, in the classroom situation, a wide variety of cultures – including learning styles – in order to be able fully to develop linguistically, cognitively, creatively, affectively and socially themselves.

It may sometimes seem that even the basic anti-culturist strategies outlined above will achieve little as long as they remain in opposition to persistent culturist practices in the larger social and educational systems. However, teachers may take heart from the fact that even within slow-moving official discourses some significant shifts of opinion have taken place during the last thirty years. Such shifts are reflected both in changes to curricular content (in all school subjects in the UK, for example, there have been important changes in curricular and pedagogic orthodoxy, both at examination and at pre-examination level), and in some of the messages emanating from central government, which at least recognise that there may be a 'culturist issue' to be addressed.

In the light of this last point, the following conclusions, presented in DfEE Research Report No. 59 (*Teaching and Learning Strategies in Successful Multi-Ethnic Schools*), may prove particularly helpful and encouraging to teachers wishing to develop anti-culturist strategies in their own schools and classrooms, in areas in which they may expect to find some official support. Among examples of successful practice in schools identified as dealing effectively with racism, stereotyping and low expectations among minority group children, Report No. 59 includes the following observations and conclusions:

- Effective schools listened to, and learnt from, students and their parents, and tried to see things from the students' points of view. They were then willing to reappraise and adapt school practices in the light of these.
- They tried to understand and work with the 'whole child'. To do this, they linked academic achievement with the mental and physical welfare of students by linking closely the pastoral and academic aspects of schooling. This involved setting up structures which enabled flexible deployment of staff to deal with issues which arose.
- In secondary schools, they understood the different kinds of pressures faced by adolescents from all groups, and worked with this understanding.

- They had codes of behaviour which applied to both students and staff, and students knew both that they would be given a fair hearing and that each student's safety and well-being was important to the school.
- They worked on strategies for preventing exclusion and provided clear written policies for dealing with negative behaviour constructively and with compassion.
- High expectations were developed through structures of accountability for staff and through close monitoring of individual achievement.
- Students of all ethnic backgrounds and with all kinds of learning needs were treated as potential high achievers. No students were given up on.
- [Schools] were sensitive to the identities of students and made efforts to include in the curriculum their histories, languages, religions and cultures.

(Blair *et al.* 1999)

Though current examination syllabuses and areas of the National Curriculum in the UK may retain much of their culturist, ethnocentric spines, and though there is much work here that teachers may feel still needs to be done, there may also be grounds for optimism that central government will continue to become more receptive to issues of culturism in schools, and that eventually, with appropriate prompting, this might lead to official re-examinations of culturist aspects of school curricula.

SUMMARY

In exploring issues of cultural bias or 'culturism' within school curricula and pedagogies, this chapter has argued the following points:

- School curricula are not 'neutral' but socially constructed. They tend to be culturally biased and therefore to operate in the interests of dominant groups within society at the expense of non-dominant groups.
- They do this by selecting and validating – through apparently 'objective' syllabuses and examination criteria – certain areas of knowledge, skills, values, modes of behaviour and forms of presenting and representing knowledge, that relate much more closely to the cultural norms and preferences of some social groups than to others.

These points have been developed through particular reference to the theoretical writings of Pierre Bourdieu and the classroom observations of Ann Taber. Consideration has been given to:

- the relevance for teachers of Bourdieu's theories of habitus and field, cultural capital and symbolic violence as a way into understanding how culturism operates within the school setting;
- the value of Taber's evaluations of her work in bilingual classrooms as a way of illustrating how students' favoured cultural practices and learning styles can be *validated* by teachers, even when they run counter to dominant cultural practices as enshrined in public syllabuses and assessment criteria.

Finally, the notion of 'multiculturalism' has been critiqued, in favour of educational anti-racism which actively challenges the curriculum bias upon which formal education is typically structured.

SUGGESTED ACTIVITIES

1. Consider some of the home–school 'cultural mismatches' that you might expect to find in your own subject area or phase. What approaches might you take to bridge the gaps, in ways that would build on rather than devalue your students' home and community cultural preferences and styles?

2. What examples can you find from within your own practice and experience of cultural bias in the curriculum? Look for examples of bias in both curriculum content and curriculum bias (e.g. the ways in which textbooks or worksheets are written and presented). What steps might you take as a classroom teacher or group of teachers to oppose or reduce cultural bias in the curriculum?

3. Bearing in mind the case study of Abdul and the observations of Ann Taber, investigate examples within your own subject specialism or age-phase of possible culture-based responses to set tasks that might be misread as examples of cognitive, affective or linguistic deficit.

4. Describe some of the steps you might take in your own classroom to (a) evaluate, (b) begin to remedy any cultural bias that might exist not in curriculum content but in pedagogy. (This might include considerations of the way the classroom is laid out, pupil groupings, and strategies for incorporating pupils' existing experience and cultural preferences into lessons.)

5. What evidence can you find of gender bias

   (a   in your own classroom practice;
   (b)   in the materials available for your use;

(c)   in examination syllabuses and (where relevant) the National
Curriculum for your subject area?

What steps might you consider taking to counteract such bias?

SUGGESTED READING

MacDonald, M. (1977) *The Curriculum and Cultural Reproduction* and
Culture, Class and the Curriculum: The Politics of Cultural Reform.
MacDonald's books are two of several groundbreaking study-books
produced by the Open University during the 1970s, aimed at producing
detailed, accessible, politically-aware summaries of key educational issues.
Other useful titles in a series that has retained its relevance during the intervening years include *The Culture of the School* (Dale 1972), *School
Knowledge and Social Control* (Whitty 1977), and *Culture, Ideology and
Knowledge* (Skilbeck and Harris 1976). Of MacDonald's two books, the first
offers a useful and challenging account of some of the issues of cultural
reproduction that we have considered in this chapter, including a more
developed account and critique of Bourdieu's theories. The second book is
recommended for reading alongside the current chapter, but also in conjunction with chapters 2 and 6, in which issues of the historical and possible
future developments and rationales of formalised curriculum and pedagogy
are considered.

Brice Heath, S. (1983) *Ways With Words: Language, Life and Work in
Communities and Classrooms*. Brice Heath uses ethnographic research techniques to explore and illustrate the ways in which the favoured cultural
forms, styles and practices of working-class students may fail, initially, to
match the favoured cultural forms, styles and practices of schools – and to
examine the impact of such 'cultural mismatches' on both the children and
their culture. Of particular interest is the account of differences between
what may be valued in story-telling practices in the home and community,
and what may be valued in story-telling in the school setting.

Cummins, J. (1996) *Negotiating Identities: Education for Empowerment in a
Diverse Society*. Cummins builds on his earlier work on the nature and potential benefits of bilingualism, to examine ways in which bilingual students
continue to be coerced and marginalised in society, offering practical as
well as political advice to teachers seeking to operate in opposition to such
marginalisations. Cummins' account of accelerated learning for bilingual
students provides an interesting comparison with other versions of accelerated learning, including that of Alistair Smith, described in Chapter 6 below.

Kress, G. (1982) *Learning To Write*. Kress's very readable book describes
in some detail the ways in which school-students are required to develop

expertise in certain culture-specific representational *genres* (that is to say, not merely to learn about certain things but to demonstrate their knowledge within certain cultural–linguistic formats and styles) if they are to succeed academically at school. As with Bourdieu, but in a style that is much more closely referenced to recognisable classroom practice, Kress argues that these genres, like the selections of skills and knowledge that comprise the school curriculum, are essentially 'arbitrary', in that they have no intrinsic right to the dominant positions they occupy.

Tizard, B. and Hughes, M. (1984) *Young Children Learning.* Ethnographic research of primary-age children leads Tizard and Hughes to show how working-class students can be disadvantaged when learned home behaviours – including linguistic etiquettes – differ from those that are taken for granted by mainly middle-class teachers. Often such children are misdiagnosed as academically, cognitively or linguistically deficient when, in many cases, they may simply be daunted by the unfamiliar cultural surroundings and values in which they suddenly find themselves.

5   Effective Practice: what makes a good teacher?

This chapter looks at three different models of good teaching: the charismatic/communicative model, the competence model, and the reflec-tive/reflexive model. It is suggested that no single model provides an adequate description of the good teacher, and that there are many different kinds of good teacher and good teaching just as there are many different kinds of good learner and good learning. For effective practice to ensue, however, it is suggested that teachers need to possess high levels of expertise across the models, and that they need also to perceive their practice as strategic, exemplary and contingent.

THE CHARISMATIC SUBJECT AND THE TEACHER AS COMMUNICATOR

'What good teachers do you remember from your own school days? What was it about those teachers that made them good?'

When applicants for courses of initial teacher education are asked such ques-tions in interview, they generally experience little difficulty in nominating particular exemplary teachers (Wragg 1974; Moore and Atkinson 1998). A difficulty ensues, however, when those same applicants are asked to *elaborate* on their choices. While it is not uncommon for applicants to recite the 'personal qualities' of fondly-remembered teachers, such as a sense of humour, a commitment to fairness, 'good communication skills' or 'infectious enthu-siasm for the subject', these are often expressed in the very vaguest of terms. Furthermore, there is seldom reference (explained partly, perhaps, by their 'invisibility' as far as the school-student may be concerned) to such things as planning, preparation, classroom management skills or assessment of students' work and progress. Always, the emphasis is on the teacher as personality – what we might call the teacher as *charismatic subject* (Moore and Atkinson 1998) – and always the implication is that good teachers are 'born' rather than 'made'.

A common feature of the notion of the charismatic teacher is that they are presented as achieving success in often unconventional ways: certainly, in ways that have little to do with such mundane matters as planning and preparing for lessons. On the contrary, the charismatic teacher is often described as coming into the classroom deliberately *un*prepared – solely reliant on his or her subject knowledge, inherent popularity, and intangible ability to enthuse and inspire students. Not uncommonly, this teacher is configured as something of an institutional rebel, taking up an oppositional stance to such things as petty school rules, and being seen to identify much more closely with the student population than with other members of staff.

Such a vision of teaching, which remains popular in cinematic and literary representations of schools and classrooms (Dalton 1999), often has the unfortunate effect of making life very difficult for *student* teachers when, in the classroom situation, they discover that they cannot emulate, or be instantly respected in the manner of, the only truly effective teacher they can remember from their own school days. While it may be possible to draw lessons from one's own teachers on how to handle difficult students, how to make work interesting and accessible, how to promote self-esteem and motivation through sensitive, constructive assessment and so on, it is usually a futile and ultimately destructive task to seek to copy their manner of self-presentation.

> It is axiomatic that, in the end, though teaching may always be something of an 'act', the successful teacher has to remain true to 'who they are'.

If the notion of the charismatic subject, with its over-reliance on 'personality' and its frequent under-reliance on technique, is potentially a very dangerous one for the beginner teacher, this is not to say that it should be rejected totally or in all its parts. Part of the nature of teaching which is often forgotten in these days of 'competences' and 'standards' is that it is very often 'expressive and emergent, intuitive and flexible, spontaneous and emotional' (Woods 1996, p. 6). The notion of the charismatic subject, in which the teacher may not only be seen to prioritise their selective personality but may also give a high and sensitive profile to the specific and variable *contexts* of teaching and learning, may accommodate notions of the expressive and emergent, the intuitive and flexible, the spontaneous and emotional far more easily and readily than some of the other notions of good teaching that we shall consider shortly. Furthermore, the notion of the teacher as charismatic subject foregrounds another essential ingredient of successful teaching, which is the ability to *communicate* clearly, purposefully and interestingly to an audience comprising individuals with very different psychological make-ups and from many different cultural backgrounds.

A more useful concept than that of the 'charismatic' teacher might, indeed, be that of the *communicative* teacher. The communicative teacher relies not so much on some difficult-to-define 'personality' but on more easily recognised and more readily imitated communication and presentational *skills*. The teacher is not only able to de-centre sufficiently to be understood by the range of students in any class, but is sensitive to the range of needs in the classroom and works at and plans effective communication strategies both before lessons (in the planning stage) and after lessons (in the evaluative stage). The communicative teacher listens carefully to students, remaining sensitive to what students say about themselves – both through spoken language and through behaviour generally – and recognising the role and impact of emotions in the classroom situation (Boler 1999). Additionally, the teacher thinks carefully about how they 'self present' – an aspect of their work which might include such issues as:

- how to position oneself physically in the classroom,
- how to display, through appropriate body-language, a genuine interest in what students have to say,
- knowing when to talk, when to listen and when to interrupt.

The teacher may *appear* 'charismatic' to the students; however, in practice they are merely displaying effective communication skills coupled with a sound understanding of and enthusiasm for whatever subject or subject area is under discussion.

If good communication, presentation and de-centring skills are positive aspects that may attach to the notion of the teacher as charismatic subject, possible negative aspects might include:

- an over-concern with one's own performance rather than with the progress and development of one's students;
- an over-reliance on high-profile 'personal' attributes rather than on less visible aspects of pedagogy to do with such things as planning, assessment and evaluation;
- a reluctance or inability to provide teachers newer to the profession with constructive, practical advice on how to develop their own practice.

One final point that needs to be made about the teacher as charismatic subject is that although the teacher's 'charisma' may appear to be embodied in and to emanate from the teacher, it is in essence an attribute that is 'conferred' upon the teacher by their students. This is what Zizek and others, after the psychoanalyst Jacques Lacan, have referred to as the 'transferential illusion', whereby a quality that one invests in another object *appears* to reside intrinsically in the object itself (see, for instance, Zizek 1989, p. 146). Bearing this in mind, it might be a useful exercise for student teachers, rather than trying to work out and emulate the 'charisma' of a particular teacher or teachers, to try to analyse why it is that the teacher's students invest charisma in the teacher in the way they do. This might involve, centrally, an identification of the particular personal and professional qualities and techniques that the students appeared to be responding to most positively.

THE COMPETENT PRACTITIONER

Although the notion of the charismatic teacher still holds much popular following, it has rarely had much of a place on courses of initial teacher education. Such courses have tended to emphasise the theoretical aspects of teaching and their relation to practice (what might be called the notion of the teacher as expert) and – more recently – the discrete *skills* of teaching, in what has come to be known as the *competences* discourse (Moore 1999b).

The notion of the 'competent teacher' has its roots in books of practical advice for teachers on such matters as controlling awkward classes and individuals, making sure that lessons are interesting, accessible and well-thought out, planning for and assessing students' work, and working constructively with colleagues (see, for instance, Marland 1975; Cohen and Manion 1977; Stephens and Crawley 1994).

Recently, the competences model of teaching has become the dominant discourse in initial teacher education, first in the USA (Henry 1989) and then, in the 1990s, in the UK. The domination of the competent teacher discourse in initial and continuing teacher development in the UK can be traced to 1992. The discourse was powerful before then; however, 1992 marks something of a turning point, in that the discourse at this point had *legitimisation* bestowed upon it with the full force of the British law. A key document and defining moment in this process was a circular dispatched by the Council for the Accreditation of Teacher Education (CATE) in the September of that year to all Higher Education Institutions in the UK providing initial teacher education courses. This circular laid out the basic requirements for all such courses clearly and unambiguously in the terms of the competences discourse, as the following extract indicates:

> The main objective of all courses of initial training is to enable students to become *competent* teachers who can establish effective working relationships with pupils. To do so, they will need to be knowledgeable in their subjects, to understand how pupils learn, and to acquire teaching skills.[. . .] It is recognised that [. . .] the acquisition of competences is not the totality of training [and] each competence is not a discrete unit but one of many whose sum makes for a confident start in teaching.
>
> (CATE 9/92, p. 9)

Emphasis in this circular was placed on key areas of competence that were to become the key 'sub-discourses' of the next six years: 'subject knowledge', 'class management' and 'assessment and recording of pupils' progress'. Since the publication of 9/92, the Council for the Accreditation of Teacher Education in the UK (CATE) has been replaced by the Teacher Training Agency (TTA). This change, however, as the new title suggests, has represented not a break from the latter-day discourse of CATE but rather a natural progression and development of it which continues to identify and prioritise 'discrete', universal skills (TTA 1998; see, too, DfEE 1997b). As such we may discern in the competences discourse a shift of emphasis away from the notion of teacher *education* traditionally favoured by universities and teachers (NUT 1976, Institute of Education 1972; Alexander *et al.* 1984; Popkewitz 1987) toward one of '*training*', which had always been more popular in the official documentation (see, for instance, DES 1981, Allen 1994). This shift of emphasis may be seen to place less importance on – and to allow for more limited coverage of – matters of teaching and learning *theory*, and a correspondingly greater emphasis on the *practicalities* of life in the classroom and the school.

Much of what is contained within the competences discourse does make relatively uncontentious good sense. Teachers do, of course, need to have sufficient subject knowledge to teach their students effectively, and they do, of course, need to be effective planners and classroom managers. Indeed, a high level of personal organisation and preparedness is generally agreed to be one of the principal requirements of good teaching. Furthermore, the notion of the teacher as the 'competent' possessor and practiser of learnable skills helps to 'demystify' the teaching process in a way that the charismatic subject discourse does not (Woods 1996, p. 19), often providing for more confident and often more effective teachers. Examples of this from the official documentation abound, of which the following demonstrates the difference between the competences discourse and that of the charismatic subject:

> For all courses, those to be awarded Qualified Teacher Status must, when assessed, demonstrate that they [. . .] use teaching methods which sustain the momentum of pupils' work and keep all pupils engaged through [. . .] matching the approaches used to the subject matter and the pupils being taught; [. . .] structuring information well, including outlining content and aims, signalling transitions and summarising key points as the lesson progresses; [. . .] clear presentation of content around a set of key issues, using appropriate subject-specific vocabulary and well chosen illustrations and examples; [. . .] clear instruction and demonstration, and accurate well-paced explanation.
>
> (DfEE 1998, p. 13)

The above represents a much clearer guide for the would-be communicative teacher than the much vaguer suggestion offered by the term 'charisma' that the successful teacher merely succeeds through the force and strength of an equally vaguely defined 'personality'.

When perceived and approached in this way, the lists of competences – more recently redefined as 'standards' – provided by the Office for Standards in Education (OFSTED) and the TTA to student teachers via their course tutors – may be seen as helpful descriptors of the qualities that all good teachers need to have, as well as providing a detailed set of criteria by which teachers know they will be assessed. This latter function, which is perhaps less discussed in debates about competences, replaces often very vague and woolly assessment criteria, that provided little external support for student teachers who were doing badly but could not fully understand why. The provision of lists of competences may thus be viewed as an advance in the areas of teacher entitlement, teacher access and equality of opportunity. In the case of national lists of competences, it may also be seen as a way of ensuring that student teachers are likely to cover the same ground and be assessed against the same criteria, regardless of where they undertake their studentship.

Institutions offering courses of initial teacher education often provide their own lists of competences for student teachers, and are perfectly at liberty to do so. However, all such lists are now required, in England and Wales, to at least include all of the areas and sub-areas of competence provided nationally by the TTA and OFSTED – a national list that is currently published and promulgated through two complementary documents: *Framework for the Assessment of Quality and Standards in Initial Teacher Training* (OFSTED/TTA 1997/98) and *Teaching: High Status, High Standards* (DfEE 1998). The latter document defines the 'standards for the award of qualified teacher status' under broad headings, each subdivided into a number of specific skills or areas. The broad areas are:

- Knowledge and understanding of subject area(s);
- Planning, teaching and class management;
- Monitoring, assessment, recording, reporting and accountability;
- Other professional requirements.

The document also details the knowledge and skills required of beginner teachers in the areas of information and communications technology (ICT), with additional, much more detailed sections for primary and secondary teachers related to the 'core' subject areas of English, mathematics and science.

If we wanted to select some of the more positive characteristics and anticipated outcomes of a competence-based approach to initial teacher education, we might include, among other things:

- encouragement and support for teachers in more effective monitoring and assessment of their students' work;
- the development of better understandings, leading to more effective practice, of the circular relationship between planning, outcomes and evaluation, whereby the success or failure of previous planning feeds constructively and critically into future planning;
- a greater emphasis on the teacher's need to keep up-to-date with developments in subject knowledge and not to over-rely on knowledge gleaned during their own previous educational experience;
- a sharper focus on the purposes of individual lessons and sequences of lessons, in terms of both whole-class and individual students' development, including a more thoughtful approach to target-setting;
- an insistence on teachers' adopting a wide range of teaching strategies and materials in order to achieve stated aims, rather than being

over-reliant (as can more readily happen within the charismatic discourse) on a narrow range of strategies and materials including the teacher's own front-of-class performance.

Difficulties with the competences model

Although potentially very useful for teachers, the discourse of the competent teacher is not without its difficulties. One obvious difficulty is the way in which it almost inevitably lends itself to misinterpretation. As we have already seen, CATE 9/92 very specifically stated that 'the acquisition of competences is not the totality of training. The criteria do not provide the entire syllabus of initial professional training', and 'each competence is not a discrete unit but one of many whose sum makes for a confident start in teaching' (CATE 1992, p. 9).

However, the inevitably list-like nature of competences (particularly those emanating from 'official' sources that seek some kind of universality), and the need to leave 'nothing out' for fear of implying that some areas of competence are more or less important than others, gives teachers and teacher educators a very clear impression that identified competences do, indeed, provide 'the entire syllabus', that the skills listed are indeed 'discrete', and that the lists are intended as finite representations of essential truths (Moore 1996). As such, they may be seen to be located within the same dominant educational discourses of selectivity and quantifiability that we have already considered in relation to the National Curriculum for schools.

It could be argued that this impression, which has been reinforced by subsequent documentation (for example, DfEE 1997b; 1998), sustains a view – consistently rejected by many teachers and teacher educators – that the ingredients of 'good teaching' can be itemised and that, subject to their being appropriately acquired, anyone can make an effective teacher. One problem with this is that many student teachers do appear – to themselves and to others – to acquire, in a satisfactory manner and to a satisfactory degree, the various competences, but still have huge difficulties in the classroom and cannot begin to understand why this should be so (Moore and Atkinson 1998).

A second problem with the competences discourse is that language – however precise and 'scientific' it may be – seldom if ever says exactly what we want it to say or, indeed, *everything* that we might want it to say (Moore 1996). It is consequently highly resistant to the kind of inventorialising that characterises the competences discourse, so that however many hours may go into their construction lists of competences will never, finally, be able to answer the question they set themselves: 'What makes an effective teacher?'

One result of this 'linguistic' problem is that statements of competence may themselves be reduced to the vague forms of language that often characterise the charismatic–subject discourse. The insistence that (DfEE 1998, p. 13) student teachers should demonstrate their teaching skills through 'stimulating intellectual curiosity, communicating enthusiasm for the subject being taught, fostering pupils' enthusiasm and maintaining pupils' motivation' is, for example, arguably much less helpful than other, more easily assessable competences, in that it gives rise to a number of unanswered questions and tends to reduce both teaching and learning to much less complex and sophisticated activities than they actually are. 'Communicating enthusiasm' in particular seems to suggest some kind of invisible, infectious, esoteric and almost spiritual quality reminiscent of the charismatic–subject discourse, while the call to 'foster enthusiasm' comes with no indication as to how best to achieve this or how the student teacher's success in this area might be assessed. (How, for instance, does one reliably measure 'enthusiasm' during the course of one lesson, let alone across a longer period of time when enthusiasm may come and go according to a wide range of circumstances and events, many of them totally beyond the teacher's reach or control?)

A third problem with the competences discourse lies in its attempted 'universality': that is, its attempt to isolate and define skills and kinds of knowledge that all teachers will need regardless of the kind of person they are or the circumstances in which they operate. While this is by no means an impossible or futile project, it becomes problematic if it does not provide some means of allowing and catering for such differences of character and circumstance – that is to say, if it overlooks the personal and responsive aspects of teaching that many commentators have placed at the heart of good teaching (Maguire 1995; Woods 1996; Moore 1999b). As most teachers will agree (Moore and Edwards 2000), there is no one model of good teaching, any more than there is any one model of the good student or the good school. It is also clear that attempts to identify the universal good teacher, student or school through measurable 'outcomes' are themselves misleading, precisely because of the contingent and idiosyncratic aspects of schooling itself – a problem recognised in the notion of 'value added', whereby raw examination results of school-students are translated into more meaningful data by taking account of such matters as the social and initial academic backgrounds of schools' students in the construction of 'league tables'.

Goudie has taken this particular issue a stage further, relating the absence of contingency and idiosyncrasy from the competences discourse to questions of *disempowerment* and the suppression of *creativity* in teaching activity:

> Deference to any prescriptive theory is out of pace with time and context and suppresses consciousness of the self as a social being; it results in conformity, and disempowers social actors from acting authentically in response to the particular situation. It also turns practice into a technical performance, debilitating the creative imagination as it interacts with external reality.
>
> (Goudie 1999, p. 60)

Goudie argues that teachers need to be encouraged to expose 'the ideology of technocratic control' implicit in the competences discourse, in order to 'have a chance to struggle over the inequity of social forces of domination and subordination' upon which formal state education systems are partly structured (ibid., p. 93).

The capacity of the competences discourse to deskill the classroom teacher or undermine their professionalism is directly related to another difficulty, recently identified by Basil Bernstein. That is its capacity to contribute to misdiagnoses of perceived educational failure, and to deflect solutions of educational difficulties away from analysis and reform of social conditions towards the blaming of individual students, teachers and schools (Bernstein 1996). To refer to an issue already discussed in Chapter 2, it does this partly by prioritising skills and knowledge which may be perceived as residing 'within' the *individual* over more complex issues of educational *processes* that may be seen as residing in the larger educational and social *systems*.

From Bernstein's perspective, the power and importance of the competences discourse for central governments is plain to see: it is both far easier and more economical to treat perceived social difficulties *symptomatically* – for example, to concentrate blame on schools and teachers for educational failure – than it is to take a causal approach which might imply a drastic readjustment in the social distribution of power and wealth. This personalisation of the difficulty, implicit in the competences discourse but disguised by its 'abstracted', universalised appearance, may have the added impact of effectively disguising broader social problems (Moore 1996): what Bernstein refers to as a pointing 'away from the macro blot on the micro context' (Bernstein 1996, p. 56).

THE REFLECTIVE PRACTITIONER

Although the competence discourse currently enjoys a position of dominance in debates about good teaching and, consequently, in the nature and structures of courses of initial and continuing teacher education, other models of good teaching have also enjoyed a rise in popularity and influence in recent years. Chief among these – if we are to judge by the literature available, by submissions to national conferences on education, and by virtue of the fact that it sustains its own academic journal – is the notion of the *reflective practitioner*.

Working in parallel with the competences discourse – sometimes in apparent opposition, sometimes in a more complementary way – the discourse of the reflective practitioner emphasises not so much the *acquisition* or development *per se* of the skills and areas of knowledge required for successful teaching, but rather the particular skills needed to *reflect constructively* upon ongoing experience as a way of developing those skills and knowledge and improving the quality and effectiveness of one's work.

Such reflection refers to the range of strategies and techniques one has at one's disposal or that one is in the process of developing; but it does so selectively, flexibly and strategically, taking full account of the particular circumstances relating to any given problem at any given time. In particular, the discourse encourages teachers and student teachers to take into account the 'whole picture' of their teaching, analysing the effectiveness of a lesson or series of lessons not simply by measurable outputs such as their students' test scores, but through an attempt to evaluate what was learned, by whom, and how more effective learning might take place in the future. As such, the reflective practitioner discourse involves careful evaluation on the teacher's part of their own classroom performance, planning and assessment, in addition to and in conjunction with evaluations of students' behaviour and achievement, in ways that seek to problematise and 'make strange' the taken-for-granted assumptions of everyday life and practice (Erickson 1986). Reflection also implies a sound understanding on the teacher's part of relevant educational *theory and research* – including theories of cognitive, linguistic and affective development – in order to enable them to address issues that are not restricted to the 'what' and the 'when' of education but also embrace questions of 'how' and 'why'.

The notion of 'reflective practice', though already current under different names in the early 1970s (see, for instance, Combs 1972; Wragg 1974), came to the fore for many teachers in the 1980s and early 1990s, through the work of such writers as Schon (1983; 1987), Valli (1992) and Elliott (1991; 1993). The work of these writers placed as much emphasis on teachers' own *evaluations* of their practice as on the planning and management skills into which such evaluations should feed. One of the central techniques recommended in the reflective practitioner discourse has been the keeping of diaries or journals by teachers and student-teachers, in which they reflect systematically on their experiences as they perceive them, keeping a record that can be returned to and re-interrogated in the light of subsequent experiences, and providing scope for the self-setting of targets and goals. The role of *initial and continuing teacher education* in these processes may be described not so much in terms of the relatively independent acquisition of skills by the teacher or student-teacher, which can then be applied to the practical setting, but rather in terms of *dialogues about practice*, held between teachers and tutors, that are aimed to render the invisible visible (see also Chapter 4 above). Smyth, for example, describes how 'clinical supervision' encourages such dialogues 'in a way that enables questions to be asked about taken-for-granted (even cherished) assumptions and practices, the formulation of alternative hypotheses for action, and the actual testing out of those hypotheses in classroom situations' (Smyth 1991, p. 3).

The reflective practitioner discourse continues to show its popular appeal through bookshop shelves (Loughran 1996; Loughran and Russell 1997; Mitchell and Weber 1996), even as it becomes increasingly marginalised by government-sponsored publications favouring the 'competent craftsperson' approach (OFSTED/TTA 1996; DfEE 1997b; 1998). In this respect, it must be said that for all its popularity with teachers who teach teachers, the reflective practitioner discourse does *not* appear to be well favoured within current 'official discourses' of teacher education. The competence category of 'evaluation of one's own teaching', for example, is not included in the most recent Teacher Training Agency documentation, being relegated in terms of position to the end of another broad area – 'Teaching and Class Management' – and in terms of wordage to '[students must demonstrate that they can] evaluate their own teaching critically and use this to improve effectiveness' (DfEE 1997b, p. 10; TTA 1998, p. 8). Such a marginalisation may be said to reinforce the notion held by some teachers that the competences discourse is anti-intellectual and anti-theoretical, and that it promotes a view of teachers as essentially 'clerks and technicians' (Giroux and McLaren 1992, p. xiii) rather than thinkers and creators.

If the competences discourse emphasises the teacher as technician and 'deliverer', whose 'internalised' skills can be easily monitored through measurable outcomes, the reflective practitioner discourse has always taken a subtler approach to teaching, recognising the centrality of much-harder-to-identify, codify and quantify skills (to do with communication, presentation, analysis, evaluation and interaction) – often promoting, for example, *counselling* skills on the part of teacher educators, and emphasising the *strategic* aspects of teaching above the acquisition of less flexible methodological approaches (Handal and Lauvas 1987). Such a difference clearly has implications not only for classroom teaching itself, but for the ways in which teacher education is conducted and for related research. The competences discourse, for example, because of its inventorial, 'self referential' nature (see Bernstein 1996, p. 73), suggests an *evaluative* response, sited within a world of skills and capabilities that already exists 'outside of' the individual. In the area of educational research, this situation prompts such questions as

- Which system of competences works best?
- Which higher education institutions implement the competences approach most effectively?

The *reflective practitioner* discourse, by contrast, suggests a qualitative research-based response, focused not on measuring success by outcome ('How many students successfully completed this or that course?', 'What gradings were courses given by OFSTED inspectorates?') but on exploring the *nature* of the teaching and learning processes that are taking place, through an emphasis on 'the processes of meaning-assignation and situation-defining' and on 'how the social world is constructed by people, how they are continually striving to make sense of the world' (Woods 1979, p. 2; see, too, Van Manen 1990).

Differences and similarities between the competences and reflective practitioner discourses

The differing research implications of the two dominant discourses in teacher education may be seen to represent a summary of the two contradictory views of human behaviour that underpin them. To approach this via a question posed by Peter Woods – 'Is teaching a science or an art?' (Woods 1996, p. 14) – the competences discourse may be said to represent a *quasi-scientific* perception of teaching and learning, firmly sited within a paradigm of educational thinking sometimes critiqued under the term 'modernism' (Moore 1998). Such a paradigm assumes 'the possibility of completeness' (Standish 1995, p. 133,) through viewing the world as 'an ordered place' and the 'elements of the world of knowledge as topologically invariant' (Hamilton 1993, p. 55). What is knowable – or what 'needs to be known' – is ultimately definable and susceptible to inventorialisation and tidy assessment: it is underpinned by a tacit assumption that there is, under passing acknowledgement of the possibility of local variations, only one right way or set of ways of doing things.

In contrast with the neat, knowable and easily describable world implied in the competences discourse, the discourse of *reflection* recognises what Goodson and Walker have called 'the messy complexity of the classroom' and its only 'partially apprehendable practice' (Goodson and Walker 1991, p. xii). This discourse gives full recognition to 'the central role that people play in the educational process and educational systems' (ibid., p. 1), legitimises a *range* of approaches and behaviours, and understands that 'much of the most expert practice in schools is based on intuitive judgement' (McIntyre *et al.* 1994, p. 57). It is a discourse that is often associated, in the philosophy of education, with the use of the term 'postmodernism' (Usher and Edwards 1994) as denoting a 'commitment to notions of process, experience and pleasure' (Green 1995, p. 402; see also Standish 1995; Hebdidge 1986; Levin 1987; Hargreaves 1993). As such, it views teaching more as art than as science, lending itself to corresponding modes of research.

Though clearly separated from one another, the two dominant discourses of competence and reflection should not be seen as oppositional. Certainly, they are not mutually exclusive, and most student teachers these days will find themselves being encouraged and helped to be both 'competent' and 'reflective'. Indeed, in some of its cruder manifestations, in which 'checklists, rankings, peer evaluations, etc.' are prioritised while 'student teachers are seldom given an opportunity to have a concrete understanding of their personalities [and therefore] find it difficult to understand *why* they react to people, situations, or circumstances as they do' (Johnson 1989, p. 340, emphasis added), the reflective practitioner discourse can overlap the competences discourse to such an extent that the two may often appear, to the student, to merge into one.

Such convergences suggest that, philosophically, the two discourses may be closer to one another than at first appears. In particular, we might suggest that each of these discourses has its roots in an Enlightenment view of social development, discussed in Chapter 2 above, that is founded on the primacy of private and collective 'reason', and of the notion of the unitary, ideal 'self'. Thus, although the competences discourse may be seen as focusing on universals, and the reflective practitioner discourse on the contingent and idiosyncratic, both have the *potential* to overemphasise a particular form of agency (that which focuses on 'self-improvement' rather than that which looks 'outward' toward reforming society), through implying the existence of 'detached', 'independent', unified identities. Just as in the competences discourse success rests on the student's responsibility, with the aid of tutors, to become 'competent', so, in the reflective practitioner discourse, it can become incumbent on the individual student to use their own reflective, rational powers to right wrongs in the classroom for which, ultimately, they are perceived responsible. In this way, within either discourse it can become an easy task to pathologise the individual student, teacher or student-teacher for any breakdowns that occur in social interaction (Walkerdine 1982, 1990).

> Such pathologising does two things. First, as has already been suggested, it shifts debate away from issues related to broader socio-economic and cultural relations. Second, through its appeal to ideal, universal 'reason', it promotes the discourse (already very familiar to teachers and students) of individual *blame*, leading to anxiety and self-doubt (see also Leat 1995).

The first of these difficulties, of course, can be addressed initially by ensuring locally that such issues are given adequate coverage as curriculum inputs on courses. The second is rather more difficult to address, since it involves a radical departure for teachers not only in how they perceive their classrooms but in how they perceive and understand themselves.

THE REFLEXIVE TEACHER

The potential difficulties of the reflective practitioner discourse have been noted by a number of commentators. Leat, for example, has suggested that the term 'reflective practice' has too easily become something of a slogan, and that consequently its capacity to offer a radically alternative concept of the good teacher or of what it takes to become a good teacher is greatly reduced (Leat 1995), while Smyth (1991, p. 3) has argued that many of the advocates of reflective practice are 'remarkably unreflexive of their own agenda'. Goudie, with reference to Habermas's work, has suggested that reflection which does not challenge its own presuppositions and the discursive-ideological bases upon which it is constructed will simply end up as another way of reinforcing dominant ideologies and reproducing dominant (and potentially exclusive) cultural practices (Goudie 1999).

Smyth's reference to 'reflexivity' not only points at the possible limitations and dangers of the reflective practitioner discourse, but also suggests a way in which the discourse can be developed to ensure its effectiveness. That development entails a move away from the concept of the rational, unified self as somehow removed from the social circumstances in which it is constructed, towards a notion of self as *constructed*, as many-faceted and as continuously developing through the passage of its own history: that is to say (Moore and Atkinson 1998) the self as a developing or unfolding *text* that may be 'read', and that may be the subject of many varied readings, both by other selves and by the 'self itself'. Such a notion is implicit in earlier accounts of *critical reflection*, such as that described by Habermas (Habermas 1972, 1974; see also Van Manen 1977; Schon 1983; Calderhead and Gates 1993).

As the above suggests, to approach pedagogy as a reflexive project is not merely to reflect upon one's practice but to reflect upon the *ways in which one reflects*, and upon one's former life-history – a history that provides both the context for and selectivity involved in the reflection. As Goudie puts this in relation to student teachers: 'By reflecting on their action in praxis, prior personal experiences are exposed for scrutiny, criticized and evaluated with respect to the enquirer's theoretical knowledge' (Goudie 1999, p. 58; see also Bogdan 1992; Knowles 1992; Goodson 1992). In similar vein, Greene's discussion of autonomy in learning, which implies the need for school-students to be as reflexive as their teachers, argues the importance of becoming 'insightful enough to know and understand one's impulses, one's motives, and the influences of one's past' (Greene 1988, p. 188). The essential difference between the reflective practitioner and the reflexive practitioner discourses may be summarised as follows: while the reflective discourse tends to focus on reflection about practice *per se*, the reflexive discourse is more inclined to focus on the *practitioner* and on the wider personal and general social contexts within which practice takes place. The reflexive teacher, like the reflexive learner, may thus ask of their own classroom behaviour not simply 'What did I do that was right or wrong, that worked or did not work?' but '*Why* do I do that which was right or wrong, that worked or did not work?' and 'How did my past and current experience of life and work *influence me* in behaving in the particular way I did or in suggesting the particular courses of action I took?'

Such questions are reminiscent of the three 'clusters of reflective activity' singled out by Boud *et al.* (1985) as being potentially productive in the reflective process: that is to say,

- returning to experience;
- attending to feelings;
- re-evaluating experience.

Such questioning may not find neat 'answers'; indeed, it is at the heart of reflexivity that it should be exploratory, that it should help to make sense of experience, rather than that it should feed directly into 'action plans'. Nor can it claim to free itself from the dominant discourses and discursive practices within which it is sited (the pre-formed structures and meanings of language itself inevitably guide and shape our 'reflexions' just as they guide and shape our 'reflections'). It may, however, help the practitioner's everyday practice by helping them to understand and to be happy with their 'self'.

The concept of the reflexive practitioner is not a new one, and can find recent support in a range of writings drawn from a variety of academic disciplines. It is often associated with the notion of multiple identities, and with 'postmodern' or 'high modern' configurations of pluralism in education, including arguments resistant to identifying the 'good teacher' or the 'definitive curriculum'. Thus, Hargreaves has talked, in words that remind us, also, of some of the issues of *culture* introduced in the previous chapter, of the 'postmodern world' in which

> multiple rather than singular forms of intelligence are coming to be recognized [. . .] multiple rather than singular forms of representation of students' work are being advocated and accepted [. . . .] Many ways of knowing, thinking and being moral, not just rational, 'logical' ones, are coming to be seen as legitimate.
>
> (A. Hargreaves 1993, p. 22)

Elsewhere, Giddens has talked of the 'reflexive project of the self, which consists in the sustaining of coherent, yet continuously revised, *biographical narratives*' (Giddens 1991, p. 5, emphasis added), while Cole and Knowles (1995, p. 131) have described teaching practice in terms of its 'multiple roles and contexts'. The centrality of 'biographical narratives' in the reflexive paradigm also finds its support in practice and research drawn directly from teacher education (see, for instance, Quicke 1988; Schon 1988).

The alternative notions of self implicit in the notion of the reflexive practitioner have given rise to new modes of practice in initial teacher education as well as to new forms of theoretical inquiry, in which teachers and student-teachers are encouraged to interrogate and critically reflect not only on their students' behaviour or upon what happened in the classroom, but also on their own behaviours – on the ways in which they responded to situations, interacted with other people, experienced emotional responses and so forth. Such reflection includes a recognition by the teacher not just of the nature and impact of their own cultural preferences on the ways in which they handle themselves and their students in the classroom, but also of the emotional 'baggage' (old and new!) that they bring with them into the classroom, whether they want to or not – baggage which, in the often highly-charged atmosphere of the school, can intrude both positively and negatively into their practice. (Negatively, for example, when the classroom becomes the social space for the playing out or repetition of family-related repressions, irresolutions and role-anxieties).

The reflexive approach encourages teachers, appropriately supported by their tutors (Combs 1972; Wragg 1974), not only to reflect critically on ongoing experiences *in themselves*, but to contextualise these experiences within previous experiences as a way of developing more effective teaching strategies (Quicke 1988; Schon 1988; Cole and Knowles 1995; Thomas 1995). Part of that activity, aimed at helping practitioners to understand more clearly 'the way in which a personal life can be penetrated by the social and the practical' (Thomas 1995, p. 5) and to make sense of 'prior and current life experiences in the context of the personal as it influences the professional' (Cole and Knowles 1995, p. 130), involves encouraging individual teachers to critique difficulties they may be experiencing in the here and now within the context of previous roles and experiences they have encountered 'outside' the classroom situation in, for example, their family life or their own schooling. Inevitably, this also introduces issues of *desire* (Hargreaves 1994; McLaren 1996) into understandings of practice:

- 'What do I want from these interactions?'
- 'What do others want of me?'
- 'What am I afraid of?'
- 'What do I want to *do* about the things I don't like here?'

With reference to Peter Woods' question as to whether teaching is a science or an art, we might say that this kind of teaching and research about teaching moves us away from the art/science dichotomy into a new area in which the question begins to lose its pertinence. As Woods concludes in response to his own question: '[Teaching] is both a science and an art – and more besides' (1996, p. 31).

Problems with reflexivity

There are, of course, obvious dangers in an approach that invites teachers to interrogate their own behaviours textually. Chief among these are

(a) that practitioners and their tutors may engage in ill-informed 'amateur psychoanalysis' that ends up benefiting nobody or even worsening an already difficult situation;

(b) that the discourse may slip into the very pathologisations implied by the other discourses we have considered, and provide another way of obscuring the 'macro blot'. Teachers may, for example, end up relocating classroom difficulties within very personal problems in their own lives, to an extent that draws them away from elaborating constructive criticisms of the wider socio-economic *systems and ideologies* within which formal teaching and learning are sited, as well as from the devising of more effective strategies for dealing with classroom difficulties and for improving the quality of learning of their students.

This particular difficulty has been pointed out by Foucault, who presents reflection and reflexivity as modes of self-surveillance leading to institutional access to and control over the individual's thoughts and actions – that is to say, a form of *institutional power* that 'reaches into the very grain of individuals, touches their bodies and inserts itself into their action and attitudes, their discourses, learning processes and everyday lives' (Foucault 1980, p. 39).

Such potential dangers call for care and common sense rather than a dismissal of the reflexive practitioner discourse itself, along with a recognition that most of the other discourses we have considered (the charismatic subject, the competent practitioner, the reflective practitioner), are also replete with dangers. Experience, furthermore, suggests that the incorporation of this additional discourse *with* those of the competent teacher and the reflective practitioner can, if properly handled, have very beneficial effects, both for teachers and student-teachers experiencing classroom difficulties and in terms of reorienting teachers towards informed criticism of wider social issues. As Kemmis argues with reference to this latter possibility: '[C]ritical reflection aims at recovering and examining the historical and developmental circumstances which shaped our ideas, institutions and modes of action, *as a basis for formulating more rational ideas, more just institutions and more fulfilling forms of action*' (Kemmis 1985, p. 146: emphasis added).

Though it continues to appeal to 'rationality', Kemmis's argument attaches a 'material' political and personal purpose to reflection; that is to say, it is aimed at improving both one's own practice *and* the wider social conditions in which that practice is located, through deconstructive activity aimed at providing better opportunities for those who suffer most as a result of institutional marginalisation and discrimination.

Reflexivity and the notions of 'manifest' and 'latent' meanings

As has already been indicated, the development of a reflexive approach to teaching is not a question of *substituting* the competences and reflective practitioner discourses with the reflexive practitioner discourse. Rather, it is a matter of adding the reflexive discourse *to* those other discourses, in a way that makes it easier and more profitable for students to 'enter', to understand and to negotiate those discourses: that is to say, in addition to any merits of its own, it is a discourse that can take on a *contextualisation* function that helps replace morbid, unconstructive 'self' criticism ('Something *in me* is wrong') with constructive, reasoned, 'action' criticism ('Something *that's being done* is wrong').

To draw a parallel with Freud's approach to the analysis of dreams, we might say that the reflexive discourse recognises and suggests *latent* or 'hidden' meanings and interpretations of classroom interactions. Gaining access to these latent meanings, through appropriate analysis and interrogation of more immediately accessible *manifest* meanings and interpretations, may subsequently enable a more effective reading of – and response to – those manifest meanings, facilitating the more effective use of available strategies as a way of helping the students through their difficulties (see also Moore 1999b).

To illustrate this with reference to Freud's dream theory, Freud suggests that the symbolic material of which dreams are made (essentially, the images, words, sounds and 'stories' of our dreams, some of which we may remember on waking), act as representatives or substitutes for hidden desires, anxieties and so forth that are normally banished from our conscious lives but that threaten to surface, disquietingly, while we sleep. The function of the dream-material is, effectively, to *disguise* those surfacing feelings so that they do not disturb our sleep and wake us. If the principal value of the dream to the dreamer lies in its capacity to protect their sleep, the potential value to the psychoanalyst lies in its capacity to be treated as a *text* whose specialised reading may provide a window on to the roots of deep-seated anxieties, unfulfilled desires and so on that may be causing the dreamer debilitating discomfort during their waking hours. (For further accounts of Freud's dream theory, see Freud 1991, pp. 77–133).

Whether or not we accept Freud's theory of the nature and significance of dreams, the notion of manifest contents and ascribed 'meanings' or readings disguising more disquieting – and potentially more helpful – 'latent' meanings is potentially a very useful one in analysing classroom behaviours and interactions. Putting this another way, it is not unfeasible that our *interpretations* of classroom events and interactions, especially where these have been dysfunctional, may serve to mask or 'suture' the actual *reasons* for what has happened.

An example of this potential usefulness is provided by the following, initially fairly innocuous-looking and routine observation of an actual student-teacher in one of her written evaluations of a lesson carried out during teaching-practice:

> 'The lesson went well, but ideally the pupils would have had a lot longer to discuss their findings in small groups. With this particular class, though, I felt I couldn't do that because they aren't disciplined enough to handle it.'

The 'manifest' meaning attached by the student to what happened and did not happen in the classroom remains 'self-referential': that is to say, it bases its understanding of events only on information available from 'the lesson itself', without, as it were, moving beyond the lesson in search of other interpretations. Not surprisingly, perhaps, it holds the students in the class essentially responsible for the teacher's decision not to allow extended groupwork, presenting and (implicitly) justifying that decision on the grounds of teacher pragmatism. In this interpretation of events, discipline itself is reified as a human quality residing in individual actors, rather than being used as a descriptor of wider symbolic and social systems and practices, in operation both in the school classroom itself and in the wider society.

There may, of course, be nothing at all wrong or misleading or unhelpful in the student-teacher's evaluation as far as it goes. However, the reflexive discourse, by introducing the possibility of additional, latent meanings, might add to the initial interpretation, providing the teacher with a broader raft of ideas on which to work and from which to develop useful strategies. Reflexivity might suggest to the teacher, for example, interpretations that are not directly and exclusively embedded in reifications of *student* behaviours, but that may have as much to do with their *own psyche* and the relationship between that and the wider symbolic and social order in which classroom activity is situated. These interpretations might include (among other things) considerations as to whether a fear of losing control might have contributed in any way to the teacher's *decision* not to allow extended group-work, the extent to which that decision may have been based on learned but uncriticised roles and behaviours made familiar in the teacher's own schooling and family upbringing, and – with reference to the wider social-symbolic order – whether, through denying opportunities for extended group-work (for whatever perceived reason), the teacher is unwittingly replicating power relations and inequalities that exist in the wider society and thus contributing to the development of coerced, compliant citizens.

If the introduction of these possible latent meanings (which can also, of course, be used to extend possible interpretations of the class's own behaviours) seem initially harsh, that harshness may quickly evaporate once it is turned to the considered development of additional teaching *strategies*, or when it has re-opened possibilities that the preliminary, 'manifest'-oriented evaluation has foreclosed. In this case, for example, the reflexive approach, aimed at exploring possible latent meanings, might end up with the teacher arriving at the same conclusion – though by a more thoughtful and wide-ranging route – that she originally came to. On the other hand, it might encourage her to look again at the possibility of developing group-work with her 'indisciplined' class, perhaps by setting it up in ways, and through using supporting materials, that minimise the risks of failure.

In conclusion, we might say that while both the competences and the reflective practitioner discourses may be of use to the teacher, it may be the reflexive discourse that fully 'activates' that usefulness, making it accessible and opening the way to a more critical engagement with the interface between personally-experienced difficulties and systemic failings.

THE TEACHER AS RESEARCHER AND THEORIST

Both the reflective practitioner discourse and the *reflexive* practitioner discourse are supported by another discourse: that of the teacher as researcher and theorist (see also Stenhouse 1975). An appreciation of educational theory – whether it be sociological, cultural or developmental – along with involvement in teacher-led educational research, can support practitioners both in interrogating and developing their practice and in articulating and sustaining educational arguments, some of which may run counter to those enshrined in official policy (Scott 2000). As Eraut argues, theory comprises 'concepts, frameworks, ideas and principles that may be used to interpret, explain or judge intentions, actions and experiences in educational or education-related settings' (Eraut 1994, p. 70) – a notion pursued by Goudie's suggestion that 'within the educational arena, teaching and research intertwine with each other to empower pedagogic interactions and to transform curricular knowledge through a deepening and expanding mode of knowing' (Goudie 1999, p. 57; see also Kincheloe 1991; M. Greene 1995; Carr 1995). In Goudie's view, teachers who are merely 'engaged in transmitting "expert knowledge" rather than constructing authentic knowledge through critical enquiry lose the desire to act or reflect'. Consequently, 'they perpetuate the inequity of power, and stagnate or stunt educational growth' (ibid., p. 60).

The form of educational research most closely linked to reflection and reflexivity in education is *action research*: research, that is, which is carried out by practitioners on their own practice in response to a perceived problem or set of problems, aimed at improving understanding of the issues and situations at stake, leading in turn to the development of more effective practice (Corey 1953, 1983; McNiff 1988; McKernan 1991).

Action research, which has been described as 'a deliberate process of emancipating practitioners from the often unseen constraints of assumptions, habit, precedence, coercion and ideology' (Carr and Kemmis 1986, p. 86) can take various forms and utilise a range of research strategies and techniques. It is always, however:

- situational, contextual, practice-based and practitioner-led
- problem-centred, interventionist, aimed at improvement
- reflexive in nature
- collaborative, participatory and collegial
- systematic and investigative
- emancipatory, empowering and critical

Action research is not, of course, the only research that teachers might wish to involve themselves in: however, it is often the most convenient to carry out and has the bonus of providing results which can be put to immediate use, either through changed practice or through developed understandings.

Many teachers may feel that in spite of the obvious professional advantages of reading theory and taking part in research projects, they are living in a time when their profession is being driven increasingly towards the technicist paradigm by government policy, and increasingly away from theory and research – with the competences discourse playing a major role in this movement. The news is not, arguably, all bad, however, with grants now available from the Teacher Training Agency for schools and teachers keen to undertake approved research projects and an abundant range of advice on the possible nature and conduct of such projects (Walford 1991; Hitchcock and Hughes 1995; McNiff *et al.* 1996). Perhaps the central struggle for the would-be teacher-researcher now is to ensure that research undertaken in schools really does contribute to understanding and generates, illustrates or contributes to useful educational *theory*.

THE TEACHER-STRATEGIST

'Fortunately', says James Cummins, 'good teaching does not require us to internalize an endless list of instructional techniques. Much more fundamental is the recognition that human relationships are central to effective instruction.' (Cummins 1996, p. 73.)

This observation takes us back both to the notion of the communicative teacher and to the 'missing elements' of the competences discourse. It also suggests that teachers need to take full account of the 'unexpected' or less easily predictable aspects of teaching and learning, that they need to be flexible in their practice, and that part of that flexibility entails thinking and working *strategically*.

Recognition of the unpredictable aspects of teaching and learning involves careful consideration of 'local' variations, be they geographical or temporal. It includes an acknowledgement that there may be perfectly acceptable differences between schools and between individual students within them, and that certain forms of policy and practice may be more appropriate in one phase of an institution's, an education service's or indeed a national or international history than at others: that is to say, it is not locked into one universal model of curriculum and pedagogy, but able to respond flexibly to changing circumstances. In addition, the recognition of such aspects of teaching and learning involves an acceptance and appreciation of perfectly acceptable *personal* variations, both in teaching style and (see Chapter 4) in the ways in which students learn and conduct themselves – again resisting a universal model of appropriate teacher and student behaviour and development.

The notion of the teacher as strategist comprises two strands. The first strand involves the construction of what might be called a pedagogic *identity*, that draws on the various discourses we have already considered: the communicative teacher, the competent teacher, the reflective teacher, the reflexive teacher, and the teacher as researcher and theorist. This identity provides the day-to-day 'character' of one's teaching style and helps provide a necessary but not restrictive coherence and continuity to one's professional work. The second strand is more *directly* connected to the notions of contingency and idiosyncrasy, in that it brings the professional identity to bear on the solving of often unanticipated problems and challenges, through resort to a range of deliberate strategies aimed specifically not at righting past wrongs but at enabling improved future practice.

The kind of strategic practice involved in this latter strand is best illustrated with reference to the feeling, that most teachers experience at various points in their career, of having let themselves or their students down in the classroom and of questioning whether they will ever be as good a teacher as they would like to be – doubts which, at their most extreme, can even prompt teachers to leave the profession (Moore and Edwards 2000). The remorse that often accompanies such reactions can be extremely painful if not always constructive. It is an adage in teaching that, although such emotions as regret and self-pity should not be denied, they will not, in the end, make things better in the future. For the temporarily demoralised teacher, such feelings have to be worked through as quickly as possible, and, when they have been worked through, replaced by what Kemmis and others might call a more 'rational' response, in which the teacher asks, as coolly as possible, questions such as:

- What specific strategies can I adopt in my future lessons that will help avoid a repetition of what went wrong last time? (i.e. What positive remedial *action* can *I* take?)
- What circumstances 'external' to the situation in question might have contributed to the difficulty, and to what extent can an understanding of those circumstances *inform* the future action I take?

Constructing strategies that draw on past experience but are firmly oriented to future practice can help to 'depersonalise' problematic situations, to manage unhappy or uncomfortable feelings, and to give the teacher confidence to face a difficult classroom situation again. This approach quite rightly places the onus on the individual teacher to try and make things work better next

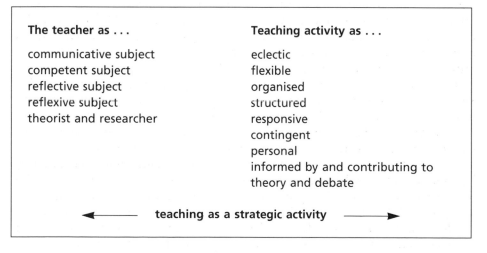

The teacher as . . .	Teaching activity as . . .
communicative subject	eclectic
competent subject	flexible
reflective subject	organised
reflexive subject	structured
theorist and researcher	responsive
	contingent
	personal
	informed by and contributing to theory and debate

◄——— **teaching as a strategic activity** ———►

Figure 5.1 The teacher as strategist

time; however, it does so within an appropriate set of contexts that enables the teacher to take *responsibility* without getting drawn into a discourse of *blame*.

To summarise, the strategic approach to teaching (Figure 5.1, above) involves drawing both on the different discourses or models of the good teacher *and* on a range of specific approaches and responses, in order to construct an appropriate professional identity that will promote a reasoned, proactive response rather than a predominantly self-blaming or reactive one, to the full range of classroom situations including those that present major difficulties. The precise strategies themselves are worked out *by* the teacher in response to the situation, and are as likely to draw on lists of competences as on the less formal, ongoing advice offered by colleagues during the course of practice.

INSTITUTIONAL SUPPORT: THE DEVELOPMENT OF THE WHOLE-SCHOOL POLICY

While individual teachers need to think strategically in their work, to draw on a range of skills and to have some clear sense of an educational philosophy that lends a sense of purpose to their work, they are likely to be more successful in this if their school – and perhaps the local education authority – has its own policy for teaching and learning and if that policy provides a sufficiently close match with the individual teacher's. Nowadays, many schools do have their own policies for teaching and learning across the curriculum, in an effort to ensure that good practice and education for good practice are promulgated in the school, that the learning experiences of students are relatively uniform as they move from subject area to subject area, and that teachers themselves continue to interrogate and learn from their own and one another's practice on a day-to-day basis. Such policies are often conceived within wider discourses and aims, such as the development of the school as 'socially-critical' (Kemmis *et al.* 1993) or as a 'learning' institution (Nixon *et al.* 1996), or the re-identification of the school as a 'whole community' rather than a group of disparate individuals. As Nias *et al.* have put this, the development of the 'whole school' involves the aspiration

> to belong to a community, to share the same educational beliefs and aims, to work together as a team, to acknowledge and activate the complementary expertise of colleagues, to relate well to other members of the group, to be aware of and involved in classes beyond one's own and to value the leadership of the school principal.
> (Nias *et al.* 1994, p. 235)

Whatever we may think of the merits and demerits of all the teachers in a school 'sharing the same educational beliefs and aims', it is clear that in the construction of the whole-school policy certain shared *principles* will need to underpin any specific strategies that are promoted and exemplified – if, that is, the policy is to provide genuine support for teachers rather than to act merely as a monitoring and surveillance device. To draw on the policy for *Teaching and Learning* in successful operation at one school, the following principles might figure prominently on any such list:

- The policy should promote universality and consistency in the sense of supporting and promulgating good practice and recognising student entitlement, yet allow for idiosyncratic differences in teaching styles and a degree of teacher autonomy.
- The policy should recognise that there is no such thing as the 'typical student', and that students in the school are likely to have a variety of learning styles as well as a variety of learning needs.
- The policy should support and promote a range of teaching approaches and strategies that teachers can put into practice as contingency demands.
- The policy should be underpinned by a philosophy, a theory and a sense of purpose as to the nature of teaching and learning and, in particular, the nature of *effective* teaching and learning (for example, a school-wide commitment to the notion of *active learning*). This should include shared views as to how cognitive, linguistic, creative, expressive and affective development occur and can be influenced by pedagogy and curriculum.
- The policy should include mechanisms whereby teachers can continue to develop professionally, through such practices as attending courses or observing and commenting on one another's teaching.
- The policy should be *provisional*, and should be regularly reviewed in the light of experience and perceived results.
- The policy should be *reflexive* in nature, seeking to challenge both its own terms of reference and the official discourses within which it is situated in the wider social and educational context.
- The policy should not be reduced to a statement of intent that resides only on the pages on which it is written. It should, rather, be a descriptive account of agreed and regularly monitored *practice* that can be witnessed on a visit to any classroom in the school.

Such fundamental principles, which may appear as a preface to the policy document in which they are described, are likely to be translated elsewhere into more refined points of policy that clearly show what institutional structures and procedures are available to support teachers in translating the policy into practice. Such refinements are unlikely to appear in the level of detail encountered within lists of teacher competences or standards, but, rather, to be suggestive of more *general* approaches and considerations that can be applied easily to the whole range of anticipated teaching and learning activities. The following example, taken from the same school's policy on Teaching and Learning, illustrates how this might work with reference to understandings of *differentiation*. The document begins by outlining the teacher's broad task in relation to this aspect of their work:

> - Differentiation must be embedded in all aspects of teaching and learning.
> - The principle of differentiation is fundamental to the success of mixed ability teaching. Work must be matched to students' attainments and abilities.
> - As well as the provision of tasks with varying degrees of complexity – i.e. core, extension and reinforcement – due consideration must be given to the variety of teaching and learning strategies used, which in themselves can make varying degrees of demand on students.

Having provided these basic guidelines, the document subsequently describes proposed whole-school support for their implementation, principally through the establishment of a 'differentiation team':

> - The differentiation team has been instrumental in raising and maintaining an awareness of the issue of differentiation throughout the school. Much emphasis has been placed on the importance of developing appropriate core, extension and reinforcement resources for teachers to use. This process needs to continue, whilst encompassing broader aspects of teaching and learning.

The brief of the differentiation team includes:

> - monitoring the progress of identified groups of students in relation to differentiation and the quality of teaching and learning
> - carrying out a training role: e.g. workshop sessions in curriculum areas
> - acting as a catalyst for curriculum development, ensuring that differentiation (including the associated teaching and learning strategies) is embedded in all schemes of work
> - acting as consultants to area teams, offering support and advice on matters relating to differentiation and aspects of teaching and learning.

The value of the whole-school policy resides partly in the promotion of consistency of practice, whereby both teachers and students 'know where they stand'. It may, for example, include not just broad advice on how to develop a positive learning environment or how to monitor learning in ways that feed constructively into pedagogy and planning; it may also contain quite specific instructions for all staff to follow, regarding such matters as the starting and ending of lessons, the implementation of a homework policy, and the carrying out of a departmental 'teaching and learning audit'. The whole-school policy, however, has a wider function than this, in that it provides the school with an opportunity to explore and develop what Bernstein (1996) calls its 'therapeutic' pedagogic identity; that is to say, it provides an opportunity for the staff of the school to explore and put into practice what *they* think good education and good teaching are about, regardless of what may come down to them in the form of official government policy.

> The whole-school policy, we might say, provides a site for the authentic voices and opinions of teachers, providing them with the platform to fashion their own educational policy and, through doing it, to develop their understandings of teaching, learning and the curriculum. Through such ownership and intellectual endeavour, support can be provided for teachers' practical efforts in ways that they may feel are not always provided in the 'official' educational discourses of central and local government.

It may not always be the case that all teachers in a school or even all parties involved in the production of whole-school policies will feel entirely supportive of all aspects of any given policy; nor will the policy be able to ignore – or even want to ignore – key aspects of official policy, including any legal requirements that may be in place. The whole-school policy remains, however, an important space for teachers to be able to reflect collectively and independently on a range of educational issues, including issues specifically related to models and philosophies of teaching and learning. It also offers the potentiality of a site within which teachers can actively *resist* public policies and *diktats* (Apple 1995), which they may feel are not in the best interests of their students.

SUMMARY

This chapter has reviewed different models of good teaching, suggesting that teachers need to be *strategic* in their work and to draw eclectically on a range of models of professional practice. The chapter has emphasised that:

- Teachers need to be effective *communicators* who are able to be reactive and spontaneous as well as proactive and well prepared.
- Teachers need to be *'competent'*, and students and their parents need to be confident of receiving the same quality of education across all

schools. However, there is a danger that the competences discourse can become all-pervasive and limit the more creative, opportunistic aspects of teaching that are also crucial to effective practice.

- Teachers need to be *reflective* of their own practice, carrying out thoughtful, constructive evaluations of their teaching in order to develop improved future practice. They also need to be wary that such reflections can, as with the competences discourse, lead to teachers over-blaming themselves for breakdowns in constructive classroom interactions. (This is particularly likely to occur when teachers reflect only on their own immediate performance, outside the context of the wider social milieu or their own life experiences.)

- It is equally important for teachers to be *reflexive*. Through a closer examination of one's responses in the context of one's personal history and its interface with life in the classroom, reflexivity seeks to explain and critique not just classroom situations but the ways in which we are constrained to experience and respond to them. Reflexivity directs the practitioner to acknowledge the complex nature of the *self* and the way in which selves are constructed through experience and through social structures. Though open to the same dangers as reflection, reflexivity, handled appropriately, may offer the teacher the best opportunity for genuine development and change.

- Teachers should perceive themselves as *researchers* and *theorists* as well as practitioners. *Action research* is a particularly valuable way for teachers to evaluate and critique their own current practice and to move in an informed and principled way towards more effective future practice. The *whole-school policy* also offers a space for reflection and action, in which teachers can prioritise their own voices away from the direct shadow of central government's policies and directives.

SUGGESTED ACTIVITIES

1. What manifestations are there in your own practice of the teaching discourses outlined in this chapter (i.e. the charismatic teacher, the competent teacher, the reflective teacher, the reflexive teacher, the teacher as researcher and the teacher as strategist)? How might a greater or lesser adherence to one or more of these discourses result in your practice becoming more *effective*?

2. Identify, summarise and justify two or more *action research* projects that might usefully be carried out by you and/or your present school.

3.   Evaluate two or more whole-school policies at your current school, against the criteria listed with the Policy for Teaching and Learning described in this chapter. In what ways might these policies be amended, updated or generally improved?

4.   Assess the importance of differentiation in formal education. How widespread is a common understanding of differentiation at your school, and how consistently are modes of differentiation put into practice across the curriculum and across staff? How might differentiation be more effectively applied, both in your own teaching and in your school in general?

SUGGESTED READING

McNiff, J. (1988) *Action Research: Principles and Practice.* Usefully read in conjunction with McNiff *et al.*'s *You and Your Action Research Project*, this book gives useful practical guidance for teachers wishing to develop their own classroom-based research projects, in a way that is accessible, realistic and understanding of the demands and constraints of classroom teaching.

Mitchell, C. and Weber, S. (1999) *Reinventing Ourselves as Teachers: Beyond Nostalgia.* One of a group of recent books, including Hargreaves' *Changing Teachers, Changing Times* (1994) and Goodson's and Hargreaves' *Teachers' Professional Lives* (1996), that helps teachers and other interested parties to re-interrogate and understand the teacher's working life in the light of changed attitudes towards education and changes in the larger socio-economic systems. *Reinventing Ourselves as Teachers* is particularly useful in its inclusion of the 'personal' aspects of professional practice, in the links it makes between critical reflection and everyday experience, and in the breadth of its illustrative material.

Richardson, V. (ed.) (1997) *Constructivist Teacher Education: Building a World of New Understandings.* At a time when teaching is dominantly configured in terms of universals such as competences and teaching standards, *Constructivist Teacher Education* usefully explores the ways in which individual teachers create their own unique explanations and understandings of events at the interface of their existing knowledge and experience and new ideas and situations encountered in the course of professional practice. The book suggests how, through awarenesses and elaborations of such meaning-making, teachers can challenge their own taken-for-granted attitudes and approaches to teaching, and progress to more complex and relevant understandings leading, in turn, to more effective pedagogies.

Scott, D. (2000) *Reading Educational Research and Policy.* Scott's book provides insightful practical support for teachers wishing to make sense of educational policy and research, partly as a way of developing their own identities as teacher-researchers. The book is particularly useful in that it provides guided extracts and examples for readers to critique as part of their professional development in this area.

6 Working With and Against Official Policy: pedagogic and curricular alternatives

This final chapter returns to the dilemmas outlined in Chapter 2, when official policy and the law appear to run counter to firmly held personal and collective views as to what constitutes good teaching practice and acceptable and appropriate models of curriculum. With particular reference to the UK National Curriculum, the chapter looks forward rather than back, exploring possible alternative models of pedagogy and curriculum for the future. While recognising that teachers wishing to promote such alternatives may need to work 'subversively' within an existing curriculum that may be fundamentally conservative and outmoded in both content and style, it is argued that at the same time teachers need to continue to lend their expert voices to public debates in ways that challenge the usefulness of the existing school curriculum in the context of a rapidly changing world.

THE IMPACT OF OFFICIAL POLICY ON TEACHING AND LEARNING

There are two broad areas in which official education policy impacts on teaching and learning. The first concerns the nature and content of imposed school curricula and syllabuses. The second concerns issues of enforced or 'encouraged' forms of pedagogy, including impacts upon such matters as class size, classroom organisation, and guidance on appropriate teaching methodologies. That is to say, there is a *curricular* impact and a *pedagogic* impact.

Central governments, of course, may often claim not to wish to interfere with matters of pedagogy (although they clearly perceive a right – and in some cases a duty – to be prescriptive on matters of curriculum). The current National Curriculum for England and Wales, for example, claims specifically to advise teachers *what* they must teach but not how they must teach it. There is arguably, however, only a partial truth in such a claim. The National Curriculum, for example, may not tell teachers explicitly how they should teach, but the nature of the curriculum content clearly does, often, imply, promote or even necessitate certain kinds of pedagogy, even as it marginalises others. Thus, if a National Curriculum specifies that young students must be able to name in grammatical terms the various parts of speech, this may appear a matter of *curriculum content* but clearly presupposes a particular model of language development that compels forms of pedagogy different from those that might be pursued by a teacher who has a fundamentally different view of language development. In this case, the teacher may feel compelled to adopt pedagogic practices (teaching the parts of speech as a means to a particular end) that run counter to preferred practice, even though the ultimate curricular aim (to ensure certain levels of linguistic competence) may be the same. Similarly, a National Curriculum that details a list of authors to be studied, along with a high level of specificity as to what aspects of those authors' work must be studied, effectively denies teachers the possibility of pursuing the kinds of pedagogy argued by Freire and others, in which learning is perceived to take place most effectively when students are implicated in the setting of their own educational agendas via their own curriculum selections.

In these cases, a curricular influence and a pedagogic influence may be seen to collide – reminding us, perhaps, that the separation of curriculum and pedagogy, like the separation of language and thought, may have some convenience-value for analytical purposes but will always remain somewhat artificial in practice.

The above are examples of public policy influencing and even changing pedagogy, through the imposition of a very prescriptive curriculum. While some teachers may regret the imposition of such change, others, of course, may welcome it. Recent research suggests that teachers are divided, both intrapersonally and interpersonally, on the value and relevance of the National Curriculum. Some teachers, for instance (Halpin, Moore *et al.* 1999–2001), see the National Curriculum as providing useful structures for teachers and students, and as helping to eliminate 'sloppy practice'. Others, by contrast, see the curriculum in their subject area(s) as restrictive, monocultural and largely irrelevant.

Working with and against official policy

It is easy to see how teachers who react positively to imposed changes may incorporate new ideas and emphases into their practice – and how they are likely to be supported in this endeavour by government agencies such as OFSTED as well as by headteachers and school governors anxious for their school to be presented in a good light within the terms of current dominant discourses of standards and accountability. It is rather harder to understand, however, how teachers who are generally *oppositional* to major government policies on education might respond, and how they might devise ways of continuing what they perceive as good practice *in spite of* the directions and restrictions being imposed on them from above. This may be a particularly difficult issue if teachers feel they are denied a voice in debates about educational practice, either within the school or within the wider policy-making forums.

It has recently been suggested in this respect (e.g. Moore and Edwards 2000) that teachers have, by and large, become less overtly political and ideologically 'driven' than they once were, preferring to categorise themselves professionally as 'eclectic' or 'pragmatic' rather than as (say) 'traditional' or 'progressive'. If this is the case, it does not follow that oppositional teachers do not continue to act subversively, or to pursue their own unsponsored agendas: rather, that teachers may have reset their sights on local rather than on national or universal sites of action. The classroom, in particular, remains a site where, in spite of increased levels of monitoring and surveillance, inventive, creative and imaginative teachers *can* still pursue and develop what they perceive as good practice while following the letter of the law and satisfying inspection criteria. (See too Eraut [1994 p. 224] on the notion of 'some individual practitioners rejecting the recommendations of their own professional body, though not transgressing its regulations'.)

> It is in these local sites, perhaps – such as the school classroom and the whole-school policy – that resistant *pedagogies* can best be pursued. Resistant *curricula*, on the other hand, although they can be pursued to an extent within individual schools and classrooms, may be best pursued – and, arguably, are being pursued – through wider challenges to the status quo, through the persistence of pressure groups or independent bodies with a professional interest in the purposes and outcomes of formal state education.

What follows is an attempt to

(a) summarise some of the resistant pedagogies that have emerged in recent years and that seem to offer genuine, radical alternatives to some of the more 'traditional' pedagogies that still dominate in official educational discourses (if not always in actual school classrooms);

(b) consider some of the alternative models of curriculum recently being proposed by a range of educationalists and educational pressure-groups, that offer radical alternatives to ongoing officially-endorsed school curricula with their emphases on discrete subject areas, pre-selected bodies of skills and knowledge, and the promotion of competition over collaboration and 'rationality' over feeling.

RESISTANT PEDAGOGIES

(1) Critical literacy

The notion of resistance to dominant educational discourses (including those enshrined in National Curricula) through local, essentially *pedagogic* action has been explored by numerous commentators, none more celebrated than Paolo Freire. Freire (1972; 1974) has argued for forms of pedagogy that teachers can engage in inside the classroom and within imposed constraints, that go beyond the recognition and valuation of multicultured students' cultural practices and experiences that we considered in Chapter 4, towards sharing with students an understanding of how – and why – such practices and experiences came to be marginalised in the first place. This kind of teaching – sometimes known as 'transformative pedagogy' – centralises *critical literacy* (McLaren 1988), which includes active criticism of the very structures within which formal learning normally takes place. Part of that criticism is enshrined in the 'substance' of lessons (the texts that are read and studied, the discussions and debates that take place, the assignments that students undertake, and so on), and part in the relationship between teacher and student, which is typically one of equalised status and shared investigation and discovery. Shor and Freire are thus able to identify a central task for schools and teachers as 'demystifying the dominant ideology' (Shor and Freire 1987, p. 168) – that is to say, as helping students to understand and 'make visible' the kinds of cultural–ideological coercions to which they are typically subjected by the state in general but also through existing pedagogies and school curricula (see, too, Shapiro 1990, p. 114).

The task of 'demystification', suggest Shor and Freire, is essentially a *pedagogic* task, to be undertaken *by* teachers *in* actual classroom situations. It is one that

> cannot be accomplished by the system. It cannot be accomplished by those who agree with the system. This [demystifying process] is the task for educators in favor of a liberating process. They have to do this through different kinds of educational action; for example, through teaching music or mathematics, teaching biology or physics or drawing, no matter.
>
> (Shor and Freire 1987, p. 168)

For Shor and Freire 'the system', including the imposed school curriculum and examination syllabuses, is powerful and monolithic, suggesting that only local subversions of it may be practicable. Their 'critical pedagogy' 'invites students to recognise and discover what is typically hidden from us' (for example, the power relations and symbolic violence underpinning the selections that make up the school curriculum), and the extent to which we actually 'co-operate in denying our own freedom' (Shor and Freire 1987, pp. 173–174). As such, it suggests presenting students with *alternative* ways of viewing the natural and social world, that challenge existing 'commonsense' or *hegemonic* views (Gramsci 1971). Such challenges might include taking an oppositional stance to a variety of social myths, such as the still-prevalent, common-sense views that homosexuality is unnatural, that capitalism is the only conceivable way of organising societies economically, or that the collections of knowledge that comprise the school curriculum are 'natural' and 'obvious' rather than cultural and biased. Although such subversions may represent an essentially pedagogic enterprise, they do not exclude, as part of that pedagogy, equally alternative selections of skills and knowledge: that is to say, they are not without a curricular aspect. Teachers wishing to combat notions of racial supe-riority, for example, might seek to de-emphasise the histories and achievements of dominant racial groups within a given society, in order to emphasise the histories and achievements of the dominated or marginalised racial groups. They may do this not simply through the manner in which they treat existing curricular content and materials, but through the introduction of a variety of 'alternative' texts.

The kinds of pedagogic subversion recommended by Freire and others do not necessarily involve revolutionary attempts at dismantling a wider social, economic and cultural *system* (the very system, it is argued, that denies students the freedom of thought, expression and opportunity). What it does attempt to achieve is the empowering of students through 'illuminating reality' – not, per-haps, to overthrow the coercive system but to recognise its manipulations and to be better able to 'confront' them. As Noam Chomsky has suggested, any attempt to overthrow the larger system through local opposition may, in any event, be doomed to failure, since: '[i]n most fields [society wants] students to be obedient and submissive [. . .]. Now teachers can try, and do break out of that, but they will surely find if they go too far that as soon as it gets noticed there'll be pressures to stop them' (Chomsky 1995, p. 141).

The power of the state to limit local subversions of national curricula and officially acceptable pedagogies, and the consequent persistence of profound conservatism in formal schooling, is echoed by a number of educationalists, including Paul Willis. In relation to the notion of 'progressivism', for example, Willis argues that any changes in education that we have witnessed have neither been brought about nor been caused by any 'real shift in basic philoso-phies' but rather by changes in the perceived needs of markets and of the dominant social classes who continue to control education (Willis 1977, p. 178). Bourdieu, too, has claimed that changes in educational systems tend to be 'morphological', affecting 'nothing essential' (Bourdieu 1976, p.115; see also Chapter 2 above), while Michael Apple has suggested that it is through quiescence that society retains its stability, and that schools consequently have a fundamentally conservative *function* in promoting such quiescence (Apple 1995). Even the presence of a relatively left-wing government, Hoare argues, has typically proved insufficient to effect radical changes in the way formal education operates, largely because it has failed to address the *content* of what is taught. Writing in 1967, Hoare suggests that:

> the Labour Party has at no time offered a global challenge to the present system. It has at most stood for its expansion and the elimination of some of its most flagrantly undemocratic features. . . . Above all, it has never attacked the vital centre of the system, the curriculum, the *content* of what is taught.
>
> (Hoare 1967, p. 40)

In an elaboration of the view that nothing much, fundamentally, has changed, Blenkin *et al.,* in an anticipation of issues of *curriculum change* that we shall turn to shortly, invoke Stenhouse's distinction between educational 'renewal' and educational 'innovation':

> Stenhouse . . . makes a clear distinction between innovation and renewal, arguing that curriculum *renewal* is a matter of updating materials, of keeping pace with developments of knowledge and techniques of teaching. Curriculum *innovation* involves changes in *premisses* of teaching – its aims and values – and consequent thinking and classroom practice. This is an important distinction to highlight, for much of what has been claimed in the name of curriculum innovation has often turned out, on closer inspection, to be curriculum renewal. A further distinction could be made between innovation and development. The former implies a *radical break* with former practice, the latter a more gradual enhancing of it.
> (Blenkin *et al.* 1992, pp. 30–31, my emphasis)

(See also Fullan 1982, on the three dimensions of educational change: the use of new materials; the use of new teaching approaches; and the alteration of teachers' philosophies or *beliefs*.)

Approaching this matter from another angle, Bruner has argued that 'educational reform confined only to the schools and not to the society at large is doomed to eventual triviality' (Bruner 1972, p. 114) – the implication here being that local action may not be as effective as is suggested by Freire and Shor, precisely because it will be overly constrained by the rules, regulations and ideologies of the larger social system.

The criticisms of formal state education put forward by Freire, Chomsky, Apple, Bourdieu and Bruner invite practising teachers to address some important questions. These might include:

- How feasible or necessary is it for teachers to militate for a change in the larger social and educational systems within which their practice is situated?
- If they *are* able and willing to militate, what form(s) might their oppositional action take?
- Does the apparent invincibility of the system, including the ways in which it judges and grades students, inevitably limit opposition to local subversions through 'transformative pedagogies'?
- If Apple's analysis is right, how do we feel about (a) reproducing or (b) resisting reproducing a 'quiescent' population?

(2) Multiple intelligences

A second, relatively recent body of theory and research to have challenged some of the more 'traditional' pedagogic practices – and the theories of learning and development that underpin them – relates to the notion of 'multiple intelligence'. This notion suggests that different people learn in different ways from one another and, furthermore, that the same person may learn different *things* in different ways. As Howe puts this: 'No two learners are the same: every person is unique' (Howe 1984, p. 87).

Theories of multiple intelligence foreground

(1)   an understanding of how the individual's learning takes place,
(2)   the production by the teacher of the appropriate classroom *conditions* for effective learning to take place.

Although the notion of multiple intelligence may not always engage in debates about the actual and possible *purposes* of formal education in the same overtly political way as the work of McLaren and Freire, it does nevertheless suggest an orientation towards formal education that may be seen as oppositional to much central policy (for example, the production of a standard National Curriculum, and the identification and ascription of 'levels of attainment') in its emphasis on the individualistic aspects of teaching and learning and in its belief in and valuation of the classroom teacher's capacity to make informed choices within the specific teaching–learning contexts and environments within which they work.

One of the foremost proponents – perhaps *the* foremost proponent – of the notion of multiple intelligence is Howard Gardner (1983, 1993), whose work will already be familiar to many readers (see also, however, Armstrong 1994; Howe 1984, pp. 87–92; and Bentley 1998).

Gardner begins by describing, critically, what he calls the 'uniform school' (1993, p. 6). In the uniform school, 'intelligence' is measured using standardised tests, suggesting that everyone's mind operates in much the same way. There is also (ibid.) 'a core curriculum, a set of facts that everybody should know, and very few electives': that is to say, an emphasis on 'absorption' rather than process, and on what Bernstein, with reference to UK schools, has called 'strong classification and framing' (Bernstein 1971b), whereby there is little or no room for negotiation and fluidity either between subject areas or within the individual subject syllabus. In the uniform school, says Gardner, 'the better students, perhaps those with higher IQs, are allowed to take courses that call upon critical reading, calculation and thinking skills' whereas the students deemed to be weaker are not; in other words, once standardised assessment procedures have been used to identify stronger and weaker learners, different curricula are effectively provided for the different students, in line with different expectations and leading to different outcomes. In this way, 'the best and the brightest get into the better colleges, and perhaps – but only perhaps – they will also get better rankings in *life*' (Gardner 1993, p. 6, emphasis added).

In place of the 'uniform school', Gardner offers 'an alternative vision [of education] . . . based on a radically different view of the mind . . . that yields a very different view of school' – that is to say, the 'individual-centred school'. The individual-centred school is constructed on 'a pluralistic view of mind, recognizing many different and discrete facets of cognition, acknowledging that people have different cognitive strengths and contrasting cognitive styles' (1993, p. 6).

In elaborating the 'different and discrete facets of cognition' and 'contrasting cognitive styles', Gardner identifies seven 'intelligences' which have 'an equal claim to priority' (Gardner 1993, pp. 8–9; see also NACCCE 1999). These are:

- linguistic intelligence (the intelligence exhibited, for instance, in writing poetry);
- logical-mathematical intelligence (the kind of intelligence investigated by Piaget, and often confused with 'intelligence' itself);
- spatial intelligence (shown, for example, by sailors, engineers, surgeons, sculptors and painters);
- musical intelligence;
- bodily-kinesthetic intelligence ('the ability to solve problems or to fashion products using one's whole body, or parts of the body');
- interpersonal intelligence ('the ability to understand other people: what motivates them, how they work, how to work co-operatively with them');
- intrapersonal intelligence (the 'capacity to form an accurate, veridical model of oneself and to be able to use that model to operate effectively in life').

(Gardner 1993, p. 9)

Gardner asserts that in most people these different intelligences work together. More controversially, perhaps, he also suggests that we may all be born with – and continue to develop – different 'intelligence profiles' (ibid., p. 9).

> While the notion of intelligence profiles may support the embracing of cognitive pluralism in the classroom, it should be noted that it also has the *potential* to support student labelling and to lead to teacher *in*flexibility. That is, the teacher may decide: 'This student thinks in such and such a way; therefore, I will not present them with an activity which, in itself, demands some other kind of thinking.' An issue for teachers here would be the extent to which they need to extend each student's intelligence 'repertoire' (see also Chapter 3 above) rather than merely focusing on intelligence varieties that they perceive each student already to possess.

This 'double potential' of multiple intelligence theory is further reflected in Gardner's view that

> the purpose of school should be to develop intelligences and to help people reach vocational and avocational goals that are appropriate to

their particular spectrum of intelligences. . . . People who are helped
to do so . . . feel more engaged and competent, and therefore more
inclined to serve the society in a constructive way.

(ibid., p. 9)

Some important questions for teachers here are:

- Does 'appropriate' imply a restricted and restrict*ive* view on the
  teacher's part of a student's learning potential?
- How can we be sure that the initial assessments of a student's 'intelligences' are any more reliable or culturally unbiased than, say, the
  results of standardised tests?
- Is 'feeling' engaged and competent the same as *being* engaged and
  competent?
- Is it a central purpose of education that people should learn to 'serve
  the society', or is this itself a problematic notion?
- What do we *understand* by 'the society'?
- What do we mean by 'constructive', and against what and whose
  criteria do we decide what is constructive and what is not?

Despite these possible problems, the notion of multiple intelligences still offers
a radically alternative model of learning that seeks to get away both from the
inflexible, monolithic curriculum and from certain forms of pedagogy that seem
intent on 'spoon-feeding' the student. It also allows for student idiosyncrasy in
a way that some 'universal' theories of learning (it could be argued that Piaget's
theories of development fall into this trap) do not, refusing to dismiss students
as backward simply because they are not getting on in the classroom.

Gardner's own contextualising critique of some models of teaching and
learning is usefully summarised in his account of 'three biases' which he believes
[Western] societies perpetuate and suffer from, both generally and specifically,
through much educational practice. These biases he terms *Westist*, *Testist* and
Bestist (Gardner 1993, p. 12).

Westist, says Gardner, 'involves putting certain Western cultural values,
which date back to Socrates, on a pedestal. Logical thinking, for example, is
important; rationality is important; but [says Gardner] they are not the only
virtues'. *Testist* 'suggests a bias towards focusing upon those human abilities
or approaches that are readily testable' – an approach which does not properly acknowledge that 'assessment can be much broader, much more humane
than it is now, and [that] psychologists should spend less time ranking people
and more time trying to help them'. *Bestist* implies the need to interrogate
what is often *perceived* as 'best' in approaches to problem-solving, and at the
same time what is *meant* by 'intelligence'. In an echo of Cummins (1996, pp.
220–24), Gardner argues with reference to this last bias:

If we can mobilize the spectrum of human abilities, not only will
people feel better about themselves and more competent; it is even

possible that they will also feel more engaged and better able to join the rest of the world community in working for the broader good. Perhaps if we can mobilize the full range of human intelligences and ally them to an ethical sense, we can help to increase the likelihood of our survival on this planet, and perhaps even contribute to our thriving.

(Gardner 1993, p. 12)

The implications of the above statement for the *future nature* of education – that is to say, an education aimed very specifically, both in terms of curriculum and pedagogy, at promoting a happier, safer, more equitable *world* – provide one very important aspect of Gardner's theory as it is put into practice. A further, equally important aspect relates to the area of teacher expertise – including assessment expertise – and how this needs to be configured and developed within the context of a meaningful educational experience that has clear relevance to the natural and social world in which learners live.

> How, for example, do we assess 'interpersonal' and 'intrapersonal' intelligence if we have not been trained to understand such intelligence and if we continue to view and evaluate all intelligence through the very narrow lenses of (say) linguistic and logical-mathematical intelligences?

(3) 'Accelerated learning'

One influential theory to have emerged from Multiple Intelligences theory is the notion of *Accelerated Learning* (see, for example, *Excellence in Schools,* DfEE 1997a). Accelerated Learning has been referred to by many commentators in support of improved methods of teaching and learning, including the teaching and learning of *bilingual students* (Cummins 1996). It is probably best known in the UK, however, through Alistair Smith's two books *Accelerated Learning in the Classroom* (1996) and *Accelerated Learning in Practice* (1998).

Accelerated Learning combines many of the techniques that might have been previously associated with 'progressive', student–centred teaching (see, for example, A. Smith 1996, pp. 9–10), and with a 'Vygotskyan' ideal of helping 'all learners . . . reach a level of achievement which currently may seem beyond them' (1996, p. 9). In doing so, it places a particularly heavy emphasis on the construction of an appropriate learning *environment* that uses recent knowledge about the structure and workings of the human *brain* to take into constructive account the various social and emotional influences – external and internal to the school and the classroom – that might affect any one student's learning either positively or negatively. At its heart is a view that teaching and learning is not simply about covering *curriculum content*, but that it is equally about teaching students to 'learn how to learn' in order that they may develop as *interested, enquiring, independent thinkers and doers* (1996, p. 9).

In common with the notion of multiple intelligences, the notion of accelerated learning recognises that different students have different preferred ways of learning and that these must be taken properly into account in the planning and teaching of lessons. (Smith quotes research to suggest – somewhat contentiously, perhaps – that in the typical classroom 29 per cent of students will be essentially 'visual learners', 34 per cent 'auditory learners' and 37 per cent 'kinesthetic learners').

Smith proposes some interesting theories, based on brain research, that offer serious challenges to many aspects of 'traditional' pedagogy as well as to the traditional curriculum. He quotes, for example, the known effects of *stress* on the human brain. Thus, in stressful situations:

> Blood flows towards the reptilian brain [the 'oldest' part of the brain, that is 'configured for survival'] and away from the higher order processing functions in the other parts of the brain. Chemicals such as adrenaline, catecholamines and cortisol are injected into the bloodstream to ensure a quick response. The heart rate increases. Blood vessels are constricted in the skin and intestines, and blood leaves these areas. The blood pressure rises and the increased supply of blood is made available to the reptilian brain. This closing down effect under perceived threat results in the control functions ['survival', 'territoriality', 'rote behaviour' etc.] . . . displacing the capacity for patterning, problem solving, creativity, flexibility, and peripheral awareness. Higher order thinking skills are displaced by survival, ritualistic and rote behaviours. An individual loses peripheral vision, focusing on the source of anxiety, resorting to behaviours learnt in early childhood.
>
> (A. Smith 1996, p. 16)

Apart from fairly obvious implications concerning the manner in which students are formally *assessed* (the stress of the examination-room, for example, would seem perversely designed to reduce the very capacities that are supposed to be being tested), it is not difficult to imagine how an understanding of these essentially physical effects – and their likely impact on behaviour and learning – can provide the teacher with a useful additional tool for analysing classroom events, for structuring future pedagogies accordingly, and even for helping students to understand why things may not be going well for them. Furthermore, it can do so in a way that circumvents 'reactive', perhaps confrontational responses to diffident learning or perceived bad behaviour. Knowing that a student who is not working, for example, or whose behaviour is generally unacceptable, may be struggling partlybecause of biological effects caused by social stress may lead to a more rational and ultimately more effective approach to the problem than simply allowing oneself to become angry, punitive or anxious. Similarly, it may suggest to the teacher that cajoling alone – perhaps followed by a more punitive approach such as exclusion from the classroom – may be an inappropriate strategy for getting the student to behave as required, and that something in the *physical* environment of the classroom may also need to be attended to, or that the student, as long as they are not interfering with other students' work and development, may just need to be 'left alone' for a period.

By way of helping the teacher to assess what, if anything, may be causing stress in a student – as well as to move towards appropriate response-strategies – Smith cites the following common causes of 'learner stress':

- disputes with parents, friends or teachers;
- victimisation, bullying, cliques, gangs, personal threats, low self-esteem, lack of self-belief, negative self-talk;
- inability to connect learning with personal goals or values;
- belief that the work is too difficult, inability to make a beginning on tasks;
- inability to understand the connections between current and past or possible future learning;
- physical or intellectual difficulty in accessing material as presented;
- poor sight or hearing;
- distractions in the learning environment;
- poor self-management and study skills.

(Smith 1996, p. 16)

Among the more interesting arguments promoted within the accelerated learning discourse are first the notion that effective teaching – *regardless of the subject discipline* – needs to be geared towards the 'whole' brain (i.e. the creative, integrative part), and not exclusively or principally, as is often the case, towards the 'left side' (the discrete, rational side); second, that there are limits to the extent to which it is desirable – or for that matter physically possible – for students to be expected to remain 'on task' for any length of time in the classroom.

The notion that effective teaching needs to be geared towards the whole brain offers an important challenge not just to pedagogy but to the current configuration of most school curricula, in which 'creative' subjects are identified and taught 'creative*ly*' and 'non-creative' ('academic') subjects are identified and taught 'academically'. If effective teaching involves the engagement of the whole brain, then clearly the whole brain must be engaged in whatever 'subject' is being studied.

Once such a principle is accepted, two challenging possibilities emerge: either the school curriculum should be reconfigured away from compartmentalised subject areas towards meeting the perceived demands – and supporting the perceived strengths – of the whole student (and consequently the whole society), or pedagogy in some subject areas should be reconfigured so that it recognises and promotes the use of the whole brain in students' engagement with the subject matter of the lessons.

The second of Smith's arguments, concerning *attention spans*, also offers a challenge to current pedagogies and curricula. Current school curricula, for example, are often typified by the teaching of discrete subject areas, in limited, relatively short blocks of time, with a specific examination content to be 'got through'. Smith's argument presents a challenge to pedagogies and curricula (including, it could be argued, the current National Curriculum for England and Wales) that are constructed on notions of linear cognitive–linguistic development and assessed – at least in part – on the extent to which individual students are seen to 'progress' during the course of any particular lesson or course of study. As Smith suggests:

> Our brain is designed for ups and downs, spurts and plateaus. It is not designed for constant attention. The terms 'on' or 'off' task are unhelpful in whole brain learning. The brain learns best when there are many beginnings and endings, when there are different types of input at different levels and when there are choices.
>
> (A. Smith 1996, p. 21)

Citing Jensen (1995), Smith suggests that:

> the maximum 'on task' time for adults is 20–25 minutes with breaks of 2–5 minutes in between. The best division time for 10 year olds is about 12 minutes of focus time with about 2–5 minutes of individual, paired or group review or play in between. A 6 year old is best with about 6 minutes of 'on task' time with about 2–3 away from task.'
>
> (ibid., p. 21)

Although the above analysis runs the risk of undermining its own argument by imposing universal patterns on individual learners and denying the possibility that different students may have different attention spans which themselves may vary according to the situation (see also Burden and Williams 1998), it does invite us to challenge the concept of 'on-taskness' as a teaching aim and as an indicator of pedagogic and learning success. It also raises serious questions about lesson planning, and specifically about how much a teacher and student can reasonably expect to 'get through' in any one lesson. Part of that questioning inevitably forces teachers to address the

> issue of what students are 'actually doing' – and what learning is actually taking place – when they appear, through all outward bodily signs, to be focused on a given task and in a fixed manner for longer periods of time than those suggested by Jensen and Smith.

In recommending broad strategies for approaching teaching and learning through reference to the 'whole brain', Smith suggests what he calls a 'whole brain learning diet' (ibid., pp. 21–22). The 'whole brain learning diet' is summarised as follows. Teaching, Smith suggests, should:

- be 'balanced' (geared to both sides of the brain);
- be 'varied' (changing tasks regularly and building in attention 'breaks');
- be 'nourishing' (*involving* students in the learning, helping them see a point and a purpose and providing positive, stimulating feedback);
- be 'tasty' (make learning – and the classroom environment in which it occurs – varied and fun, appealing to all the five senses);
- 'use the recipe book' (be well planned and properly evaluated, with plans and goals shared with the students);
- 'talk to the diners' (use student reviews and evaluations to improve future teaching).

The notion of accelerated learning might be viewed by some teachers with a certain degree of scepticism, not least because of its clear connections, in certain of its manifestations at least, with the theories of behaviourists such as Skinner (see Chapter 1 above). There is also a danger that, in its emphasis on the physical workings of the brain (we might call this its fundamentally *psycho-physiological* emphasis) it may too easily forget the *cultural* dimensions of teaching and learning – that there might, for example, be cultural reasons behind perceived poor performance and behaviour that are not directly connected with the physical nature of the brain at all as Smith and others present it. This lack of a cultural dimension might also prove problematic in some of the practical suggestions provided by some accelerated learning theorists for creating a learning-friendly classroom *environment*. The suggestion, for example, that background classical music might appropriately stimulate the brain may well have some validity, and has certainly helped some teachers and students working in otherwise difficult situations; however, it rather overlooks the possibility that for many students such music may be anathema, or that it may serve only to remind them of the huge cultural gap between themselves and the institution within which their learning takes place, and to confirm – by virtue of their *absence* from the classroom – the 'inferiority' of their own cultural preferences.

It is, perhaps, too early to make proper judgements as to the value of accelerated learning theory, either *in toto* or in its various aspects and manifestations. The best current advice, perhaps, is to treat the theory with an open mind, as one way among many of analysing classroom needs and behaviours and of establishing a positive learning environment for all one's students. Aspects of the theory that might prove particularly useful in practice include:

(a)   placing pedagogic emphasis on understanding – and responding to – learning rather than on what is to be learned;
(b)   recognising and valuing *difference* – albeit in a sometimes limited way – between student and student.

It is through this emphasis on the individual learner rather than on what is to be learned that, in spite of its behaviourist aspects, the theory appears to suggest what are still sometimes known as progressive forms of pedagogy. Whatever else we might say about accelerated learning, it does offer an alternative 'scientific' educational discourse to the current dominant discourse of competences, with its emphasis on discrete areas of knowledge and performance and its universalist tendencies. As such, accelerated learning theory – along with notions of multiple intelligences and education for critical literacy – can be viewed as part of a larger body of argument and research that seems to demand a radical reappraisal of both curriculum and pedagogy in our schools.

CHALLENGING THE CURRICULUM

(1) Areas of experience

I have grouped the above pedagogies under the term 'resistant', not because their proponents have presented them in this way, but because they seem to offer radical alternatives to the kinds of pedagogy often sanctioned by central government. As such, they need to be explored and evaluated by teachers – including student-teachers – within the context of broader questions about what, fundamentally, education should be about and how we ensure as teachers that our educational purposes are most effectively turned into educational achievements. In addition to these 'pedagogic alternatives', we also need to be critically aware of possible alternative or oppositional *curricula* and the extent to which these may better support our educational aims.

The school curriculum as we know it is so well established – so 'naturalised' – that teachers might be forgiven for feeling that any challenge to it is futile. Though the National Curriculum for England and Wales, for example, is relatively new, the principles on which it is based are not. A simple example of this unchanging nature of the curriculum relates to the way in which set collections of knowledge and skills are identified and then divided for teaching and learning purposes into subject areas – a process in existence long before the advent of the National Curriculum at the start of the 1990s. To quote Edwards and Kelly on this point, the National Curriculum has been 'cosmetic, quantitative rather than qualitative in its thrust' (Edwards and Kelly 1998, preface). Teachers critical of the curriculum, however, can take heart – first from a general democratic principle, second from the fact that oppositional voices clearly do exist, and that those voices are neither without influence nor easily dismissed as foolish.

The *democratic* principle concerns the fundamental right within democracies for debate, for difference and for disagreement. Indeed, it could be argued that the strength of a democracy can be measured by the extent to which it encourages and allows debate, difference and disagreement even as it moves towards some form of agreement by consensus. Educators and educationalists opposed to the structure, content and style of the school curriculum should not feel they have to apologise for such opposition, or indeed to have to justify that opposition any more forcefully than its proponents justify their support. Rather, they should reassure themselves that society and its structures are subject to repeated and endless change, and that their oppositional voices may be fundamentally important in the perpetuation of such fluidity.

Those taking an oppositional stance to current national curricula can also comfort themselves in the knowledge that they are not alone. The voices of opposition to current school curricula are many and various, including, as we shall see, both teacher-educators and bodies normally associated with matters other than the content and style of formal state education. Increasingly, there has been in these voices something of a consensus about what is wrong with current school curricula and how they might be changed for the better. That consensus suggests that school curricula as we know them tend to be based on

- outdated socio-economic needs,
- outmoded views of the learning and educational processes,
- a reluctance to change themselves to meet either the individual's or humanity's needs in the present or in the immediate future (Cummins 1996; Moore 1999a).

Such voices also question, frequently, the extent to which the curriculum is in tune with a modern society 'which is characterized by rapid technological change and the moral consequences of such change, which is ethnically diverse, which must recognize value-pluralism and which is consequently subject to cultural, moral and spiritual uncertainty' (Edwards and Kelly 1998, p. xiii; see, too, Hargreaves 1994, p. 3).

Many of these oppositional voices have been further characterised by what might be called an experiential turn; that is to say, there has been an argued resurrection of the notion that schools should not be essentially about the commodification, brokering and (from the student's viewpoint) 'purchasing' of knowledge, but that it should be more about learning itself: learning that is social, affective, creative and cognitive. Those arguing for such a curriculum suggest that it should be based on and structured around not discrete, preselected skills and items of 'knowledge', but rather on the present, past and possible future lived experiences of human beings themselves. The revised curriculum might begin not with *what* should be learned (the curriculum as a list of skills and knowledge to be 'taught and acquired'), but rather with a notion of how learning takes place and a desire to help pupils develop as active, social and independent learn*ers* for whom education is not exclusively located in the school itself but rather 'infuses every sector [of society], linking together individuals, communities and institutions through diverse, overlapping networks of learning relationships' (Bentley 1998, p. 187). This curriculum, contextualising the *individual's* development and needs within humanity's development and needs, might engage pupils and teachers in large questions such as *What is it to be a human being? How do we ensure that, in the future, humanity continues to develop, to prosper and (perhaps) to improve?*

The suggestion that school curricula should be based on experience rather than on commodified knowledge is not new, and was, indeed, the subject of a UK Department of Education and Science (DES) publication in 1977. This publication – *Curriculum 11–16* – produced by independent inspectors of education (HMIs), posited a revised school curriculum for England and Wales based upon the 'broad areas of experience that are considered to be important to all pupils' (1977, Supplement: see also DES 1976). These areas were:

- aesthetic/creative;
- ethical;
- linguistic;
- mathematical;
- physical;
- scientific;
- social/political;
- spiritual.

(The 'technological' was added later.)

The argument for a curriculum based on areas of experience rather than on discrete areas of subject knowledge went hand in hand with the notion of an 'entitlement' curriculum – leading to the subsequent HMI publication *Curriculum 11–16: Towards a Statement of Entitlement* (DES 1984).

Although the HMI publications of 1977 and 1984 have become somewhat marginalised within more recent official educational discourses, the ideas are still current within 'unofficial' discourses, and indeed may be ready to re-emerge as a more powerful oppositional voice to current official curricular policy. In their (1998) book *Experience and Education*, Edwards and Kelly use the HMI publications as a starting-point for their own argument for alternative, experience-based school curricula, presenting the case through a range of essays written by teachers with experience across the range of subject areas offered by current curriculum models.

Edwards and Kelly begin with the notion of an 'adjectival' curriculum (Edwards and Kelly 1998, preface): that is to say, 'one which will *de*scribe rather than *pre*scribe the kinds of educational experience to which all young people have an entitlement in a democratic society'. As Edwards and Kelly argue (ibid., p. xv):

> [T]he main significance of employing adjectives rather than nouns to delineate the several dimensions of such a curriculum is that they can be seen as describing different aspects of what is essentially a single entity, the developing experience of the individual, rather than as discrete elements to be kept forever apart. An adjectival curriculum, unlike a substantive curriculum, cannot be so readily viewed as an agglomeration of separate entities; it is what they all add up to which constitutes education in the full sense and which also constitutes the entitlement of every individual in such an education. For the entitlement is, or should be, to a coherent set of experiences, not to a heterogeneous conglomerate whose cohesiveness is left to chance.

For Edwards and Kelly, the notions of the adjectival curriculum and the entitlement curriculum are inevitably and inextricably bound up with the current and possible future nature of democracy, since:

> [i]n a genuinely democratic society educational provision must go beyond the demands of economic success and social control; it cannot consist merely of forms of vocational preparation and training in obedience; it must, above all things, offer social and political empowerment and opportunities for personal enrichment.
>
> (ibid., xv)

Edwards and Kelly suggest that attempts, following the 1976 and 1977 HMI publications, to introduce an experience-based curriculum failed essentially because they attempted to *superimpose* such an approach on to a subject- and content-based curriculum that remained fundamentally unchanged. For Edwards and Kelly, the experience-based 'entitlement curriculum' demands a radical change in the way in which the curriculum is conceived, organised and presented if it is to undergo the desired transformation. While the current National Curriculum for England and Wales is *presented* as an entitlement curriculum, they suggest, it is constrained from being so by its very content and structure. In their view, a genuine form of personal education, for example, 'must be more than a bolt-on afterthought of curriculum planning' (ibid., p. xiii), demanding, rather, a new curriculum entirely that 'requires an intellectual sophistication, an administrative flexibility, a trust in the professionalism of teachers and, above all, a commitment to democratic ideals at a level far beyond that shown – or, indeed, not shown – in current policies' (ibid., p. 18).

The notion that current school curricula place too much emphasis on knowledge at the expense of understanding, that they are culturally monolithic when they should be culturally pluralistic, that they should promote co-operation within a context of global security and equity rather than competition within an increasingly outmoded context of global fragmentation and patriotism, and that they should promote critical, independent thinkers able to participate equally critically in democratic processes rather than merely reproducing dominant cultures through the shared 'possession' of certain bodies of knowledge and culture-specific skills, has been voiced many times in educationalist circles. Betts, for example, in an article headed 'Ten practices for principals that impact student learning', includes the following markers for teachers seeking to provide their students with genuine empowerment through the development of learning skills:

- ensuring that fifty per cent of all problems students are asked to solve have no obvious 'right' answers;
- ensuring that the curriculum requires students to 'find' and define problems as frequently as they are required to solve them;
- using models from real-world products to set standards of excellence;
- eliminating practices that promote competition among students.

(Betts 1999, p. 31)

Elsewhere, Ross (1998) has provided the following set of 'alternative proposals' for a revised National Curriculum for the Arts:

1) The arts in schools should be expected to work together (opposition to falsely created subjects and subject boundaries);
2) Progression/Assessment in the arts is qualitative rather than quantitative (opposition to discourses of quantification and linearity);
3) The arts must figure in the curriculum as creative and expressive experiences, nurturing and extending individual critical perception (opposition to the limits and limitations of the basics discourse and its technicist approach, and to the discourse of teacher as 'deliverer' of skills/knowledge);
4) Arts education is an *identity* project which brings together public and private experience, individual and collective action, in the making and handling of 'feeling' forms (opposition to curricular 'universality', with an emphasis on authenticity and the development of the individual and collective 'voice');
5) The arts in schools must be conceived within a festival framework: committed to the twin principles of hope and redress (opposition to the notion of the curriculum as a controlling, reproductive device, in favour of education as empowering students to see possibility and to know how to militate for change: see also Greene [1995, p. 177] on a curriculum at whose centre is 'the reflective taking of initiatives . . . the moving toward what cannot be precisely predicted but what is often thought of as possibility');

6)   To teach the arts requires an understanding of the pedagogy of joy, and the courage to cherish the untouchable (opposition to education as coercive and mundane, emphasising the pleasures of teaching and learning and the spirituality of human experience).

(taken from Ross 1998, pp. 126–142)

As with Edwards and Kelly, Ross stresses the creative, constructive aspects of teaching and learning, resisting the reduction of the former to sombre technicism and of the latter to the acquisition of certain limited skills and the memorising of certain selected information that may have little practical purpose outside the classroom walls – a similar view to that enshrined in the following attempt (Moore 1998) to describe a possible 'transitional' curriculum, that might facilitate and characterise the link between 'traditional' subject-based curricula and new, experience-based curricula:

- It [the 'transitional curriculum'] is fundamentally and actively political, in a way that the development of functional and cultural literacies or the 'handing down' of selected skills and facts is not. By consequence, it demands (Freire 1972, 1974; Giroux and Simon 1988) a 'critical pedagogy' which challenges existing curricula and pedagogies as well as the cultural–ideological assumptions that underpin them.

- It resists a linear, 'hierarchical' literacy and knowledge development in which the 'basics' always precede the complexities and in which the complexities only come much later and then not to everyone.

- It encourages the development of practice, and seeks to promote students' development not merely within the terms of current dominant discourses but through an understanding that there may be other, equally valid discourses through which to examine, express and make use of our experiences of life.

- It celebrates cultural, linguistic and perceptual difference – and promotes pleasure in that difference – rather than pathologising it.

- It promotes a specific view of citizenship and democracy that has at its centre informed, radical criticism. Its persistent question is not 'How can education make this country more prosperous?' but 'What do we need to learn – and to learn to do – in order to make the *world* a happier, safer place for all who inhabit it?'

- It calls into serious question, partly through the development of cross-curricular projects, the fragmented, subject-based curriculum, which offers such 'a poor basis from which to frame courses of transforming social action that stand a reasonable chance of being effective' (Lankshear 1993, p. 55). Through questioning definitions of subject areas, and focusing on making sense of the world through interrogations of the representations by which we experience it, it concentrates less on 'what is' than on 'what might be' – or 'what ought to be'. In this, it promotes a particular approach to a full range of texts that is concerned not so much with the business of ordering such texts in terms of their perceived value, but rather on fostering 'a radicalizing mentality, both intellectual and political, which is applicable to all texts' (Brooker 1987, p. 27).

(2) Stressing the cultural and the creative

In terms of challenging the structure, content and nature of the current National Curriculum in England and Wales, Ross's is not the only critical voice to have emerged from the area of the creative arts – a fact which is not surprising, perhaps, given the manner in which the arts continue to be marginalised by the 'basics discourse' and the opposition posed by both examination syllabuses and the National Curriculum to educators' efforts to render their practice more genuinely pluralistic. Recently, for example, the government-established National Advisory Committee on Creative and Cultural Education (NACCCE) has produced a lengthy report – *All Our Futures: Creativity, Culture and Education* – aimed at ensuring 'that the importance of creative and cultural education is explicitly recognised and provided for in schools' policies for the whole curriculum, and in government policy for the National Curriculum' (NACCCE 1999, p. 192). Among the NACCCE report's recommendation for the Whole Curriculum, it offers the following six points of action for *schools*:

- Head teachers and teachers should raise the priority they give to creative and cultural education; to promoting the creative development of pupils and encouraging an ethos in which cultural diversity is valued and supported.
- The development plans of schools should make explicit reference to provision for creative and cultural education, including: *the pattern of provision in the formal and informal curriculum*; the opportunities for contact with outside specialists; and with the community and cultural organisations.
- Head teachers should conduct an audit of the quality and nature of opportunities for creative and cultural education for all the pupils in their schools, *including the balance of the curriculum in all Key Stages*.
- School plans for staff development should include specific provision to improve teachers' expertise in creative and cultural education.
- There should be a greater emphasis in schools on *formative assessment*: i.e. assessment that is intended to improve the day-to-day quality of teaching and learning.
- Option systems at Key Stage 4 should be designed to maintain breadth and to avoid narrow specialisation.

(ibid., p. 192, emphases added)

This call for action, with its focus on the development of the individual student within a broader revision of the developmental needs of human *societies*, is supported by a recognition of the need for a reassessment of the context of such action in the form of government policy. In a plea for a return to 'balance' and 'breadth' in the National Curriculum, the report calls for the Department for Education and Employment (DfEE) to include, in its immediate review of the National Curriculum, greater consideration of the creative and cultural aspects of the school curriculum, that specify 'the knowledge, skills and values which young people should acquire; . . . the principles of organisation of the National Curriculum to facilitate these outcomes; . . . the principles of teaching and learning through which they will be realised.' (ibid., p. 193).

In an echo of the HMI 'Areas of Experience' referred to above (p. 165), the report calls for a 'more fundamental review of the structure and balance of the National Curriculum beyond 2000' which will give 'full consideration . . . to achieving parity between the following discipline areas throughout key stages 1–4 *as a matter of entitlement*:

- language and literacy;
- mathematics and numeracy;
- science education;
- arts education;
- humanities education;
- physical education;
- technological education'.

(ibid., p. 196. For a useful critique of the report, see Buckingham and Jones 2000.)

> As with the HMI proposals made over twenty years earlier, the NACCCE report proposes an altered emphasis in the shape, nature and content of the school curriculum, towards notions of entitlement and areas of experience, away from the prioritisation of a body of skills and knowledge to be decided externally and with overdominating reference to the perceived needs of national business and industry.

(3) Putting learning and teaching first

Both the HMI paper and the NACCCE report present strong critiques of current school curricula that compartmentalise skills and knowledge and that appear to marginalise or devalue the creative elements of learning (see also the observations made about the 'modernist', 'Enlightenment' curriculum in Chapter 2 above). In doing so, these critiques seem to imply a shift away from the 'traditional' model of formal state education, which begins with deciding *what* should be taught (what is most commonly understood by the term 'curriculum') and only then with considering *how* it should be taught (what is most commonly understood by the term 'pedagogy'), towards a new kind of model which begins by prioritising teaching and learning and places the old-style curriculum in an essentially *supportive* role.

This revised model of curriculum is illustrated in the recent RSA (Royal Society of Arts) publication *Opening Minds: Education for the 21st Century* – a document which both critiques current curricular and related pedagogical practice, and makes tentative suggestions as to what a revised 'alternative' school curriculum might look like (RSA 1999; see also Thornton 1999). Taking as its starting point an issue we have already considered in Chapter 2 – that is to say, the widespread perception that there is a growing divide between the current school curriculum and the experiences and demands of the 'outside world' – *Opening Minds* shifts debates about perceived school *failures* away from pedagogy towards curriculum, which it configures as being fundamentally out of date, fragmented, slow to react, and ill-conceived.

In place of the current dominant curricular practice of the coverage and absorption of skills and information via discrete subject areas, the RSA paper recommends the abandonment of subject areas, with their emphasis on external marking and control, to be replaced by a renewed focus on student learning and (repeating the NACCCE's plea for a recognition of and faith in teachers' professionalism) on teacher assessment. In mounting its argument, *Opening Minds* invites a re-opening of debates as to what are – or should be – the *purposes* of education, suggesting an emphasis on *understanding and doing* (rather, that is, than 'acquiring' a body of knowledge), that makes appropriate use of the new technologies to promote flexible learning and teaching styles, to release creative energy rather than to promote social control, and to produce independent rather than 'receptive' learning. As Bayliss summarises this approach: 'We would be putting teachers back in control of the curriculum, as being there to help people learn rather than to teach in the traditional sense.' (Valerie Bayliss, quoted by Karen Thornton in the *Times Educational Supplement* 1999, 18–6–99, p. 10.)

> A central implication of all the alternative curricula we have considered in this chapter is that rather than begin with decisions – or with debates about decisions – as to what the 'taught content' of the school curriculum should be, and then to fashion pedagogy and curricular organisation accordingly, we should revisit the larger questions first – 'What do we want formal state education to *achieve*?', 'How do we best help our students to become effective, co-operative and independent *learners*?' – and *then* to fashion our content and curricular organisation accordingly: that is to say, a reversal of the curricular principles on which current formal education tends to be structured.

This is not, of course, as straightforward a matter as the above may seem to imply. What the HMI, NACCCE and RSA reports all indicate, for example, is the inseparability of pedagogy and curriculum in the practical – rather than the theoretical – world, and the difficulty of deciding when pedagogy is curriculum and when curriculum is pedagogy. To take one illustrative example of this difficulty, we might consider the question of whether an emphasis on *critical literacy* (see above) is essentially a matter for curriculum or for pedagogy or for both. Is it, for example, a matter of

- treating existing curriculum content in a particular (pedagogic) *way* (i.e. problematising existing content-choice and related materials; for example, interrogating, with students, history and geography syllabuses as classist, sexist and racist, or getting students to critique science and maths syllabuses in terms of how they support some people's interests and purposes at the expense of others')?
- introducing a different *kind* of curriculum altogether? (e.g. rejecting the subject- and content-based curriculum for a critical, concepts- and experience-based model)?
- or altering curriculum 'inputs' within an unchanging curricular *model* (i.e. introducing 'spaces' for critical literacy development within an existing subject- and content-based curriculum that continues to be presented unproblematically)?

Furthermore, if we do decide to promote critical literacy as the main focus of our *teaching*, does critical literacy itself *become* our *curriculum*?

WORKING WITH AND AGAINST OFFICIAL POLICY

This chapter has considered some criticisms of current curriculum content and structure, including those that present dominant curriculum models as outmoded and out of touch with the needs of people and societies as we enter the twenty-first century. It has also considered the suggestion that in terms of the overall structure and content of formal education, pedagogy needs to be prioritised more than it currently is. Further consideration has been given to the argument that existing subject- and knowledge-based curricula might be replaced by curricula whose content is based on areas of experience and concept development. (This is not to say, of course, that 'knowledge' would disappear from the curriculum; merely that selections of knowledge would cease to be the principal *basis* on which the curriculum was constructed.)

As has already been indicated, a central problem for teachers sympathetic to these views is that they still have to work within the terms and constraints of the curricula that are given. In some countries, indeed, such as England and Wales, they are legally obliged to work within the constraints of *national curricula* which may allow for very little flexibility in terms of course content. Given such a situation, teachers critical of current curriculum models – and concerned about the 'knock-on' effects of such models on their pedagogic practice – may need to consider two courses of action. The first involves an assessment of the degree to which preferred pedagogic practices and curriculum content can be incorporated within and alongside curriculum content and constrained pedagogic practice. In some subject areas this may prove relatively unproblematic. In the secondary English curriculum in the UK, for example, teacher-led reforms in curriculum content – themselves based on carefully argued defences of certain models of language and learning development and related pedagogic practice – have contributed in no small measure to the construction of the official National Curriculum for English (Moore 1998). In this case, teachers may well find certain aspects of the National Curriculum objectionable or inconvenient; however, there is evidence (Halpin, Moore *et al.* 1999–2001) that they are still, in broad terms, able to pursue the pedagogic practices and models of language development that they favour and that they believe are in their students' best interests. Their main difficulty lies in working out how they can *manage* curriculum content and curricular emphases towards which they are far less favourably inclined, and whose forced inclusion may reduce the time available for pursuing preferred curricular content or which may impinge on preferred pedagogic practices and theories of language and learning development. Examples here are the imposition of compulsory tests (SATs) for fourteen-year-olds on a prescribed Shakespeare play, and the nomination of a list of sanctioned authors, some of which must be studied during the course of the five compulsory years of secondary education. The challenge for teachers here is to teach the prescribed authors in *ways* which feel comfortable and in a manner which allows for the study of other, non-nominated authors (including authors writing in 'non-Standard' forms and styles of English), and in ensuring that an enforced pedagogic mode of 'teaching to tests' is embedded in a preferred pedagogic mode of encouraging enjoyment, understanding and appreciation of set texts through direct appeals to experience and imagination, small-group discussion, creative text-based activity and so on. While these compromises are normally achievable, there is often a cost. In the case of English, for example, many departments have felt themselves forced 'back' from mixed-ability teaching to setting their students by the content and form of tests and examinations.

In some subject areas, and in some phases of education, the incorporation of unpopular curricular elements and implied pedagogies may be (even) less easily achieved than in English. As has already been indicated, many secondary-school subject specialists feel that they are being overly constrained by curricula whose sheer volume of prescribed content denies them opportunities either for investigative work or for pursuing desired but 'unofficial' curriculum content of their own (for example, the development of genuinely multi-ethnic, anti-racist, anti-sexist curriculum aspects in, say, geography, history, science, mathematics or art, or more open, exploratory, design-based work in design & technology [Halpin, Moore *et al.* 1999–2001]). While such teachers might usefully open up formal discussions with (for example) parallel subject departments in other schools, or via relevant subject interest-groups, as a way of developing incorporative strategies, there may well remain severe limits on the extent to which such incorporations are possible. In these cases, teachers may feel that, while having to live with curricula and pedagogies that they are in many respects unhappy with, a space and a forum needs to be found – or created – to present principled, well-argued cases against existing curriculum policy in favour of alternatives that they feel are more equitable, more relevant and more effective.

The publication of such documents as *All Our Futures* and *Opening Minds* indicates that such informed opposition is neither isolated nor without influential support. Indeed, teachers depressed by the apparent lack of attention paid to their views through the consultation processes carried out by central governments may find some comfort and strength in the publication of these documents that argue the case for alternative policies. Changes to the basic structures of educational curricula, especially if they really do support and promote the interests of the already-powerful at the expense of the habitually disempowered, will clearly not happen overnight, and teachers will no doubt continue to have to work – as they have very successfully worked in the past – within systems which they perceive as fundamentally and unsettlingly flawed. In the mean time, it is important that practitioners do not become defeatist or dismissive about the possibility and desirability of a resurrection of debates that they already feel they may have lost. While we clearly do need to argue about how best to operate within the *current* education order and the current constraints that are thrust upon us, we must also remain wary of talking of lost causes, reminding ourselves that in education, as in life generally, things have a habit of coming round again as long as we remember to nudge them in the right direction.

SUMMARY

This chapter has reviewed some 'alternative' or 'resistant' pedagogies and models of curriculum; that is, pedagogies and curricula that offer a radically different view of what education should be for and how its aims should be accomplished.

The alternative pedagogies looked at have emphasised:

- *Critical Literacy,* which actively encourages teachers to interrogate the taken-for-granteds of everyday life, including the nature of the school curriculum itself;
- The notion of *multiple intelligences,* that argues for an abandonment of fixed ideas of 'ability' in favour of a more pluralistic view of intelligence and greater flexibility of teaching methods;
- *Accelerated learning*, which invokes recent understandings of the workings of the human brain to challenge dominant classroom practices and forms of assessment, prioritising the importance of the physical and social learning environment.

The alternative models of curriculum have included:

- The development of curricula that begin with students' own *experiences* rather than with the imposition of an externally-fixed body of knowledge and skills;
- The development of curricula that emphasise *creativity,* communication and appreciation rather than 'acquisition';
- The development of curricula which begin with educational *purposes* (e.g. developing students as independent and effective learners, developing students as responsible, critical citizens, and so on) *rather than* the acquisition of certain skills or bodies of knowledge, and decide subsequently what skills and knowledge will best support the achievement of those purposes.

SUGGESTED ACTIVITIES

1. What significant changes, if any, have taken place to (a) curriculum content and style, (b) officially sanctioned pedagogies in your age-phase or subject area during the last thirty years? To what extent do you see these changes as fitting in with or working in opposition to your own *current* teaching philosophy and style and those favoured by teachers at your school? Do you perceive these changes as representing, generally, a step forward or a step back?

2. How suited is the current curriculum to recent Government initiatives such as the planned prioritisation of education for democracy and citizenship or the cross-curricular themes (including environmental education) of the early 1990s? With reference to your own age-phase or subject area, consider the extent to which such initiatives can be 'grafted on' to existing curricula, or whether they demand a more radical revision. What might such a revision look like?

3. Starting from scratch, and eliminating any existing models of curriculum with which you are familiar including that currently at work in most UK schools, summarise how a curriculum for the twenty-first century should, in your view, look. A useful starting point for such an activity might be to identify what you perceive as the needs of today's young people in the context of the social and natural world in which they will be growing up.

SUGGESTED READING

Edwards, G. and Kelly, A.V. (eds) (1998) *Experience and Education: Towards an Alternative National Curriculum.* This collection of essays, of interest to teachers in all phases of education, critiques current curriculum policy and associated pedagogic implications, from a range of perspectives and across a variety of subject areas. Together, the essays provide a persuasive argument for educational reform that bases curriculum structure and content on experience rather than on discrete areas of knowledge and skills. The book provides a useful basis for teachers wishing to explore curriculum issues further and to articulate more effectively their concerns with current curriculum policy.

Gardner, H. (1993) *Multiple Intelligences: The Theory in Practice.* Like his earlier *Frames of Mind: The Theory of Multiple Intelligences* (1983), this book provides a useful summary of the theory of multiple intelligences and its practical implications. While readers will need to approach the book critically, bearing in mind the reservations already made in this chapter, Gardner still stimulates many important questions and debates about the nature of learning, its implications for teaching, and its cultural sitedness – although perhaps more might have been made of this last characteristic. The book offers a helpful starting-point for teachers wishing to explore more fully and personally the different ways in which their students think and learn as a way to developing more sympathetic and effective pedagogies.

Smith, A. (1996) *Accelerated Learning in the Classroom* and (1998) *Accelerated Learning in Practice.* Smith's two volumes, both of which are readable and helpfully presented, provide the ideal starting-point for teachers wishing to discover more about the notion of accelerated learning, and to evaluate related pedagogic techniques through their own practice. They also provide an important context through which to consider interpretations of accelerated learning emanating from the 'official recontextualising field' and the impact of these on public policy.

References

Alexander, R.J., Craft, M. and Lynch, J. (eds) (1984) *Change in Teacher Education*. New York: Praeger

Allen, G. (1994) *Teacher Training: The Education Bill 1993/4: Research Paper 94/58*. London: House of Commons Library

Appel, S. (1995) 'The unconscious subject of education.' *Discourse* Vol. 16, No. 2: 167–190

Apple, M. (1979) *Ideology and the Curriculum*. London: Routledge

Apple, M. (1980) 'Curricular form and the logic of technical control: building the possessive individual.' In Barton, L., Meighan, R. and Walker S. (eds) *Schooling, Ideology and the Curriculum*. Lewes: Falmer Press, pp. 11–28

Apple, M. (1995) *Education and Power* (2nd edition). New York and London: Routledge

Armstrong, T. (1994) *Multiple Intelligences in the Classroom*. Alexandria, Virginia: Association for Supervision and Curriculum Development (ASCD)

Arnold, M. (1909) 'The function of criticism.' In Arnold, M. *Essays Literary and Critical*. London: Dent, pp. 1–25

Arnold, M. (1932) *Culture and Anarchy*. London: Cambridge University Press

Barnes, D. (1976) *From Communication to Curriculum*. Harmondsworth: Penguin

Barnes, D. (1986) 'Language in the secondary classroom.' in Barnes, D., Britton, J. and Torbe, M. (1986) *Language, the Learner and the School* (3rd edition). Harmondsworth: Penguin, pp. 9–88

Bentley, T. (1998) *Learning Beyond the Classroom*. London and New York: Routledge

Bernstein, B. (1965) 'A sociolinguistic approach to social learning.' in Gould J. (ed.) *Social Sciences Survey 1965*. Harmondsworth: Penguin, pp. 144–168

Bernstein, B. (1971a) *Class, Codes and Control, Vol.1*. London: Routledge and Kegan Paul

Bernstein, B. (1971b) 'On the classification and framing of knowledge.' In Young, M.F.D. (ed.) *Knowledge and Control*. London: Collier-Macmillan, pp. 47–69

Bernstein, B. (1977) *Class, Codes and Control, Vol. 3*. London: Routledge and Kegan Paul

Bernstein, B. (1996) *Pedagogy, Symbolic Control and Identity*. London: Taylor and Francis

Betts, B. (1999) 'Ten practices for principals that impact student learning.' *The International Educator*, Feb. 1999: 31

Blair, M. and Bourne, J., with Coffin, C., Creese, A. and Kenner, C. (1999) 'Making the Difference: Teaching and Learning Strategies in Successful Multi-Ethnic Schools.' *DfEE Research Briefs*, Research Report No. 59. London: Department for Education and Employment

Blenkin, G., Edwards, G. and Kelly, A.V. (1992) *Change and the Curriculum*. London: Paul Chapman

Bogdan, R. (1992) 'Being different: the autobiography of Jane Fry.' In Goodson, I. (ed.) (1992) *Studying Teachers' Lives*. London: Routledge

Boler, M. (1999) *Feeling Power: Emotions and Education*. New York and London: Routledge

Boud, D., Keogh, R. and Walker, D. (eds) (1985) *Turning Experience into Learning*. London: Croom Helm

Bourdieu, P. (1971) 'Intellectual field and creative project' in Young M.F.D. (Ed) (1971) *Knowledge and Control*. London: Collier-Macmillan, pp. 161–188

Bourdieu, P. (1976) 'Systems of education and systems of thought.' In Dale, R., Esland, G. and Macdonald, M. (eds) *Schooling and Capitalism*. London: Routledge and Kegan Paul for Open University, pp. 192–200

Bourdieu, P. (1977) *Outline of a Theory of Practice*. Cambridge: Cambridge University Press

Bourdieu, P. (1990a) *In Other Words*. Cambridge: Polity Press

Bourdieu, P. (1990b) *The Logic of Practice*. Cambridge: Polity Press

Bourdieu, P. and Passeron, J-C. (1977) *Reproduction in Education, Society and Culture*. London and Beverley Hills: Sage

Bourdieu, P. and Wacquant, L.J.D. (1992) *An Invitation to Reflexive Sociology*. Cambridge: Polity Press

Bower, G.H. and Hilgard, E.R. (1981) *Theories of Learning* (5th edition). Englewood Cliffs, New Jersey: Prentice Hall Inc.

Brice Heath, S. (1983) *Ways With Words: Language, Life and Work in Communities and Classrooms*. Oxford: Oxford University Press

Britton, J. (1969) 'Talking to learn'. In Barnes, D., Britton, J. and Torbe, M., *Language, the Learner and the School* (3rd edition). Harmondsworth: Penguin, pp. 89–130

Britzman, D. (1999) 'Lost subjects, contested objects: towards a psychoanalytical theory of learning.' Unpublished seminar paper, Institute of Education, University of London, 22 June

Brooker, P. (1987) 'Why Brecht? or js there English after cultural studies?' In Green, M. in association with Hoggart, R. (eds) *English and Cultural Studies: Broadening the Context*. London: Murray for the English Association, pp. 20–31

Bruner, J. (1963) *The Process of Education*. New York: Vintage Books

Bruner, J. (1966) *Towards a Theory of Instruction*. London: Oxford University Press

Bruner, J. (1972) 'Poverty and Childhood.' In *The Relevance of Education*, op. cit., pp. 132–161

Bruner, J. (1972) *The Relevance of Education*. Cambridge, Mass.: Belknap Press

Bruner, J (1986) *Actual Minds, Possible Worlds*. London: Harvard University Press

Bruner, J. (1996) *The Culture of Education*. Cambridge, Mass.: Harvard University Press

Buckingham, D. and Jones, K. (2000) 'Modest proposals and cultural creativity: ideals and political realities in "All Our Futures" and "Making Movies Matter".' *The English and Media Magazine* 41: 11–16

Bullock, A. *et al.* (1975) *A Language For Life*. London: HMSO

Burden, R. and Williams, M. (eds) (1998) *Thinking Through the Curriculum*. London: Routledge

Calderhead, J. and Gates, P. (1993) *Conceptualizing Reflection in Teacher Development*. London: Falmer Press

Capel, S., Leask, M. and Turner, T. (1995) *Learning To Teach in the Secondary School: A Companion to School Experience*. London: Routledge

Carr, W. (1995) *For Education: Towards Critical Educational Inquiry.* Buckingham: Open University Press

Carr, W. and Kemmis, S. (1989) *Becoming Critical: Education, Knowledge and Action Research.* London: Falmer Press

CATE (Council for the Accreditation of Teacher Education) (1992) *Circular 9/92.* London: CATE

Chomsky, N. (1995) 'A dialogue with Noam Chomsky.' *Harvard Educational Review* 65: 127–144

Coard, B. (1971) *How the West Indian Child is Made Educationally Sub-normal in the British School System.* London: New Beacon

Cohen, L. and Manion, L. (1977) *A Guide to Teaching Practice.* London: Methuen

Cole, A.L. and Knowles, J.G. (1995) 'Methods and issues in a life-history approach to self-study.' In Russell, T. and Korthagen, F. (eds) *Teachers Who Teach Teachers.* London: Falmer Press, pp. 130–154

Combs, A.W. (1972) 'Some basic concepts for teacher education.' *Journal of Teacher Education* 23 (Fall): 286–290

Corey, S. (1953) *Action Research to Improve School Practice.* New York: Columbia University

Cummins, J. (1984) *Bilingualism and Special Education: Issues in Assessment and Pedagogy.* Clevedon: Multilingual Matters

Cummins, J. (1996) 'Babel babble: reframing the discourse of diversity.' In *Negotiating Identities: Education for Empowerment in a Diverse Society.* California: CABE, pp. 219–240

Dale, R. (1972) *The Culture of the School.* Milton Keynes: Open University Press

Dalton, M.M. (1999) *The Hollywood Curriculum: Teachers and Teaching in the Movies.* New York, Bern, Berlin, Bruxelles, Frankfurt/M., Wien: Peter Lang

Dash, P. (1998) 'Critical studies, diaspora and museum education.' *Journal of Museum Ethnography* 10: 79–86

Davies, D. (1998) 'Scientific experience.' In Edwards, G. and Kelly, A.V. (eds) *Experience and Education: Towards an Alternative National Curriculum.* London: Paul Chapman, pp. 46–62

DES (Department of Education and Science) (1976) *Curriculum 11–16.* London: HMSO.

DES (Department of Education and Science) (1977) *Curriculum 11–16.* London: HMSO

DES (Department of Education and Science) (1981) *Teacher Training and the Secondary School.* London: HMSO

DES (Department of Education and Science) (1984) *Curriculum 11–16: Towards a Statement of Entitlement.* London: HMSO

DES (Department of Education and Science) (1992) Government White Paper: *Choice and Diversity: a New Framework for Schools.* London: HMSO

Dewey, J. (1932) *Human Nature and Conduct.* Carbondale: Southern Illinois University Press

Dewy, J. (1939) *Freedom and Culture.* New York: Putnam.

DFE (Department for Education) (1995) *English in the National Curriculum.* London: HMSO

DfEE (Department for Education and Employment) (1997a) *Excellence in Schools.* London: HMSO

DfEE (Department for Education and Employment) (1997b) *Annex A to Teacher Training Circular 1/97: Standards for the Award of Qualified Teacher Status.* London: DfEE

DfEE (Department for Education and Employment) (1998) *Teaching: High Status, High Standards*. London: DfEE

Donaldson, M. (1978) *Children's Minds*. Glasgow: Fontana/Collins

Doyle, B. (1989) *English and Englishness*. London: Routledge

Dunn, R. (1987) 'Do students from different cultures have different learning styles?' *International Education* 16(50): 3–7

Eagleton, T. (1983) *Literary Theory*. Oxford: Blackwell

Edwards, D. and Mercer, N. (1987) *Common Knowledge: the Development of Understanding in the Classroom*. London: Routledge

Edwards, G. and Kelly, A.V. (1998) *Experience and Education: Towards an Alternative National Curriculum*. London: Paul Chapman

Edwards, G., George, R., Halpin, D., Jones, C. and Moore, A. (1999) 'Tradition and Teachers' Professional Identities: Theory, Research and Critique.' Paper presented at the Annual Conference of the British Educational Research Association, University of Sussex: Falmer, 2–5 September 1999

Edwards, V. (1987) 'Clever people speak proper.' *The Guardian*, 5 May 1987: 13

Elliott, J. (1983) *Action Research: a Framework for Self-evaluation in Schools*. Cambridge: Cambridge Institute of Education

Elliott, J. (1991) *Action Research for Educational Change*. Milton Keynes: Open University Press

Elliott, J. (1993) 'The relationship between "understanding" and "developing" teachers' thinking.' In Elliott, J. (ed.) *Reconstructing Teacher Education*. London: Falmer Press

Eraut, M. (1994) 'The acquisition and use of educational theory by beginning teachers.' In Harvard, G. and Hodkinson, P. (eds) *Action and Reflection in Teacher Education*. New Jersey: Ablex Publishing Corporation

Erickson, F. (1986) 'Qualitative methods in research on teaching.' In Wittrock, M. (ed.) *Handbook of Research on Teaching*. New York: Macmillan, pp. 119–161

Ernest, P. (1998) 'Questioning school mathematics.' In Edwards, G. and Kelly, A.V. (eds) (1998) *Experience and Education*. London: Paul Chapman, pp. 20–45

Fairclough, N. (1989) *Language and Power*. London: Longman

Flower, F.D. (1966) *Language and Education*. London: Longmans, Green and Co. Ltd

Fordham, S. (1990) 'Racelessness as a factor in black students' school success: Pragmatic strategy or pyrrhic victory?' In Hidalgo, N.M., McDowell, C.L. and Siddle, E.V. (eds) *Facing Racism in Education*, Reprint Series No.21, *Harvard Educational Review*. 232–262

Foucault, M. (1972) *Archaeology of Knowledge*. London: Tavistock Publications

Foucault, M. (1980) *Power/Knowledge: Selected Interviews and Other Writings 1972–1977*. London: Harvester Press

Freire, P. (1972) *Pedagogy of the Oppressed*. Harmondsworth: Penguin

Freire, P. (1974) *Education for Critical Consciousness*. London: Sheed and Ward

Freud, S. (1991) *The Essentials of Psycho-Analysis*. London: Penguin

Fullan, M. (1982) *The Meaning of Educational Change*. Toronto: OISE Press

Gardner, H. (1983) *Frames of Mind: The Theory of Multiple Intelligences*. New York: Basic Books

Gardner, H. (1993) *Multiple Intelligences: The Theory in Practice*. New York: Basic Books

Giddens, A. (1991) *Modernity and Self-identity: Self and Society in the Late Modern Age*. Cambridge: Polity Press

Gillborn, D. and Gipps, C. (1996) *Recent Research on the Achievements of Ethnic Minority Pupils*. London: HMSO

Giroux, H. (1988) 'Critical theory and the politics of culture and voice: Rethinking the discourse of educational research.' In Sherman, R. and Webb, R. (eds) *Qualitative Research in Education: Focus and Methods.* London: Falmer Press, pp. 190–210

Giroux, H. (1992) *Border Crossings: Cultural Workers and the Politics of Education.* New York and London: Routledge

Giroux, H. and McLaren, P. (1992) 'Introduction.' In Stanley, W.B. *Curriculum for Utopia: Social Reconstructionism and Critical Pedagogy in the Postmodern Era.* New York: State University of New York Press, pp. xi–xv

Giroux, H. and Simon, R. (1988) 'Critical pedagogy and the politics of popular culture.' *Cultural Studies* 2(3): 294–320

Goleman, D. (1996) *Emotional Intelligence.* London: Bloomsbury

Goodson, I. (ed.) (1992) *Studying Teachers' Lives.* London: Routledge

Goodson, I. and Hargreaves, A. (1996) *Teachers' Professional Lives.* London: Falmer Press

Goodson, I. and Walker, R. (1991) *Biography, Identity and Schooling.* London: Falmer Press

Gorman, R.M. (1972) *Discovering Piaget. A Guide for Teachers.* Columbus Ohio: Charles E. Merrill

Goudie, E. Mun Har (1999) *Student Teachers' Experiences of the Art and Design Curriculum: A Transformative Pedagogy.* Unpublished PhD Thesis, Institute of Education, London University

Gramsci, A. (1971) *Selections from the Prison Notebooks,* ed. and trans. Q. Hoare and G. Nowell Smith. London: Lawrence and Wishart

Green, B. (1995) 'Post-curriculum possibilities: English teaching, cultural politics and the post-modern turn.' *Journal of Curriculum Studies* 27(4): 391–409

Greene, M. (1988) *The Dialectic of Freedom.* New York: Teachers' College Press

Greene, M. (1995) *Releasing the Imagination.* San Francisco: Jossey Bass

Habermas, J. (1972) *Knowledge and Human Interests.* Trans. J.J. Shapiro, London: Heinemann

Habermas, J. (1974) *Theory and Practice.* Trans. J. Viertel, London: Heinemann

Halpin, D., Moore, A., Edwards, G., George, R. and Jones, C. (1999–2001) 'Pedagogic Identities and the Consumption of Tradition.' ESRC-funded research project, Goldsmiths, University of London.

Halpin D. and Moore A. (forthcoming) 'Maintaining, reconstructing and creating tradition in education' *Oxford Review of Education* 26(2)

Hamilton, D. (1993) 'Texts, literacy and schooling.' In Green, B. (ed) (1993) *The Insistence of the Letter: Literacy Studies and Curriculum Theorizing.* London: Falmer

Handal, G. and Lauvas, P. (1987) *Promoting Reflective Teaching: Supervision in Action.* Milton Keynes and Philadelphia: Society for Research into Higher Education/Open University Press

Hargreaves, A. (1993) 'Professional development and the politics of desire.' In Vasquez, A. and Martinez, I. (eds) *New Paradigms and Practices in Professional Development.* New York: Teachers College Press

Hargreaves, A. (1994) *Changing Teachers, Changing Times: Teachers' Work and Culture in the Postmodern Age.* London: Cassell

Hebdidge, D. (1986) 'Postmodernism and "The Other Side".' *Journal of Communication Enquiry* 10(2): 78–98

Henriques, J. *et al.* (eds) (1998) *Changing the Subject: Psychology, Social Regulation and Subjectivity.* London: Routledge

Henry, M.A. (1989) 'Change in teacher education: focus on field experiences.' In Braun, J.A. Jr (ed.) (1989) *Reforming Teacher Education: Issues and New Directions*. London and New York: Garland Publishing Inc.

Hitchcock, G. and Hughes, D. (1995) *Research and the Teacher: A Qualitative Introduction to School-Based Research*. London: Routledge

Hoare, Q. (1967) 'Education Programmes and Men.' *New Left Review* 32: 40–52

Howe, M.J.A. (1984) *A Teachers' Guide to the Psychology of Learning*. Oxford and New York: Blackwell

Hughes, R. (1993) *Culture of Complaint: A Passionate Look into the Ailing Heart of America*. New York: Warner Books

Hull, R. (1988) *The Language Gap*. London and New York: Methuen

ILEA Afro-Caribbean Language and Literacy Project in Further and Higher Education (1990) *Language and Power*. London: Harcourt Brace Jovanovich

Institute of Education, London University (1972) *Education and the Training of Teachers: Statement on the James Report*. London: Institute of Education

IPPR (Institute for Public Policy Research) (1993) *Education: A Different Version*. ('Alternative White Paper'). London: IPPR

Jenkins, R. (1992) *Pierre Bourdieu*. London: Routledge

Jenks, C. (1993) *Culture*. London and New York: Routledge

Jensen, E. (1995) *Brain Based Teaching and Learning*. San Diego, CA.: Turning Point

Jessel, J. (1999) 'Study: some guiding principles.' In Herne, S., Jessel, J. and Griffiths, J. (eds) *Study to Teach: A Practical and Theoretical Guide to Studying in Teacher Education*. London: Routledge

Johnson, B. (1989) 'Developing preservice teachers' self-awareness: an examination of the professional dynametric program.' In Braun, J.A. Jr (ed.) (1989) *Reforming Teacher Education: Issues and New Directions*. New York and London: Garland Publishing Inc.

John-Steiner, V. and Souberman, E. (1978) 'Afterword.' In Vygotsky, L.S. (1978) *Mind in Society*. Cambridge, Mass.: Harvard University Press, pp. 121–133

Kanpol, B. (1994) *Critical Pedagogy: An Introduction*. Westport, Conn.: Bergin and Garvey

Kelly, A.V. (1998) 'Personal, social and moral education in a democratic society.' In Edwards, G. and Kelly, A.V. (eds) *Experience and Education: Towards an Alternative National Curriculum*. London: Paul Chapman, pp. 161–177

Kemmis, S. (1985) 'Action research and the politics of reflection' in Boud, D., Keogh, R. and Walker, D. (eds) *Reflection: Turning Experience into Learning*. London: Kogan Page, pp. 139–163

Kemmis, S., Cole, P. and Suggett, D. (1983) *Towards the Socially-Critical School*. Victorian Institute of Secondary Education

Kincheloe, J.L. (1991) *Teachers as Researchers: Qualitative Inquiry as a Path to Empowerment*. London: Falmer

Knowles, J.G. (1992) 'Models for understanding pre-service and beginner teachers' biographies.' In Goodson, I. (1992) *Studying Teachers' Lives*, London: Routledge

Krashen, S. (1982) *Principles and Practice in Second Language Acquisition*. Oxford: Pergamon Press

Kress, G. (1982) *Learning To Write*. London: Routledge and Kegan Paul

Kyriacou, C. (1986) *Effective Teaching in Schools*. Oxford: Blackwell

Labov, W. (1972) 'The logic of nonstandard-English.' In Giglioli, P.P. (ed.) *Language and Social Context*. Harmondsworth: Penguin, pp 179–215

Lacan, J. (1977) *Ecrits*. London: Tavistock

Lacan, J. (1979) *The Four Fundamental Concepts of Psycho-Analysis*. London: Penguin

Lambert, D. and Lines, D. (2000) *Understanding Assessment: Purposes, Perceptions and Practice*. London: Falmer

Langford, P. (1979) *Beyond Piaget – Recent Theories of Concept Development and their Significance for Teaching*. Bundoora Victoria, Australia: La Trobe University Centre for the Study of Urban Education

Lankshear, C. (1993) 'Curriculum as literacy: reading and writing in "New Times".' In Green, B. (ed.)(1993) *The Insistence of the Letter: Literacy Studies and Curriculum Theorizing*, London: Falmer, pp. 154–174

Lawton, D. (1975) *Class, Culture and Curriculum*. London: Routledge

Leat, D. (1995) 'The costs of reflection in initial teacher education.' *Cambridge Journal of Education* 25(2): 161–174

Levin, D.M. (1987) *Pathologies of the Modern Self: Postmodern Studies in Narcissism, Schizophrenia and Depression*. New York: New York State University Press

Levine, J. (1983) 'Going back to the mainstream', *Issues in Race and Education*, Summer 1983, pp.1–3

Lewis, M. and Wray, D. (1994) *Writing Frames: Scaffolding Children's Non-fiction Writing in a Range of Genres*. Exeter: Exeter Extending Literacy Project

Lewis, M. and Wray, D. (1998) *Writing Across the Curriculum: Frames to Support Learning*. Reading: University of Reading 'Reading and Language Information Centre'

Lloyd, P. and Fernyhough, C. (eds) (1999) (4 Vols) *Lev Vygotsky: Critical Assessments*. London: Routledge

Loughran, J. (1996) *Developing Reflective Practice: Learning about Teaching and Learning Through Modelling*. London: Falmer

Loughran, J. and Russell, J. (eds) (1997) *Teaching About Teaching: Purpose, Passion and Pedagogy in Teacher Education*. London: Falmer

Lucas, T. and Katz, A. (1994) 'Reframing the debate: the roles of native languages in English only programs for language minority students' *TESOL Quarterly*, 28(3): 537–562

MacDonald, G. (1976) 'The politics of educational publishing.' In Whitty, G. and Young, M. (eds) (1976) *Explorations in the Politics of School Knowledge*. Driffield: Nafferton Books

MacDonald, M. (1977) *Culture, Class and the Curriculum: The Politics of Curriculum Reform*. Milton Keynes: Open University Press

MacDonald, M. (1977) *The Curriculum and Cultural Reproduction*. Milton Keynes: Open University Press

MacDonald, M. (1980) 'Schooling and the reproduction of class and gender relations.' In Barton, L., Meighan, R. and Walker, S. (eds) (1980) *Schooling, Ideology and the Curriculum*. Lewes: Falmer Press, pp. 29–50

Maguire, M. (1995) 'Dilemmas in teaching teachers: the tutor's perspective.' *Teachers and Teaching* 1(1): 119–131

Marland, M. (1975) *The Craft of the Classroom*. Oxford: Heinemann Educational

Marx, K. (1977) *Selected Writings* (ed. D. McLellan) Oxford: Oxford University Press

McCarthy, D. (1930) *The Language Development of the Pre-School Child*. Minneapolis: University of Minnesota Press

McGregor, V. and Moore, A. (1999) *Secondary English: Distance-Learning Materials for Returners to Teaching*. Goldsmiths, University of London

McIntyre, D., Hagger, H. and Burn, K. (1994) *The Management of Student Teachers' Learning*. London and Philadelphia: Kogan Page

McKernan, J. (1991) *Curriculum Action Research: A Handbook of Methods and Resources for the Reflective Practitioner*. London: Kogan Page

McLaren, P. (1988) 'Culture or Canon? Critical Pedagogy and the Politics of Literacy.' *Harvard Educational Review* 58(1): 211–234

McLaren, P. (1996) *Critical Pedagogy and Predatory Culture.* New York: State University of New York Press

McLure, J.S. (1986) *Educational Documents: England and Wales 1816 to the Present Day.* London: Methuen

McNiff, J. (1988) *Action Research: Principles and Practice.* London: Routledge

McNiff, J., Whitehead, J. and Lomax, P. (1996) *You and Your Action Research Project.* London: Routledge

Mitchell, C. and Weber, S. (1996) *Reinventing Ourselves as Teachers: Private and Social Acts of Memory and Imagination.* London: Falmer Press

Mitchell, C. and Weber, S. (1999) *Reinventing Ourselves as Teachers: Beyond Nostalgia.* London: Falmer Press

Moore, A. (1995) 'The linguistic, academic and social development of bilingual pupils in secondary education: Issues of diagnosis, pedagogy and culture.' Unpublished PhD Thesis, Milton Keynes: Open University

Moore, A. (1998) 'English, fetishism and the demand for change.' In Edwards, G. and Kelly, A.V. (eds) *Experience and Education: Towards an Alternative National Curriculum.* London: Paul Chapman, pp.103–125

Moore, A. (1996) ' "Masking the Fissure": some thoughts on competence, reflection and closure in initial teacher education.' *British Journal of Educational Studies* 44(2): 200–211

Moore, A. (1999a) *Teaching Multicultured Students.* London: Falmer

Moore, A. (1999b) 'Beyond reflection: contingency, idiosyncrasy and reflexivity in initial teacher education.' In Hammersley, M. (ed.) (1999) *Researching School Experience: Ethnographic Studies of Teaching and Learning.* London and New York: Falmer, pp. 134–152

Moore, A. and Atkinson, D. (1998) 'Charisma, competence and teacher education.' *Discourse* 19(2): 171–81

Moore, A. and Edwards, G. (2000) 'Compliance, Resistance and Pragmatism in Pedagogic Identities.' Paper presented at the Annual Conference of the American Educational Research Association, New Orleans, 24–28 April 2000

Mussen, P.H. (1970) 'Piaget's theory.' In *Carmichael's Manual of Child Psychology* Vol. I (3rd Edition). New York: Wiley

NACCCE (National Advisory Committee on Creative and Cultural Education) (1999) *All Our Futures: Creativity, Culture and Education.* London: NACCCE

NCC/NOP (1991) *Teaching, Talking and Learning in KS3.* National Curriculum Council/National Oracy Project UK

Nias, J., Southworth, G. and Campbell, P. (1994) 'Whole school curriculum development in the primary school.' In Hargreaves, A. (1994) *Changing Teachers, Changing Times: Teachers' Work and Culture in the Postmodern Age.* London: Cassell

Nixon, J., Martin, J., McKeown, P. and Ranson, S. (1996) *Encouraging Learning: Towards a theory of the learning school.* Buckingham and Philadelphia: Open University Press

NUT (National Union of Teachers) (1976) *Teacher Education: The Way Ahead.* London: National Union of Teachers

OFSTED/TTA (Office for Standards in Education/Teacher Training Agency) (1996) *Framework for the Assessment of Quality and Standards in Initial Teacher Training 1996/97.* London: OFSTED

OFSTED/TTA (Office for Standards in Education/Teacher Training Agency) (1997/98) *Framework for the Assessment of Quality and Standards in Initial Teacher Training (Revised).* London: OFSTED

Ogbu, J.U. (1992) 'Understanding cultural diversity and learning.' *Educational Researcher* 21(98): 5–14

Ord, F. and Quigley, J. (1985) 'Anti-sexism as good educational practice: What can feminists realistically achieve?' In Weiner, G. (ed.) (1985) *Just a Bunch of Girls*. Milton Keynes: Open University Press, pp. 104–119

Paechter, C. (1998) *Educating the Other: Gender, Power and Schooling*. London: Falmer Press

Perera, K. (1984) *Children's Writing and Reading: Analysing Classroom Language*. Oxford: Blackwell

Perera, K. (1987) *Understanding Language*. York: National Association of Advisers in English

Peters, R.S. (1966) *Ethics and Education*. London: Allen and Unwin

Piaget, J. (1926) *The Language and Thought of the Child*. London: Routledge

Piaget, J. (1962) *Appendix to Vygotsky's Thought and Language – 'Comments on Vygotsky's Critical remarks Concerning "The Language and Thought of the Child" and "Judgement and reasoning in the Child"'.* Quoted in Barnes (1976) p. 80

Piaget, J. (1971) *Biology and Knowledge*. Edinburgh: Edinburgh University Press

Piaget, J. (1975) *The Development of Thought*. Oxford: Blackwell

Piaget, J. and Inhelder, B. (1969) *The Psychology of the Child* (trans. H. Weaver). London: Routledge and Kegan Paul

Pitt, A. (1999) 'The play of the personal in education.' Seminar paper, Institute of Education, University of London, 22 June 1999.

Playfair, L. (1870) 'On Primary and Technical Education.' Quoted by Selleck (ed.) (1968), p. 15

Plowden Report (1967) *Children and Their Primary Schools*. Central Advisory Council for Education: HMSO

Popkewitz, T.S. (ed) (1987) *Critical Studies in Teacher Education: Its Folklore, Theory and Practice*. London: Falmer Press

QCA (Qualifications and Assessment Authority) (1998) *Education for Citizenship and the Teaching of Democracy in Schools: Final Report of the Advisory Group on Citizenship*. London: QCA

Quicke, J. (1988) 'Using structured life histories to teach the sociology and social psychology of education.' In Woods, P. and Pollard, A. (eds) *Sociology and Teaching*. London: Croom Helm

Raleigh, M. (1981) *The Languages Book*. London: Inner London Education Authority English Centre

Reid, J., Forrestal, P. and Cook, J. (1989) *Small Group Learning in the Classroom*. Scarborough: Chalk Face Press

Richardson, V. (ed.) (1997) *Constructive Teacher Education: building a world of new understandings*. London: Falmer

Rosen, H. (1972) *Language and Class: A Critical Look at the Theories of Basil Bernstein*. London: Falling Wall Press

Ross, M. (1998) 'The aim is song: towards an alternative national curriculum.' In Edwards, G. and Kelly, A.V. (eds) (1998) *Experience and Education*. London: Paul Chapman, pp. 126–142

RSA (1999) 'Opening Minds: Education for the 21st Century' (RSA 1999)

Schon, D.A. (1983) *The Reflective Practitioner: How the Professionals Think in Action*. New York: Basic Books

Schon, D.A. (1987) *Educating the Reflective Practitioner*. San Fransisco: Jossey-Bass

Schon, D.A. (1988) 'Coaching reflective teaching.' In Grimmett, P.P. and Erickson, G.L. (eds) *Reflection in Teacher Education*. British Columbia: Pacific Educational Press

Scott, D. (2000) *Reading Educational Research and Policy*. London: Falmer

Scott Baumann, A., Bloomfield, A. and Roughton, L. (1997) *Becoming a Secondary School Teacher*. London: Hodder and Stoughton

Selleck, R.J.W. (ed.) (1968) *The New Education 1870–1914*. London: Pitman

Shapiro, H. Svi. (1990) *Between Capitalism and Democracy: Education Policy and the Crisis of the Welfare State*. New York: Bergin and Garvey

Shor, I. and Freire, P. (1987) *A Pedagogy for Liberation*. New York: Bergin and Garvey

Siegel, L.S. and Brainerd, C.J. (eds) (1978*) Alternatives to Piaget: Critical Essays on the Theory*. New York: Academy Press

Simon, B. (1974) *The New Nations and the Educational Structure, 1780–1870*. London: Lawrence and Wishart

Sinclair, J. and Coulthard, R. (1975) *Towards an Analysis of Discourse: The English Used by Teachers and Pupils*. London: Oxford University Press

Skilbeck, M. and Harris, A. (1976) *Culture, Ideology and Knowledge*. Milton Keynes: Open University Press

Skinner, B.F. (1953) *Science and Human Behaviour*. New York: Macmillan

Skinner, B.F. (1974) *About Behaviourism*. London: Cape

Smith, A. (1996) *Accelerated Learning in the Classroom*. Stafford: School Network Educational Press Ltd.

Smith, A. (1998) *Accelerated Learning in Practice*. Stafford: School Network Educational Press Ltd,

Smith, L. (ed.) (1996) *Critical Readings on Piaget*. London: Routledge

Smyth, W.J. (1991) *Teachers as Collaborative Learners: Challenging Dominant Forms of Supervision*. Milton Keynes: Open University Press

Spender, D. (1980) *Man Made Language*. London: RKP

Spender, D. (1982) *Invisible Women: The Schooling Scandal*. London: Writers and Readers

Standish, P. (1995) 'Post-modernism and the education of the whole person.' *Journal of Philosophy of Education* 29(1): 121–136

Stenhouse, L. (1975) *An Introduction to Curriculum Research and Development*. London: Heinemann

Stephens, P. and Crawley, T. (1994) *Becoming an Effective Teacher*. Cheltenham: Stanley Thornes Ltd

Stubbs, M. (1976) *Language, Schools and Classrooms*. London: Methuen

Taber, A. (1978) 'Art in a multicultural school.' *New Approaches in Multiracial Education,* 7(1): 1–5

Taber, A. (1981) 'Art and craft in a multicultural school.' In Lynch, J. (ed.) *Teaching in the Multicultural School*. London: Ward Lock Educational, pp. 57–75

TTA (Teacher Training Agency) (1998) *National Standards for Qualified Teacher Status*. London: Teacher Training Agency

Thomas, D. (1995) 'Treasonable or trustworthy text: reflections on teacher narrative studies.' In Thomas, D. (ed.) (1995) *Teachers' Stories*. Buckingham: Open University Press

Thompson, J. (1990) *Ideology and Modern Culture: Critical Social Theory in the Era of Mass Communication*. Cambridge: Polity Press

Thorndike, E.L. (1914) *The Psychology of Learning*. New York: Teachers' College Press

Thornton, K. (1999) 'RSA "revolution" would tear up the curriculum.' *Times Educational Supplement* 18 June 1999: 10

Tizard, B. and Hughes, M. (1984) *Young Children Learning*. London: Fontana

Torbe, M. (1976) *Language Across the Curriculum: Guidelines for Schools*. Fort William: NATE

Torbe, M. 'Language across the curriculum: policies and practice.' In Barnes, D., Britton, J. and Torbe, M. (1986) *Language, the Learner and the School* (3rd edition) pp. 131–166.

Trudgill, P. (1983) *On Dialect*. Oxford: Blackwell

Usher, R. and Edwards, R. (1994) *Postmodernism and Education*. London: Routledge

Valli, L. (ed.) (1992) *Reflective Teacher Education*. New York: State University of New York Press

Van Manen, M. (1977) 'Linking ways of knowing with ways of being practical.' *Curriculum Inquiry* 6: 205–228

Van Manen, M. (1990) *Researching Lived Experience: Human Science for an Action Sensitive Pedagogy*. New York: Sunny Press

Vygotsky, L.S. (1962) *Thought and Language*. Cambridge, Mass.: MIT Press

Vygotsky, L.S. (1978) *Mind in Society*. Cambridge, Mass.: Harvard University Press

Wacquant, L.J.D. (1989) 'Towards a reflexive sociology: A workshop with Pierre Bourdieu.' *Sociological Theory* 7

Walford, G. (ed.) (1991) *Doing Educational Research*. London: Routledge

Walkerdine, V. (1982) 'A psycho-semiotic approach to abstract thought.' In Beveridge, M. (ed.) *Children Thinking Through Language*. London: Arnold

Walkerdine, V. (1990) *Schoolgirl Fictions*. London: Verso

Wallen, M. (1989) 'Write across the curriculum: summing up and pointing forward.' In *Writing and Learning* (National Writing Project). Walton-on-Thames: Thomas Nelson and Sons/SCDC, pp. 91–95

Warnock Report (1978) *Special Educational Needs*. London: HMSO

Weiner, G. (ed.) (1985) *Just a Bunch of Girls*. Milton Keynes: Open University Press

Whitty, G. (1977) *School Knowledge and Social Control*. Milton Keynes: Open University Press

Wiles, S. (1985a) 'Learning a second language.' *The English Magazine* 14: 20–23

Wiles, S. (1985b) 'Language and learning in multi-ethnic classrooms: Strategies for supporting bilingual students.' In Wells, G. and Nicholas, J. (eds) *Language and Learning: An Interactional Perspective*. London: Falmer Press, pp. 83–94

Williams, R. (1981) *Culture*. London: Fontana.

Willinsky, J. (1993) 'Lessons from the literacy before schooling 1800–1859.' In Green, B. (ed.) (1993) *The Insistence of the Letter: Literacy Studies and Curriculum Theorizing*. London: Falmer, pp. 58–74

Willis, P. (1977) *Learning To Labour*. Farnborough: Saxon House

Witkin, R. (1974) *The Intelligence of Feeling*. London: Heinemann

Wood, D. (1998) *How Children Think and Learn*. Oxford: Blackwell

Woods, P. (1979) *The Divided School*. London: Routledge and Kegan Paul

Woods, P. (1996) *Researching the Art of Teaching: Ethnography for Educational Use*. London: Routledge

Wragg, E.C. (1974) *Teaching Teaching*. Newton Abbot: David and Charles

Wright, J. (1985) *Bilingualism in Education*. London: Issues in Race and Education

Young, M.F.D. (1958) *The Rise of the Meritocracy*. London: Thames and Hudson

Young, M.F.D. (1971a) 'Introduction: knowledge and control.' In Young, M.F.D. (ed.) *Knowledge and Control*. London: Collier-Macmillan, pp. 1–17

Young, M.F.D. (1971b) 'An approach to the study of curricula as socially organized knowledge.' In Young, M.F.D. (ed.) *Knowledge and Control*. London: Collier-Macmillan, pp. 19–46

Zizek, S. (1989) *The Sublime Object of Ideology*. London: Verso

Index

accelerated learning 3, 158–63, 174
accommodation 7–8
achievement motivation 26
action research 139, 146
active learning 13, 14, 19, 30, 143
anti-culturist strategies 105, 113–14, 115–16
Apple, Michael 92, 153, 154
Arnold, Matthew 50, 57, 91
arts 167–8, 169
assessment
  continuous 53
  formative 17, 30, 169
  multiple intelligences 157, 158
  quantitative 57
  self-fulfilling prophecy 20–1
  stress effect on 159
  symbolic violence 104
  of teachers 124–5, 171
assimilation 7, 8
attention spans 161–2

Barnes, Douglas
  curriculum 33
  exploratory/transmissive teaching 39–40
  language 65, 66, 73
  learning 8, 9, 15
Baumann, Scott 26
Bayliss, Valerie 171
behaviourism 5, 30, 162, 163
Bernstein, Basil
  cultural capital 98
  educational failure 128
  framing 155
  linguistic codes 84–5
  middle classes 58
  pedagogic identity 42–3, 145
Bestist bias 157
Betts, B. 167
bilingual students 6, 66–9, 82, 84, 117, 158

biographical narratives 134
Blenkin, G. 153–4
Boud, D. 133
Bourdieu, Pierre
  cultural issues 63, 91, 92, 103, 117
  educational changes 53, 153
  habitus 94–7, 98–9, 105
  pedagogic action/authority 99–100
Brainerd, C.J. 11, 12, 13
Brice Heath, S. 83, 92
Britzman, D. 27
Bruner, Jerome
  culture 47–8
  educational reform 154
  learning 1, 4, 22–5, 30–1
  reform 53
Bullock Report (1975) 36, 74–5, 80, 81, 85

Capel, S. 109, 110
capitalism 50
Carr, W. 51
CATE see Council for the Accreditation of
  Teacher Education
charismatic model of teaching 120–2, 126,
  127
child-centredness 3, 8, 12
  see also student-centred approaches
Chomsky, Noam 153
'citizenship sessions' 41, 42
cognitive psychology 23
Cole, A.L. 134
collaborative learning 19
communication 39
communicative teaching 121–2, 124, 140,
  145
competence model of teaching 123–8,
  130–2, 136, 138, 140, 145–6
concept development 6, 15, 70
consistency of school policy 143, 144–5

constructivism 5, 39
content-process debate 38–40
contingent aspects of teaching 3–4, 12, 24, 127, 140, 143
control 40, 64, 70, 73–4
Cook, J. 77
Coulthard, R. 72
Council for the Accreditation of Teacher Education (CATE) 123–4, 126
creativity 127, 169, 175
crime 54–5
critical literacy 53, 62, 86–8, 151–4, 172, 174
critical pedagogy 168
cued elicitation 71–2, 73
cultural capital 97, 98, 100, 101, 103–4
cultural diversity 46–7, 168
cultural education 169
cultural issues
    accelerated learning 162
    bias 91–119
    Bruner 22, 24, 25, 30–1, 47–8
    language 82, 83, 84
    learning and development 12, 27, 29
    Skinner 6
cultural literacy 62, 86–7
cultural reproduction 63, 97, 99
Cummins, James 23, 46–7, 53, 110, 140, 157
curriculum
    accelerated learning 160–1
    alternative models 149, 151, 163–72, 175
    anti-culturist strategies 113–14
    change 153–4
    cultural bias 53, 92–4, 97, 98–100, 111–12, 116–17
    Enlightenment influence 51, 52–3
    experienced-based 164–6, 175
    language across 74–86
    official policy 149–50, 172–4
    pedagogic identities 42–3
    purposes of education 33, 34–5, 44–8, 51, 57, 59–60
    social reproduction 40
    see also National Curriculum

DARTs (Directed Activities Related to Texts) 79
Davies, Dan 46, 51
decentred pedagogic identity 43
democracy 164, 166, 168

demystification 152
development
    Bruner 23–4, 25
    language 70, 71, 74–5
    Piaget 8–11, 12, 13, 14, 30, 64
    Skinner 5
    student needs 107
    theory 28–9
    Vygotsky 15–16, 17, 18–19
Dewey, John 45, 51–2, 94
dialects 82, 84–6, 105
dialogic teacher–student relationships 3, 16, 19
diaries 129
differentiation 94, 107–10, 144
discipline 40, 73, 137–8
disempowerment 127
Donaldson, Margaret 4, 18, 64
Doyle, B. 33
Dunne 109

economic purposes of education 53–6, 57
Edwards, Derek 69, 70–4
Edwards, G. 163, 165–6
emotions 122, 141
empowerment 27, 38, 55, 83, 86, 167
English 41, 74–5, 76, 173
    cultural preference 96
    'standard' 63, 83–6, 93
Enlightenment 46, 51–3, 54, 57, 59, 131–2
enthusiasm 126–7
entitlement curriculum 165, 166, 170
equal opportunities 109
Eraut, M. 139, 151
Ernest, Paul 40
ethnic minorities 93, 94, 96, 109, 112–13
    see also multiculturalism
evaluation of teachers' own work 129, 130
examinations see public examinations
experienced-based curriculum 164–6, 175
exploratory teaching 37, 39, 45

fields 94–7
Fisher, H.A.L. 55
Fordham, S. 112
formal discipline 17–18
Forrestal, P. 77
Foucault, Michel 63, 136
Freire, Paulo 150, 151–2, 153, 154
Freud, Sigmund 136–7
Fullan, M. 154
functional literacy 62, 86–7

Gardner, Howard 155–8
gender bias 114–15
genres of language 63, 81–3, 87
Giddens, Anthony 134
Gillborn, D. 113
Gipps, C. 113
Giroux, Henry 48–9, 99, 111, 112
Goodson, I. 131
Goudie, E. Mun Har 127–8, 132, 133, 139
Greene, M. 133
group-work 3, 37, 38, 77, 138

Habermas, Jurgen 132, 133
habitus 94–7, 98–9, 105
Hamilton, D. 46
Hargreaves, A. 134
Herbart, 17–18
high culture 51, 52, 54
Hoare 153
Howe, M.J.A. 155
Hughes, M. 83, 92
Hughes, Robert 48
Hull, Robert 44–5, 65, 73

identity
    cultural 112–13, 116
    pedagogic 42–3, 140, 145
    professional 140, 142
individual-centred school 155–6
inequality 49, 50, 54, 55, 91, 127–8
institutional support 142–5
instrumental motivation 26
instrumental pedagogic identity 43
intersubjective learning theories 25
intrinsic motivation 26

Jenkins, R. 95, 96, 99
Jessel, J. 2

Katz, A. 110–11
Kelly, A.V. 163, 165–6
Kemmis, S. 136, 141
Knowles, J.G. 134
Kress, G. 82–3, 87–8, 92

Labov, William 83, 85, 92
Lacan, Jacques 122
Langford, P. 13
language 62–90
    cultural factors 92
    of curriculum 44
    instructional framework 110
    Vygotsky 15, 16

latent meanings 136–8
learning
    accelerated 158–63, 174
    Bruner 1, 4, 22–5, 30–1
    conflict with purpose of education 37
    experienced-based curriculum 165
    language 62, 63–4, 69, 74–6, 80, 88
    models 1–32
    multiple intelligence 155, 157
    Piaget 1, 2, 7–14, 23, 30, 157
    skills 18, 38–9, 45, 167
    Skinner 1, 4–7, 30, 73
    theories 35–6
    Vygotsky 1, 3, 4, 14–22, 30, 76
learning difficulties 5
Leat, D. 132
Levine, Josie 66–7
linguistic repertoires 75, 76, 83, 88, 103
listening 76–8
literacy
    critical 53, 62, 86–8, 151–4, 172, 174
    empowerment 38, 86
Lowe, Robert 55–6
Lucas, T. 110–11

McCarthy, Dorothea 16
McLaren, P. 86–7
marking knowledge as significant and joint
    71
Mercer, Neil 69, 70–4
meritocracy 92
middle class
    curricular bias 92, 93, 96
    influence on educational agendas 58
    language 84, 85
mixed-ability teaching 44, 144, 173
modernism 46, 131
Moore, A. 6, 67
Morrell, J.D. 54, 55
motivation 6, 25–8, 30
multiculturalism 108, 111, 112–14, 117
multilingual classrooms 110–11
multiple intelligence 3, 109, 134, 154–8, 174

National Advisory Committee on Creative
    and Cultural Education (NACCCE)
    169–72
National Curriculum 149–50, 163–4, 166,
    169–70
    competences discourse 126
    conflict with best practice 42
    critique of 46
    cultural bias 103, 104, 116

English 41, 42, 63, 76, 83–4, 173
   learning theories 1
   levels approach 3, 17, 28, 155
   linguistic competence 62
   purpose of education 38
   reading 80
   small-group discussions 77
   social reproduction 40
   staged development 11, 13, 30
   Vygotsky 20–2
   writing 81
National Writing Project (1985–89) 80, 81
Nias, J. 142

objectivist learning theories 25
Office for Standards in Education (OFSTED)
   29, 124–5, 150
official purposes of education 34–6, 37–8,
   41, 45, 49
OFSTED *see* Office for Standards in
   Education
'on task' time 161–2
oral work 76–7
outcome measurement 127, 130

Paechter, C. 114–15
paraphrase 72
pathologising 27, 84–5, 132, 135
pedagogic action 99–100
pedagogy
   curriculum influence on 34, 35, 45,
     171–2
   official policy 149–50, 172–4
   Piaget 8, 12, 13–14
   resistant 151–63
   Skinner 5
   Vygotsky 16, 17, 22
performance-competence problem 12–13
personality of teacher 120, 121, 124
Piaget, Jean
   child-centredness 3
   critiques of 4, 11–14, 22, 24, 64–5
   intelligence 18, 156
   learning 1, 2, 7–14, 23, 30, 157
   linguistic experiment 64–5
   motivation 26
   Plowden Report 36
   Vygotsky comparison 15
Pitt, A. 27
planning 120–1, 123, 124, 125
Plowden Report (1967) 36
policy
   curricular review 170

language 75, 88
   learning theories 2, 36
   middle-class influence 58
   official 149–51, 172–4
   Piaget influence 14
   purposes of education 33–4
   whole-school 142–5, 146
political issues
   Bruner 24
   critical literacy 88
   purposes of education 36, 38, 58
   transitional curriculum 168
positive reinforcement 4
postmodernism 131, 134
poverty 24, 55, 93
power relations 88, 95–6, 138, 152
presupposition 72–3
principled knowledge 70–1
progressivism 5, 153, 158, 163
prospective pedagogic identity 43
proximal development 16–17
psychoanalysis 27, 135, 137
public examinations
   cultural bias 96, 103, 104, 111
   memorising of facts 35
   pass grades 7
   reform 53
   standard English 83
purposes of education 33–61, 171, 175

racism 47, 105, 115, 153
readiness 12, 13
reading 76, 78–80
reasoning 10
reconstruction 72
reflective model of teaching 128–32, 134,
   136, 138, 146
reflexive model of teaching 132–8, 143,
   146
Reid, J. 77
reproduction *see* cultural reproduction; social
   reproduction
research 129, 138–40, 146
resistant pedagogies 151–63
retrospective pedagogic identity 42–3
rewards 4, 5, 6, 7, 26
rights and responsibilities policy 5
ritual knowledge 70–1, 87
Rosen, Harold 85
Ross, M. 167–8, 169
rote learning 15, 70
Royal Society of Arts (RSA) 171
RSA *see* Royal Society of Arts

school effectiveness 58
Schools Council Project 78, 79, 80
self-fulfilling prophecy 20–1
self-presentation 121, 122
Shor, I. 152, 154
Siegel, L.S. 11, 12, 13
Sinclair, J. 72
skills
    basic 35, 37, 38, 86
    communication 121–2
    competences discourse 123–4, 125, 126–7
    critical literacy 87
    cultural factors 109
    language 63, 66, 74–6, 85, 86, 88
    learning 18, 38–9, 45, 167
    reflective teaching 128, 130
    relevance to outside world 45, 46, 48
    social 56
Skinner, Burrhus Frederic 1, 4–7, 25–6, 30, 73, 162
Smith, Alistair 158–62
Smyth, W.J. 129, 132–3
social class 40, 49–50, 55–6, 82, 91–3, 96
    see also middle class; working class
social engineering 49, 91
social factors
    educational failure 128
    reflexivity discourse 133, 135, 136, 146
    socio-cultural context 3–4, 24, 29
    Vygotskian learning 15–16, 22, 30
social motivation 26
social myths 152
social reproduction 40, 54
speaking 75, 76–7
Spender, D. 114
spiralling 23
staged development 9–11, 13, 14, 28, 30, 64
standards 124–5
Standish, P. 46
Stenhouse, L. 154
strategy 140–2
stress 159–60
student-centred approaches 8, 27, 39, 67
    accelerated learning 158
    English teaching 76
    Vygotsky 16
    see also child-centredness
subversive teaching practices 149, 151, 152–3
symbolic violence 98, 100, 101, 104, 152

Taber, Ann 106–9, 113, 114, 117
talking 20, 75, 76–7
teacher education 3, 11, 123–4, 125–6, 129–30, 134
Teacher Training Agency (TTA) 123–4, 125, 130, 140
teacher–student dialogic relationships 3, 16, 19
technicism 139, 167, 168
Testist bias 157
texts 78–9, 93, 96, 105, 168–9
theory 2, 129, 138–9, 140
therapeutic pedagogic identity 43, 145
Thompson, J. 98
Thorndike, E.L. 4, 17–18
Tizard, B. 83, 92
Torbe, Mike 75
transferential illusion 122
transitional curriculum 168–9
transmissive teaching 13, 39–40
TTA see Teacher Training Agency

uniform school 155

validation 71
vocabulary 66, 79, 81
Vygotsky, Lev
    Bullock Report 36
    language 63
    learning 1, 3, 4, 14–22, 30, 76
    rote learning 70

Walker, R. 131
Walkerdine, Valerie 18
Wallen, Margaret 80
Warnock Report (1978) 8, 36
Westist bias 157
whole-school policy 142–5, 146
Williams, Raymond 91
Willis, Paul 112, 153
Woods, Peter 33, 131, 135
working class
    curricular bias 92, 93, 96
    language 83, 84–5
    purposes of education 55, 56
writing 20, 76, 80–6

Young, Michael 45, 92

Zizek, S. 122
zone of proximal development 16–17